HISTORIC
YELLOWSTONE NATIONAL PARK

HISTORIC YELLOWSTONE NATIONAL PARK

The Stories Behind the World's First National Park

BRUCE T. GOURLEY

Guilford, Connecticut

An imprint of Globe Pequot, the trade division of
The Rowman & Littlefield Publishing Group, Inc.
4501 Forbes Blvd., Ste. 200
Lanham, MD 20706
www.rowman.com

Distributed by NATIONAL BOOK NETWORK

British Library Cataloguing in Publication Information available

Library of Congress Cataloging-in-Publication Data
Names: Gourley, Bruce T., author.
Title: Historic Yellowstone National Park : the stories behind the world's
  first national park / Bruce T. Gourley.
Description: Guilford, Connecticut : Lyons Press, [2022] | Includes
  bibliographical references and index. | Summary: "Explores the most
  interesting moments in the park's history, including the slices of life
  in Montana and Wyoming that provide an idea of what life was like for
  those who chose to explore this gloriously beautiful corner of the
  United States"— Provided by publisher.
Identifiers: LCCN 2021024238 (print) | LCCN 2021024239 (ebook) | ISBN
  9781493059218 (paperback) | ISBN 9781493059225 (epub)
Subjects: LCSH: Yellowstone National Park—History. | Yellowstone National
  Park—Biography.
Classification: LCC F722 .G68 2022 (print) | LCC F722 (ebook) | DDC
  978.7/52—dc23
LC record available at https://lccn.loc.gov/2021024238
LC ebook record available at https://lccn.loc.gov/2021024239

∞™ The paper used in this publication meets the minimum requirements of American National
Standard for Information Sciences—Permanence of Paper for Printed Library Materials, ANSI/
NISO Z39.48-1992.

CONTENTS

CONTENTS

CHAPTER FOURTEEN: Mysteries of Life and the Universe:
How Yellowstone's Thermal Waters Unlocked a Scientific

Acknowledgments

The history of Yellowstone National Park is storied, extensive, and complex. Crafting a brief narrative of the famed park's natural and human history is a daunting endeavor. I am deeply indebted to two individuals who helped me navigate the deep and wide terrain.

Lee H. Whittlesey, now retired, was Yellowstone's fourth National Park Service historian. The dean of Yellowstone historians, he is a prolific author of the park's history. Lee read my manuscript, pointed out deficiencies, and set me straight on a number of occasions—encouraging me all along the way.

Elizabeth A. Watry, an outstanding western historian and Yellowstone historian, as well as a prolific author, also read my manuscript, graciously providing clarity on a variety of subject matters. She also encouraged me to include opening quotes for each chapter.

For their assistance with identifying and obtaining images, I am indebted to Larry Lancaster and Jack Davis, avid collectors of, and deeply knowledgeable about, historical Yellowstone images, postcards, and posters.

In addition, I am most grateful for the excellent work of the Globe Pequot editorial and production team of Rick Rinehart, Meredith Dias, and Joanna Beyer.

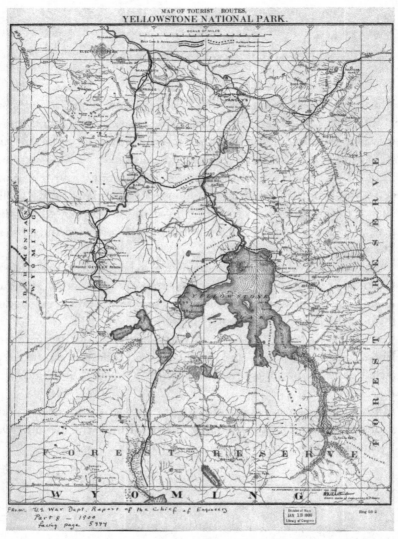

This map of Yellowstone National Park, produced by the US Department while the park was under the administration of the US Army, depicts "tourist routes" in the year 1900. Note that today's Tower-Roosevelt Junction area is labeled as "Yancy's," a misspelling of John Yancey, proprietor of an early hotel (1882–1906) near the junction that failed to withstand the test of time. LIBRARY OF CONGRESS, UNITED STATES WAR DEPARTMENT, OFFICE OF THE CHIEF OF ENGINEERS. G4262.Y4 1900 .U5 TIL.

INTRODUCTION

A LAND OF ENDURING FASCINATION AND MYSTIQUE, YELLOWSTONE National Park is a place like no other.

Upon this ancient landscape of geysers, mountains, canyons, and waterfalls that are still being sculpted by volcanic forces that originated long ago, the past, present, and future have converged. For many generations Indigenous peoples traveling through and living in this remarkable place perceived a spiritual connection to the land and its wildlife. Following decades of gradual discovery of the region's wonders by Euro-Americans, the US government in 1872 set aside Yellowstone as the people's park, and as a refuge for endangered animals.

Weathering an initial period of uneven management, Yellowstone thereafter benefited from the guardianship of the US Army and the National Park Service. Over the years many remarkable and devoted individuals have carefully stewarded this vast, 2.2-million-acre landscape.

Serving the public's interest, a tourist infrastructure unique to this wilderness park, including early iconic hotels and stagecoaches, has evolved and accommodated hundreds of millions of visitors from throughout the world. On the preservationist front, the modern conservation ethic took root in Yellowstone, sprouted into a movement, and matured into holistic ecosystem management. Enlarging frontiers of human knowledge, scientific inquiry into the geological and biological secrets of Yellowstone continues to enhance our understanding of Earth and expand our horizons of life.

This is the story of a Wonderland unparalleled in magic and majesty.

CHAPTER ONE

The Rhythms of Wonderland

*[O]ur greatest national heritage is nature itself, with all its complex-
ity and its abundance of life . . .*

—GEORGE M. WRIGHT,
NATIONAL PARK SERVICE BIOLOGIST, 1933[1]

IN THE HEART OF WINTER ATOP A HIGH MOUNTAIN PLATEAU BATHED IN
scenic beauty, a battle for life unfolds. The days are short and perilous, the
nights long and unforgiving.

It is the season of the wolf.

For months the bitter cold remains, with snow and ice blanketing
the Yellowstone plateau. Vegetation, dormant and often buried, offers
only scant nutrition for ungulates. For all animals, fat is the currency of
survival.

While bears safely shelter in hibernation and live off the fat stored in
their bodies, elk remain upon the landscape, exposed. Winter is their ulti-
mate test. Their body fat diminishing from day to day, that which sustains
them during the harshest of seasons is also life-giving food for wolves.

Ever vigilant, wolf packs stalk the most vulnerable of elk, the species critical to their winter survival. A wolf pack's proximity to an elk
herd causes the ungulates to expend valuable energy in maintaining distance from their hunters. Shadowing the herd, the carnivorous canids are
patient predators.

Their bodies weary of constant movement, a herd of elk allows a
wolf pack to draw too close. Sensing opportunity, the wolf pack charges,

In Yellowstone's Lamar Valley, a coyote trots through winter's snow. COPYRIGHT
BRUCE GOURLEY

setting the already weakened herd into slow-moving flight through deep snow. Spread out, the wolves on a run approach from multiple directions, disorienting the fleeing herd. Within moments, one young elk, smaller and weaker than the others, falls slightly behind.

Pivoting, the individual wolves from differing directions charge hard through the snow, confusing their prey. From behind, the first wolf lunges and grabs one of the elk's hind legs in its powerful jaws, bringing the animal to a standstill. Within seconds, off to the side a second wolf hurls itself upon the hapless animal, burying its teeth deep into the neck of the wounded elk. In another moment, the remaining members of the pack arrive. Each grasping a part of the elk in their jaws, they pull the animal to the ground.

Furious in their hunger, the wolves tear hunks of meat from the yet-living body of the young elk. Overwhelmed and unable to resist, the elk's final moments of life are grisly and bloody. Pausing in flight, the elk herd looks backward upon the carnage. One life, rapidly ripped to shreds, feeds the wolf pack for another day. Safe for a time, the elk herd moves on.

Night falls on a bloody patch of snow, bones, and fur.

On the clearest days of the winter solstice, fewer than nine hours of sunlight kiss the vast snowscape of this land of brutal survival juxtaposed with dazzling beauty and today known as Yellowstone National Park.

With the passing of the winter solstice, a brief period in which the Earth's axis is tilted neither toward nor away from the sun, the planet's tilt reverses, shifting back toward the sun. Measured in mere seconds the first day, more life-giving energy arrives upon Yellowstone's remote wilderness.

Although six months of increasing daylight begins, bitter cold remains for about three more months, the sun's rays too feeble to break winter's spell. Some days snowstorms blanket the entirety of the Yellowstone plateau, obscuring sky and landscape alike. At other times flakes drift down leisurely from overcast skies. Howling windstorms often signal a transition in weather patterns. Suspended above the ground on some sub-zero, clear sunny days, tiny ice crystals shimmer and sparkle like playful diamonds in miniature. On the snow-covered ground, stationary ice

Near the Grand Canyon of the Yellowstone River a grizzly searches for a meal after a long winter season. COPYRIGHT BRUCE GOURLEY

crystals blink in flashes of silver as the blazing sun to the south slings low across the deep blue sky.

A primordial quietness bathes the winterscape of Yellowstone's mountain-ringed valleys. Seemingly stretching forever, the silence from time to time is broken by the distant howl of wolves. Witnessed by few humans ancient or modern, the magnificence of the winter landscape in this remote corner of the world is unmatched. A cathedral of nature evoking reverence, winter in Yellowstone is also baptized—from predatory wolf kills to death by freezing on the part of weakened animals, fish, and birds alike—with bloody, life-giving sacrifices.

In a world of extreme cold, life, apart from the rush of the wolf hunt, moves in slow motion. While seeking scant food, ungulates instinctively conserve precious calories, each movement acting like a sacred act of sustenance.

A soft swishing sound is that of a shaggy beast buried chest deep in the snow and resolutely swinging its massive head from side to side like a pendulum. Left, right, left, right. With each arc a small indentation in the whiteness grows deeper. This is the lot of the American bison—commonly known as buffalo—in the winter Wonderland of Yellowstone. Its head crusted with ice but a thick protective winter coat keeping its body warm, the bison searches for dormant vegetation yielding scant but necessary sustenance. Each day of survival in the depths of winter is a quiet victory.

But listen closely, for the bison is not alone. Drifting across the quietness with astonishing clarity is a rhythmic grinding noise. It is a bighorn sheep, a connoisseur of different fare. Nimbly the bighorn stands upon a sun-exposed rocky promontory, the uneven terrain sparse with snow but off limits to the tank-like bison. Big glassy eyes fixated in the distance, the bighorn methodically chews on tough vegetation often avoided by other ungulates.

Down below in the meadow, a softer sound, almost mesmerizing, is that of a coyote steadily trotting in the snow. Like a small, tan boat sailing upon a white ocean, the coyote's legs sink and rise, its movements sending small sprays of white powder briefly airborne. Suddenly the canid pauses, its body rigid and attentive. Ears trained downward,

A newborn elk calf observes the world from beneath the shelter of its mother's body. COPYRIGHT BRUCE GOURLEY

it discerns the movements of a rodent beneath the snow. Honing in on the exact location, the coyote awaits, motionless and silent. The tension released, in a motion swift and precise the hunter leaps upward, a ballet dancer hovering midair on nature's vast stage. Downward the coyote deftly dives, nose first, eyes fixated, a furry arrow plunging into the snow. In the blink of an eye and a splaying shower of blurry whiteness it reemerges. Success? Sometimes. In this case, yes. A warm, tasty morsel is swiftly consumed. A small beating heart ceases, a larger life is nourished. On the coyote floats across the sea of whiteness in search of prey beneath its feet.

Other ungulates, too, live in this remote enclave where winter lingers for many months. Deer graze on shrubs and trees above the snow, while antelope prefer lower elevations with little snow cover, and hence easier access to grasses. Moose, large creatures of solitude astride remarkably long legs, tramp through deep snow and dine on leafy trees and shrubs.

Near the Firehole River a mother bison and calf stand near one another.

In dens underground or in clefts or caves, some mammals large and small find refuge for the winter in varied states of torpor or hibernation. Largely sleeping with their bodies nourished by reservoirs of fat, their heartbeat and respiration rate slow dramatically, accompanied by a drop in body temperature. From chipmunks to grizzlies, winter dormancy is a successful survival strategy for certain mammals.

On the other hand, some small to mid-sized mammals in Yellowstone sport thick winter coats and remain active during the winter months, including animals as diverse as squirrels, lynx, bobcats, and otters. In addition to providing warmth, the fur coats of weasels, snowshoe hares, and jackrabbits turn white during the winter months, offering camouflage from predators. Some other small furry mammals, including varieties of mice, travel and live beneath the snow, insulated and, to some degree, protected. Wolves, coyotes, and foxes remain active atop the snowscape, their thick winter coats providing warmth.

While furry mammals deploy a variety of techniques for winter survival, beneath the ice-covered surfaces of rivers and lakes, trout and other species of fish move slowly and rest often, struggling to survive. Birds living year-round in Yellowstone deploy their own defensive strategies for conserving heat during the winter months. Some roost with their heads tucked into their thick rear feathers. Grouse spend winter nights burrowed beneath the snow for insulation. Many fish and birds do not survive the harshest of winter conditions during which temperatures drop to 50 degrees below Fahrenheit or lower.

Even as Yellowstone's diverse wildlife utilize a variety of methods to survive the harsh winter months, winter's reign in Wonderland is checked by an even more powerful force: extreme heat.

As shallow as two to three miles beneath Yellowstone's landscape and billions of years in the making, molten rock churns and roils. The hottest substance on planet Earth, magma ranges between about 1,300 and 2,400 degrees Fahrenheit. Radiating upward, heat from the magma, cooling slightly as it rises, is absorbed by solid rock. Still traveling upward, intense heat radiates from rocks and boils water in underground reservoirs. Superheated water in turn channels the quickening vertical ascension of water-borne energy through the cracks and tubes that connect the underground cauldrons to surface water above.

Emerging from this subterranean complex of magma, rock, water, and fissures is a dazzling display of thermal activity: geysers, hot springs, mudpots, and fumaroles (vents emitting volcanic gasses) numbering approximately fourteen thousand by current estimates. Within the vast area of Yellowstone's caldera—the underground volcanic perimeter wherein near-surface magma heats ground-level water above—thermal features generate micro domes of warmth, holding at bay the coldest of winter weather.

Here at the juncture of extreme fire and ice is a unique and magical sub-world shrouded, shifting, supernatural. Boiling water rockets skyward, geyser eruptions clothed in billowing steam. Falling back to Earth the once scalding droplets of moisture descend through colder air. Some splash back into the hot reservoir of water or upon nearby warm ground. But even in the gentlest of breezes many stray this way or that, tiny particles of liquids by the thousands freezing and sculpting nearby trees or brush, or the occasional bison, into ice-coated ghosts playing hide-and-seek in a cloud of steam. Within the dome of warmth near non-erupting hot springs, large ungulates sometimes seek refuge, a danger-filled landscape upon which a misstep risks scalding or death.

In seasonal time winter recedes, daylight gradually claiming more hours each day than nighttime. Day by day more energy-giving sunlight lingers upon the landscape. At lower elevations and ever so slowly snow and ice melt one drip at a time. Patches of green appear, a return of spring. Their hibernation period over, famished grizzlies, versatile omnivores, compete with wolves for winter-killed carcasses. Not picky in their quest for nutrients, the bears also dine on grasses, insects, and earthworms.

For mammals the cycle of new life arrives as mature females pregnant during the winter months now give birth. Buffalo and elk calves, quickly mobile following birth, frolic within the safety of the herd. Wolf and coyote pups as well as fox kits cautiously venture from their dens. Bear cubs, clumsy and playful, stay close to their protective mothers, climbing trees for fun or when danger approaches. Also in trees, bird chicks in nests and hollows hatch and grow, in their initially helpless condition fed

Deep in the heart of winter, Mammoth Hot Springs Lower Terrace is blanketed in heat and ice both. COPYRIGHT BRUCE GOURLEY

continuously by diligent parents. Down below in slowly warming rivers and lakes trout fingerlings emerge from eggs.

As the ice recedes, a watery landscape marks the return of warm weather. Downward and downward from mountains and in canyons waterfalls thunder and plunge and cascade, some driven by seasonal snowmelt, others flowing year-round. Meandering rivers and creeks spill over their banks. Rains darken skies and nourish life. Grasses, brush, and trees absorb life-giving sunlight. Other than for momentary snowstorms, the once vast whiteness retreats to recessed shadows and mountain peaks. Beginning in the low elevations and marching upward, wildflowers bloom in brilliant yellows, blues, pinks, reds, and purples. Geysers and hot springs display their splendor. With no two exactly alike, some exhibit a change in behavior during the wetness of spring and early summer. Shrouded in steam in the coolness of early morning, geysers on clear sunny days throw water upward or sideways in glorious displays. The sun's rays transform microbial-filled hot pools into rainbows of brilliant color.

Summer arrives, but it is short-lived upon this high mountain plateau. Ungulates graze almost constantly, packing into their bodies nutrients needed for the cycle of life in this challenging environment. Grizzlies, the most versatile of eaters, hunt, fish, scavenge, dig, or even browse for their food. From bison and elk to smaller game, wolves hunt widely, their summer prey more expansive than their winter diet of elk. Coyotes and foxes hunt small game and—alongside magpies—scavenge what they can, often opportunistically dining on winter kill carcasses, sometimes with grizzlies or wolves lurking nearby. From innate memory bison, feeding on lush grasses, traverse generational corridors through forests and meadows, over hills and across rivers. Rubbing against trees they shed their winter coats bit by bit, tufts of thick brown hair no longer needed. Otters swim and splash and sun. Fish feed voraciously. Birds of prey hunt fish and rodents. Ducks and Canada geese abound, and lesser numbers of pelicans, sandhill cranes, and trumpeter swans ply waterways and marshy regions.

A month or so after the summer solstice the sun, still near its zenith, bears down at its hottest. Depending on elevation, rain can become scarce. Brief thunderstorms bearing little moisture hurl lightning bolts from the heavens that sometimes ignite wildfires. Flowers slowly wilt. Some grasses and bushes fade into a dry sea of browns. Others transform into brilliant orange or red hues. Weeks pass. Bit by bit, nights grow cooler. From small rodents to grizzly bears, mammals eat continuously, storing up as many calories as possible. Wolf packs remain ever on the hunt. From young elk and bison to trout and berries and more, grizzlies forage on a smorgasbord of high-fat food.

A passing storm leaves behind a momentary crown of snow atop mountain peaks. As the weather cools, mammals begin growing thick seasonal coats. Mating season arrives. As if on cue and driven by a seasonal spike of testosterone, the rut begins. Bison and elk bulls become aggressive as they compete for the right to mate with cows. Bulky and forceful, male bison butt heads and throw their weight around. Crowned with pointed antlers and ever alert, mature and strong bull elk clash and crash head first with young challengers eager but less armored. Among bison and elk alike some bulls too old and weak to hold their own are forced off the battlefield for the first time. This is the beginning of the shadow years of their existence, a time increasingly alone and vulnerable to predators. But aging predators, too, are susceptible to aspiring claimants. The dethronement of an alpha wolf means banishment from the safety of the pack and a lonesome and dangerous journey in the unforgiving wilderness of the Yellowstone plateau.

In the fading sunlight of fall aspens undergo their own rapid transformation. Fluttering stands of green give way to shades of yellow that under the right fall conditions briefly peak in flaming brilliance. Sometimes within a week, bright yellow foliage transforms into rasping browns and grays, the leaves quickly stripped away by gusting winds. Snows grow more frequent, spanning from peaks to meadows. For a short while longer the sun's rays melt the whiteness, but all too soon the fading warmth of days becomes shorter and shorter. Soon, the cold can no longer be held back.

Upon mountains, in meadows, under trees, and apart from thermal basins the snow is here to stay. Winter in Yellowstone has returned.[2]

CHAPTER TWO

Volcanoes and Glaciers

A Landscape Sculpted by Fire and Ice

The glacial winter came on. The sky was again darkened, not with dust and ashes, but with snow which fell in glorious abundance, piling deeper, deeper, slipping from the overladen heights in booming avalanches, compacting into glaciers, that flowed over all the landscape, wiping off forests, grinding, sculpturing, fashioning the comparatively featureless lava beds into the beautiful rhythm of hill and dale and ranges of mountains we behold to-day; forming basins for lakes, channels for streams, new soils for forests, gardens, and meadows.
　　　　　　　　—JOHN MUIR, NATURALIST AND FOUNDER
　　　　　　　　　　　OF THE SIERRA CLUB, 1901[1]

IF THE STORY OF EARTH WERE SCALED INTO A PERIOD OF TWENTY-FOUR hours, humans entered the picture at approximately the last minute. The place that came to be known as Yellowstone National Park, on the other hand, has partially existed in some form for most of the planet's history. Although the mountains now comprising the Greater Yellowstone Ecosystem—some thirty-four hundred square miles of wilderness interspersed with urban areas and centered in and expanding far beyond the park—are geologically young, some of the rocks within the park's peaks and in nearby mountain ranges are among the oldest on Earth.

While time travel is often the stuff of futuristic science fiction, geology is, in a literal sense, the scientific window into our planet's past. Mountains in particular offer great insights into Earth's earliest days. From below the Earth's surface thrust upward by violent tectonic forces long ago, mountains laden with sub-surface rock strata contain some of Earth's oldest rock formations. A short distance south of Yellowstone National Park, the majestic peaks of Grand Teton National Park provide a glimpse into this ancient past.

Estimated to be approximately 4.6 billion years old, Earth, formed from dust and gas orbiting the sun, initially bore no resemblance to that of the present day. During an immense period of time from the planet's formation to about 541 million years ago, the Precambrian Period witnessed dramatic change in slow motion. For the first half-a-billion years or so—the Hadean Era—no life existed in a torrid environment of oceans of liquid rock, erupting volcanoes, lava flows, and meteor strikes within a poisonous atmosphere saturated with carbon dioxide.

In this hellish environment the planet slowly cooled. Earth's crust hardened and oceans evolved from atmospheric water vapor. Rocks formed, marking the beginning of geological history in the period known as the Archean Era, a span beginning about four billion years ago and lasting some 1.5 billion years. Roughly 3.8 billion years of age, the most ancient rocks in the Teton mountains are from the early Archean Era. They are among the oldest rocks on the planet, remnants of Earth's early solid crust that became the North American continent.

The Tetons' most ancient rocks, predating the emergence of life forms on Earth, took shape amid a planetary landscape of ongoing volcanic activity and toxic atmospheric conditions. In time, chemical-powered cells emerged in primordial seas, leading to the first terrestrial life form: single-celled microscopic bacteria about 3.4 billion years ago. Eventually these simple bacteria exhausted the supplies of toxic atmospheric chemicals. Seeking a new source of energy, they adapted to and harnessed the sun's power. Through photosynthesis they released oxygen into the ancient seas and hence into Earth's atmosphere.[2]

Today's mountainous regions of Yellowstone National Park's northernmost area between Mammoth and the western edge of the Lamar Valley contain Precambrian Period / Archean Era metamorphic rock. Some of the oldest rocks in the park, formed approximately 2.5 billion years ago, may be viewed along the Lamar Canyon immediately to the west of the Lamar Valley.[3]

Eventually, bacterial release of oxygen into the atmosphere by way of ancient seas kickstarted the final two billion years of the Precambrian Period. Enabled by climbing atmospheric oxygen levels, the emergence of expanding and abundant life forms marked the Proterozoic Era. Bacteria proliferated and diversified. Approximately 1.8 billion years ago eukaryotes emerged, simple life forms with cellular nuclei, including multicellular algae. In the last one hundred million years of the Precambrian Period the first known animals, soft-bodied sea-dwelling organisms, appeared in modern-day southern Australia.

Within a relatively short geological span, life mushroomed during the Paleozoic Era between 541 and 252 million years ago, a rapid proliferation sometimes referred to as an explosion of evolution. Adapting, expanding, and spreading throughout marine environments, life eventually migrated to land. First in the form of leafless plants and invertebrate animals, the latter similar to centipedes, life then progressed from air-breathing fish to the introduction of vertebrate amphibians. Next, some life forms evolved away from dependence upon watery environments for reproduction, leading to seed-bearing ferns and primitive reptiles reproducing by means of hard-shelled eggs. During this time landmasses drifted together, eventually forming the Pangea supercontinent, which over time fragmented. Pangea's breakup, in turn, formed the Atlantic Ocean and the Indian Ocean between approximately 180 to 140 million years ago. North America then separated from Europe some eighty million years ago.

Modern-day Yellowstone National Park bears witness to the Paleozoic Era in rock formations in the park's northwest and northeast corners, as well as in a few areas in the extreme south-central portion of the park, beginning immediately eastward of the South Entrance station.

In these ancient times life's rapidly increasing pace during the Mesozoic Era (approximately 237 to sixty-six million years ago) produced the dinosaurs as well as an abundance of marine animals, mammals, and flying animals, the latter including pterosaurs and birds, as well as a remarkable diversity of plant life. Subsequently the debris from a massive meteor impact in present-day Mexico blocked the atmosphere and reduced photosynthesis. It is widely believed this event led to the extinction of the dinosaurs. As in earlier periods of geological history, Yellowstone also contains evidence of the Mesozoic Era. In this instance, rock formations paralleling the age of the dinosaurs can be spotted in the park's extreme northwestern section to both the east and west of Mammoth, and the south-central region to the east of the South Entrance station.

Much more than mere rock formation, however, characterized present-day Yellowstone National Park during the ancient Paleozoic and Mesozoic periods. Some 550 million years ago a Paleozoic sea covered the park. Yellowstone's fossil record indicates that early invertebrates such as corals, bryozoans, brachiopods, trilobites, gastropods, and crinoids lived in the shallow sea waters. Studies indicate that a dozen or more ancient seas alternatively flooded and receded across the park region during the course of hundreds of millions of years. Land dinosaurs during the Paleozoic Era roamed in the broad vicinity of Yellowstone, leaving an extensive fossil record in present-day Montana and Wyoming. Fossils from the age of dinosaurs have been found in Yellowstone, including dinosaur bone fragments, dinosaur eggshells, turtle bones, and fish scales, teeth, and vertebrae.[4]

Following the period of recurring oceans and overlapping with the age of the dinosaurs, gradual mountain-building in successive phases of plate tectonics and faulting occurred in the relatively flat landscape of the Yellowstone area. Formed first in the present-day park, the Gallatin range to the west began uplifting about 150 million years ago, reaching its highest altitude approximately forty million years ago. As the Gallatin's peaks reached their high point, the Beartooth range along the park's northern perimeter took shape. Both mountain ranges formed as upthrusts lifted diversely aged rocks of the Precambrian to Mesozoic Eras upon one another in jumbled layers, exposing ancient strata. The latter stages of the Gallatins' upthrust and the parallel formation of the Beartooths took place during the larger formation of the whole of the Northern Rocky Mountains along a north-south axis.

As the landscape evolved, massive volcanic activity approximately fifty million years ago formed the Absaroka range in Yellowstone's eastern and southeastern sections. Absaroka volcanic rocks are visible today at Barronette Peak near Yellowstone's Northeast Entrance and along

An ancient petrified tree stands as testimony to Yellowstone's violent volcanic past. COPYRIGHT BRUCE GOURLEY

the roadway north of Dunraven Pass. Bunsen Peak near Mammoth is the eroded remains of an Absaroka volcano. Evidence of the Absaroka volcanic sequence is also preserved in petrified tree trunks on Specimen Ridge. One study of Specimen Ridge's exposed rocks identified twenty-seven distinct forest layers that left an imprint of petrified trees including chestnut, oak, sycamore, walnut, magnolia, and other warm-weather trees currently found in the southern United States.[5]

Several thousand feet of lava rock and ash covered Yellowstone following the cessation of the Absaroka volcanic activity approximately forty million years ago. At this juncture Yellowstone's perimeter as presently viewed began taking shape. Lofty mountain ranges encircled and marked the Yellowstone plateau. The interior, on the other hand, remained a land of fire. Covered in debris and drained by streams, active volcanoes dotted a gritty landscape bathed in a warm climate. During this era and farther to the southwest, a separate and highly active cluster of volcanoes emerged about 16.5 million years ago near the juncture of present-day Nevada, Oregon, and Idaho. For millions of years intense volcanic activity in Yellowstone and to the distant southwest occurred in tandem. In Yellowstone, major periods of volcanic activity took place about nine million years and 8.7 million years ago. Simultaneously during this era, plate tectonics slowly pushed the southernmost volcanic field across an expansive shallow magma field in a northeasterly direction toward Yellowstone. The movement of crust over magma created a series of calderas (cauldron-like craters left behind by the emptying of a magma chamber) over a five-hundred-mile-long trajectory beginning in southern Idaho and arriving in Yellowstone about 2.1 million years ago.[6]

The arrival and alignment of the shallow magma bed beneath mountainous Yellowstone ushered in the next phase of the park's geological sculpting. The newly arrived and vast shallow reservoir of magma, infused with explosive materials far more powerful than the previous Absaroka volcanic period, soon triggered a massive explosion. Occurring perhaps two million years ago, the volcanic explosion ejected material six thousand times greater than the 1980 Mount St. Helens eruption. Perhaps the largest volcanic eruption in Earth's history, the ancient event created a vast caldera in the park's central region. Over time the underground reservoir refilled, leading to a second major but smaller volcanic eruption atop the caldera some 1.3 million years ago. The process repeated itself yet again as a refilled magma chamber erupted for a third time, approximately 640,000 years ago, forming the current Yellowstone caldera, an area roughly thirty by forty-five miles in size. Some eighty much smaller eruptions followed, one taking place about 174,000 years ago and forming the West Thumb of Yellowstone Lake. This extended period of volcanic eruptions finally ceased about seventy thousand years ago, bringing an end to active lava flows in Yellowstone.[7]

Evidence of lava flows, primarily from the 640,000-year-old eruption, are visible today throughout much of the Yellowstone caldera. Rhyolite, the predominant type of hardened lava, is easily visible along the Firehole Canyon drive. Even more spectacular are ledges of basalt, a second type of hardened lava, lining the Grand Canyon of the Yellowstone near Tower Fall. Shaped like columns, bands of basalt hug the west side of the road immediately north of Tower Fall and are also visible across the canyon to the east.[8]

Following the major eruption of 640,000 years ago, Yellowstone gradually grew cooler in the absence of additional major volcanic events. Amid the cooling a major period of glaciation occurred, and the Bull Lake glaciers covered Yellowstone from about 160,000 to 151,000 years ago. Afterward a new cycle of warm weather, driven by renewed but smaller-scale volcanic activity, arrived upon the high mountain plateau.

Early Yellowstone photographer William Henry Jackson captured this 1871 image of columns of volcanic breccia (rock) near Tower Falls. LIBRARY OF CONGRESS, PRINTS & PHOTOGRAPHS DIVISION, LC-USZ62-61814

During this warm period the Grand Canyon of the Yellowstone River began forming as hydrothermal activity weakened the rhyolite, eventually reaching the present depth of twelve hundred feet approximately ten thousand years ago. As the Grand Canyon formed another cooling period arrived, triggering a new era of glaciers. The Pinedale Glaciation, forming between twenty-one thousand and fifteen thousand years ago, lasted until approximately thirteen thousand years ago.[9]

More is known about the Pinedale event than the prior glaciations. During the Pinedale Glaciation two massive icefields formed in the high mountains just beyond Yellowstone's perimeter, one to the southeast and one to the north. From the south a large glacier moved northward and eventually settled into the basin that is now Yellowstone Lake. From the north a second glacier flowed southward into the present-day Yellowstone and Lamar River valleys. Smaller glaciers traveled along the eastern and northwestern areas of the park. Eventually present-day Yellowstone Lake became a mountain of ice thousands of feet in height, and glaciers covered some 90 percent of the entire park. During the heart of this last ice age in Yellowstone only the western edge of the park remained ice free, along with perhaps a few of the park's highest peaks.

Yellowstone's landscape today bears witness to glaciations, the more recent Pinedale event most visible. As warm weather returned to the region and melted the Pinedale glaciers, the retreating ice masses left behind a reshaped landscape. Indentations scooped out by retreating glaciers formed valleys and lakes, including the Hayden Valley and the southern portion of Yellowstone Lake (the northern portion of Yellowstone Lake, by contrast, was formed by volcanic processes). Scooped out earth, in turn, formed mounds of soil and rock. Glacial kames, hills or mounds deposited by retreating glaciers, include the Porcupine Hills and Twin Buttes in Fountain Flats. Layered rock debris left in the wake of the glaciers, known as moraines, are visible today along the Madison River between the park's West Entrance and Seven Mile Bridge, as well as in the Lamar Valley. Glacial till, debris less formed than kames and moraines, is visible in the Hayden Valley. Glacier-transported large boulders, known as erratics, are visible in areas including Tower Fall, Canyon, and the Lamar Valley.[10]

Throughout the glacial era, Yellowstone's volcanic activity remained, albeit subdued. Today, buried molten rock, or magma, from Yellowstone's most recent volcanic eruptions of sixty thousand to seventy-five thousand years ago lurks mere miles beneath the surface of thermal areas within the caldera. Rainwater and snowmelt flows downward through fractures and faults into subterranean pools near rocks heated by the magma. The hot rocks superheat the water to at least 465 degrees Fahrenheit according to some studies, generating immense pressure. Rising to the surface through cracks, channels, and tubes, the boiling water either releases pressure gradually, resulting in a surface hot spring, or releases pressure suddenly, erupting as a geyser. Mudpots (hot springs with viscosity) and fumaroles (dry vents releasing steam) round out the four types of thermal features fed by Yellowstone's vast underground network of magma, heated rock, and heated water.

Due to the yet unsettled nature of the caldera, including frequent and typically minor earthquakes, Yellowstone's thermal basins, no two alike, remain in flux collectively and individually. While numbering in the thousands annually in modern times, most earthquakes do not visibly impact the park's hot springs and geysers. An exception, the 7.3-magnitude 1959 Hebgen Lake earthquake centered some twenty-five miles west of Yellowstone temporarily altered the activity of hundreds of hydrothermal features within the park. In the broader historical context, radiocarbon studies indicate that Yellowstone's largest thermal area, the Upper Geyser Basin, has witnessed continuous hydrothermal activity following the end of the Pinedale Glaciation to the present day.[11]

Bearing witness to the Earth's early years, the landscape of today's Yellowstone National Park was formed by extended and recurring episodes of intensive volcanic activity followed by alternating warm periods of lesser volcanic activity and cool periods of glaciation. In the latter stages of this three-billion-plus years, the park's landscape emerged in modern form: mountains rose, lava flows sculpted distinctive features, the Grand Canyon of the Yellowstone River took shape, glaciation carved out valleys and lakes, and thermal basins formed.

The retreat of glaciers and formation of thermal basins also heralded other changes. Previously and far from the Yellowstone plateau, the warming of Earth created an environment suitable to mammals, their numbers and diversity exploding following the extinction of dinosaurs. In this environment the mammalian tree gave rise to early prehumans around 4.5 million years ago. For millions of years thereafter through periods of warm and cold climates mammals evolved further, different species adapting to local climates. Eventually, the final retreat of large-scale glaciers from most of North America ushered in modern fauna and lured migratory mammals, including groups of hunter-gatherer humans, to the mysterious high mountain plateau that is Yellowstone.

To these early mammals and peoples of the Yellowstone region our attention now turns.

CHAPTER THREE

Indigenous Peoples

Yellowstone Prior to the Arrival of Euro-Americans

*Most visitors to the park have no idea that hunter-gatherers were an
integral part of this landscape for thousands of years.*
—DOUG MACDONALD, PROFESSOR OF
ANTHROPOLOGY, UNIVERSITY OF MONTANA[1]

EVOLVING YET INCOMPLETE, THE STORY OF THE ORIGINS AND EARLY
development of humanity in the Yellowstone region remains in flux.
Enabled by ever-advancing technology and methodologies, twenty-first
century archaeologists, researchers, DNA scientists, and data analysts
reach further and further backward in time in an ongoing quest to recon-
struct our ancient past. From data currently available an outline can be
sketched of an early human presence in the Yellowstone region. Future
advances in DNA analysis and additional archaeological discoveries will,
in time, expand and refine the historical recounting of a still murky past.

Millions of years after our human ancestors emerged in the tree of
life, modern humans migrated out of Africa about sixty thousand years
ago. From there they rapidly expanded across the planet, reaching North
America near present-day Austin, Texas, by about sixteen thousand years
ago, if not earlier. Some three thousand years later humans arrived on the
Yucatán Peninsula farther to the south. Within a few hundred years thereafter and far northward humans also arrived in proximity to modern-day
Livingston, Montana, at a site about seventy-five miles north of Yellowstone National Park. The skeletal remains of these early Paleo-Americans
("paleo" is Greek for "old" or "ancient") near Austin, Texas, on the Yucatán

Peninsula, and north of Yellowstone share DNA of a common Asiatic ancestor: an early American people group known as the Clovis culture. Early Western Hemisphere Paleoindian hunter-gatherers, Clovis peoples are the ancestors of modern Native peoples of the North, Central, and South Americas.[2]

Clovis-culture peoples, like other human groups across the planet prior to about twelve thousand years ago, roamed in search of sustenance. Fashioning sharp weapons they tracked and killed animals small and large alike. Armed with bifacial (two-sided), fluted (grooved) projectiles— Clovis points—they expanded across much of the Americas in search of food as the last ice age slowly receded. Perhaps the Clovis hunter-gatherer group who left evidence of their presence near Yellowstone some 12,700 years ago set foot somewhere in northern Yellowstone's lower-elevated landscape. Or maybe the ice and snow during North America's last ice age yet remained too daunting.

As the climate in modern-day Yellowstone continues warming, receding high-mountain snow-cover continually reveals additional archaeological evidence of early human activity in the park. From these ongoing discoveries the story of human presence in Yellowstone comes further into focus.

Based on what is presently known, by around eleven thousand years ago Clovis peoples were traveling across Yellowstone, evidenced by the dating of a Clovis point of that age made from Yellowstone obsidian. Volcanic rock with a glassy sheen, the hard black substance was obtained from Obsidian Cliff, an area between present-day Mammoth Hot Springs and Norris Geyser Basin. Recent archaeological finds reveal that Native peoples traveling in Yellowstone routinely harvested obsidian, crafting and sharpening the durable rock into powerful weapons known as Folsom points. A Yellowstone obsidian Folsom point dated at approximately 10,900 years ago, as well as many other artifacts dating from roughly eleven thousand to ten thousand years ago, have been found along the shores of Yellowstone Lake. Knapped with stone, obsidian Folsom points served both as a knife and a projectile. Prized for their high quality, Yellowstone obsidian Folsom points were useful for hunting elk and other large mammals in the Yellowstone region and became a staple of a large

Passing through the Dakota Plains, some early tourists to Yellowstone National Park encountered Indigenous peoples in fashion similar to this image captured in 1880 in Aberdeen, Dakota Territory. LIBRARY OF CONGRESS, PRINTS & PHOTOGRAPHS DIVISION, LC-DIG-DS-14181

North American trade network spanning distant people groups through-out the continent.[3]

In post-glaciated North America, early nomadic Native peoples encountered fauna and flora in transition. Other than in Alaska, mammoths and saber-toothed cats, unsuited for the warming climate and pressured by the growing presence of humans, declined and went extinct around ten thousand years ago. Fossils in ancient post-glaciated Yellowstone National Park include those of rodents, rabbits, bats, canids (the dog family), felids (the cat family), mustelids (the weasel family), bears, deer, elk, bison, reptiles, and birds, among others. Native peoples in the Yellowstone area responded to the decline of large game by altering their meat diets. An archaeological site on the shore of Yellowstone Lake dated to 9,350 years ago yielded Folsom points with traces of blood from large-to small-sized game animals including bison, bear, elk, deer, bighorn, and rabbit. Collectively, archaeological sites in the park dating from the period between ten thousand and four thousand years ago reveal evidence of a food diet consisting not only of animals, but also of vegetation such as camas, bitterroot, sunflower, sagebrush, wild onion, balsamroot, and more.[4]

Meanwhile, Alpine tundra, once common in Yellowstone, also declined in the warmer climate. In its stead whitebark pine forests emerged around eleven thousand years ago. At the same time, sediment-laden valleys, the rich soil deposited by retreating glaciers, transitioned to lush grasses and sagebrush, while aspens and firs emerged in rocky areas of the park. In time lodgepole pine forests replaced the whitebark pines, only to decline as Douglas firs spread across much of Yellowstone by about sixty-five hundred years ago. Still later lodgepoles made a comeback and are now the predominant tree in the park.[5]

Having discovered Yellowstone thousands of years prior to the arrival of Euro-Americans, nomadic Native Americans mined obsidian, fished, camped, and hunted, including on the shores of Yellowstone Lake. As the millennia passed the park's vegetation changed, evolving by about 5000 BCE into its current form. More large megafauna in North America became extinct, including the prehistoric bison native to the Yellowstone region, survived by the modern Plains bison that evolved into existence about 2500 BCE.

Long after these changes evidenced by archaeological discoveries, oral histories have placed the Salish people in Yellowstone about 1000 BCE. During this era the ancestors of many contemporary tribes—including Blackfeet, Coeur d'Alene, Nez Perce, Shoshone, Perce, and Bannock—traversed the park on established trails en route to hunting grounds. By about 500 CE Native peoples in the Yellowstone area and throughout the larger Rocky Mountain region transitioned to utilizing more advanced weaponry. Evidence of bow and arrow weaponry has been identified at large sheep traps in mountainous regions, as well as at bison corral-sites on the plains. Meanwhile, the oldest human remains recovered in the park, a woman buried alongside a dog near present-day Fishing Bridge, have been dated to approximately two thousand years ago.[6]

Much more is known about Native peoples of Yellowstone from the fifteenth through eighteenth centuries. Many of the Plateau Indian tribes continued traversing the park via long established ancestral trails. Some tribes associated with Yellowstone lived near the park: the Crow to the east, Blackfeet to the north, and Shoshone, Bannock, Utes, and others to the west. Some western Native Americans annually crossed the park on their way to hunt buffalo on the plains. Meanwhile, according to oral histories, Kiowa peoples arrived in the Yellowstone region around 1400 CE. One tribe, the Sheepeaters, or Tukudika, followed the migration of bighorns, adapted to high altitudes, and lived in Yellowstone. Bighorns provided both food and tools for the Sheepeaters.[7]

Among Native Americans obsidian remained popular for the fashioning of weapons and tools, as well as for purposes of trade. From mammals to fishes, Yellowstone also served as a source of food. Meanwhile, far away to the southwest as the Euro-American presence in North America expanded, some Native peoples obtained horses from the white newcomers, enabling rapid travel over the great distances comprising the vast American West. Crow peoples, having acquired horses, perhaps arrived in Yellowstone at this time, followed by the Lakota Sioux.[8]

Particularly intriguing to Native peoples were the hot springs and geysers, oddities of geography found nowhere else in North America. Archaeologists have identified some 150 tepee sites near geysers. Native peoples regularly visited the geyser basins, utilizing the thermal springs for medicinal, religious, and other purposes. The Shoshone soaked bighorn sheep horns in hot springs prior to crafting them into bows. Crows believed the thermal areas were home to benevolent spirits, while Native peoples at large perceived great spiritual power amid the geysers and hot springs. Thanks to years of painstaking research on the part of anthropologists Peter Nabokov and Lawrence Loendorf, a partial record of some of the names that Native peoples used in referring to present-day Yellowstone National Park has been recovered. The Crow alternatively referred to the park as the "land of the burning ground" or "land of vapors." They referred to geysers as "Bide-Mahpe" (translated "sacred or powerful water"). Yellowstone's steaming landscape was described as "smoke from the ground" by the Flatheads and "many smoke" by the Blackfeet. To the Crow Yellowstone was "the place of hot water." The Bannocks certainly knew of the thermal regions, but simply referred to the park as "buffalo country."[9]

Early Native peoples frequently visited present-day Yellowstone National Park. According to oral tradition, the Crow people alternatively referred to the park as the "land of the burning ground" or "land of vapors." Geysers, such as Lower Geyser Basin's White Dome Geyser pictured here, were "Bide-Mahpe," translated as "sacred water" or "powerful water." COPYRIGHT BRUCE GOURLEY

Altogether some twenty-six modern-day tribes trace ancestral connections to Yellowstone National Park. Addressing the big picture of Indigenous peoples' presence within the park since the era of mammoths and mastodons, Yellowstone anthropologist Doug MacDonald says, "The big myth about Yellowstone is that it's a pristine wilderness untouched by humanity. Native Americans were hunting and gathering here for at least 11,000 years."[10] Representative of larger biases among white Americans, however, park officials for many years, especially in the late nineteenth century, purposefully failed to adequately honor or even acknowledge Native Americans' ancient historical presence in Yellowstone.

Conflicts between Native peoples and Euro-Americans long predated the establishment of Yellowstone as a national park in 1872. Euro-Americans, coveting Native lands and simultaneously fearing the otherness of Native peoples, utilized superior weaponry to subjugate

Indigenous communities. Over the course of nearly three centuries Euro-Americans' hostility toward Native Americans took the form of wars, genocide, removal of Indigenous peoples from their lands, and suppression of traditional beliefs. Simultaneously the newcomers transmitted deadly diseases among Natives who lacked immunity to European-borne illnesses. Their numbers greatly reduced by warfare and diseases and their traditional lands stripped away through treachery and violence, Native Americans by the late nineteenth century were largely and forcefully confined to less commercially desirable lands under the administration of the US government. Ironically, the original boundaries of the Crow Reservation, a vast expanse of some thirty million acres set apart in 1851, encompassed the eastern and northern portion of what became Yellowstone National Park.[11]

Yellowstone's establishment arrived near the culmination of this extended campaign of dehumanizing, slaughtering, and confining remaining Native peoples on remote western lands. The signing of the 1872 Yellowstone Act took place while some Native peoples yet lived peacefully on the shores of Yellowstone Lake and along the Yellowstone and Madison Rivers. But apart from remote Yellowstone, the 1874–75 Red River War in Texas against Southern Plains Indians and the 1876 Battle of Little Bighorn in Montana against Sioux and Cheyenne warriors signaled escalating efforts on the part of the US government to subdue and confine Native peoples. Following the defeat of the US Army at Little Bighorn, tensions and running skirmishes among western Indigenous peoples making last stands for their freedom against encroaching white settlements further heightened fear among white Americans. At the same time, Euro-Americans' near eradication of bison, the animal most vital to the Plains Indians' way of life, upended Native society and culture. Finally, the December 29, 1890, massacre by the US Army of 150 natives near the Pine Ridge reservation of South Dakota effectively broke remaining resistance to white power.[12]

Victorious in conquering Native peoples in the West, whites employed "tame" Indians from reservations to model tribal dress, customs, and dances before audiences of western railroad travelers, including vacationers, en route to Yellowstone. Many Euro-American visitors perceived Indigenous Americans as curiosities living on the margins of, yet detached from, an Americanized West. Although Native peoples frequented Yellowstone into the early twentieth century, some stories told by Euro-Americans falsely claimed Indigenous peoples historically avoided the park out of fear of geysers, hot springs, and other thermal features. Not until the 1990s did the National Park Service, led by researchers Nabokov and Loendorf, begin in large measure systematically incorporating cultural history into interpretive narratives, thereby finally embracing, preserving, and communicating Yellowstone's Native American heritage long lacking in written histories of the park.[13]

Now, through ethnographic, archaeological, and anthropological studies translated into interpretive displays throughout the park and books for sale in gift shops, today's park visitors can readily learn the story of Yellowstone National Park's first discoverers and inhabitants. But there is more.

"When people look at Yellowstone," anthropologist Doug MacDonald writes, "they should see a landscape rich with Native American history, not a pristine wilderness. They're driving on roads that were Native American trails. They're camping where people camped for thousands of years."[14]

CHAPTER FOUR

Adventurers, Explorers, and Visionaries

Incredible Stories of the Yellowstone Plateau

The largest of these wonderful fountains, projects a column of boiling water several feet in diameter, to the height of more than one hundred and fifty feet.
—WARREN ANGUS FERRIS, FUR TRAPPER, 1834

IN THE PRESENT-DAY CONTIGUOUS UNITED STATES OF AMERICA, EARLY European immigrants and their descendants by the eighteenth century pushed westward from the East Coast, eastward from the West Coast, northward from Mexico, and southward from Canada. While advancing without invitation into the homelands of Plains Indians, from fear of the wilderness and Native peoples they built protective forts. In this ever-constricting vise natives of the interior West, increasingly angry and hostile toward the invaders, struggled to maintain their thousands of years of freedom, culture, and traditions.

Deep within the interior West, ringed by mountains and rising high into the sky was the remarkable place of wonders that would one day become Yellowstone National Park. As destiny would have it, the Yellowstone plateau, long traversed and utilized by Native peoples, would become the last geographical holdout from white discovery, the final terra incognita on maps, the prize most dazzling but ever elusive as Euro-Americans for over a century ventured ever deeper into the western wilderness.

Fur-trading Frenchmen from Canada first approached the western mountains encircling the mysterious plateau. In search of pelts Frenchman Pierre Gaultier de La Vérendrye in the late 1730s ventured west of

Lake Superior onto the Canadian prairie. Searching for a rumored River of the West alleged to reach the Pacific Ocean, Vérendrye accompanied by his sons traveled westward and southward, in 1738 reaching Mandan country on the Upper Missouri River in present-day North Dakota. Continuing westward in 1742/43 sons Louis-Joseph and François left Fort La Reine and traveled up the Missouri as far as the Yellowstone River, becoming the first recorded white men to see the Rocky Mountains.[1]

More than five decades passed, however, until the first documented reference to the Yellowstone River, the massive waterway originating in the heart of the Yellowstone plateau. In the late spring of 1795 French explorer Juan Fotman visited and traded in Mandan/Hidatsa villages in the Dakotas. There he met a fellow Frenchman, by the last name of Menard, living among the Native peoples. Descending the Missouri River to St. Louis following his trade mission, Fotman met with Zénon Trudeau, lieutenant governor of Upper Louisiana (the present-day American Midwest). Trudeau recorded the interview, adding in writing Fotman's account of his conversation with "old" Menard. West of the Mandan villages there "was a beautiful river that had its source on the slope of a high cliff" in the "Rocky Mountains," Menard had confided to Fotman.[2]

One year later fur trader Jean Baptiste Truteau, working for the Missouri Company of St. Louis and also familiar with Menard, reported more information about the mysterious river. Truteau wrote that Menard spoke of a remote "large river, called the river of the Yellowstone, which is almost as broad and deep as the Missouri." Crows lived near the river's lower reaches, while "several other savage nations that are still unknown to us" dwelled "high up" in the mountains near the river's source. Truteau's telling is the first known written account of the name "Yellowstone."[3]

Also at this time another Frenchman traveling in the region referred to the river as the "Rock or Crow" River. Tying the two names together, the Minataree tribe described the mysterious river as "Mi tse a-da-zi," literally translated into French as "Roche Jaune" or "Pierre Jaune," and into English as "Rock Yellow River." In 1797 explorer and geographer David Thompson, an Englishman, referred to the river as "Yellow Stone," a phrase believed to indicate the towering yellow sandstone formations near the headwaters of the river. During the following decade, explorers Meriwether Lewis and

William Clark during their pathbreaking 1803–1806 expedition to the Pacific coast alternatively used the English and the French translations of "Yellow Stone." On their return eastward in 1806 in present-day Montana the expedition split up. Taking a more southern route, Clark's contingent reached the Yellowstone River some fifty miles north of present-day Yellowstone National Park and near the present town of Livingston. Clark followed the river to its confluence downstream with the Missouri River. Along the way Indians informed Clark that a great lake—Yellowstone Lake—existed at the headwaters of the river.[4]

Three years thereafter Clark added a notation to his expedition journal, a note pertaining to the Yellowstone plateau, and a quote of unknown origins and misleading claims. "At the head of this [Yellowstone] river the nativs [sic] give an account that there is frequently herd a loud noise, like Thunder, which makes the earth Tremble, they State that they seldom go there because their children Cannot sleep—and Conceive it possessed of spirits, who were averse that men Should be near them." In reality many Native Americans frequented the geyser basins, and at least some identified the thermal areas as home to good spirits. Even so, by the late nineteenth century Clark's spurious story of Native peoples' fear of the region would become part of white people's Yellowstone lore, a tale useful for soothing visitors' fears of Native peoples.[5]

Meanwhile, John Colter, a member of the Lewis and Clark Expedition, returned to the Yellowstone region in 1807–1808 to trade furs with regional Indian tribes. Colter failed to document his travels, leaving historians to work from unreliable secondary records in their efforts to piece together his possible route. Some historians conclude that Colter from the south crossed the Tetons northward into present-day Yellowstone National Park. Passing along the western shore of Yellowstone Lake, he followed the Yellowstone River to the Tower Fall area. From there he perhaps ventured eastward into the Lamar Valley and exited the park into the nearby Absaroka/Beartooth Mountains. Regardless of the accuracy of this possible route, it seems likely that Colter did wander into the park at some point, the first white man to do so.[6]

By this time fur trading had evolved into a major economic activity in the American West. In the early nineteenth century a proliferation

Fur trappers, gold seekers, and explorers in the Yellowstone region struggled to comprehend and verbalize the numerous and strange thermal wonders they witnessed. Boiling water and mud sometimes evoked comparisons to hell. COPYRIGHT BRUCE GOURLEY

of English fur trading companies increasingly gained market share from the French-Canadian North West Company. But the vast public appetite for beaver hats and coats came with a terrible price: decimated beaver populations on the Great Plains to the east and in the Pacific coastal region westward. Seeking new sources of beaver pelts, in growing numbers trappers ventured into the imposing Rocky Mountains. There they discovered the towering peaks and fertile valleys of the "Snake country," today known as Jackson Hole and home to Grand Teton National Park. From Jackson Hole some trappers ventured northward into present-day Yellowstone National Park, marking the beginning of five decades of an evolving, colorful, and fantastical discovery of the region by white men.

Handed down orally, some early stories of trappers' experiences in the Yellowstone region were eventually published after the fact as second-hand accounts, including the story of Canadian Donald McKenzie. A veteran of the fur trade, McKenzie was among the first to venture into

Yellowstone following Colter's trek. In the vicinity of "Snake country" McKenzie in 1819 found "Boiling fountains, having different degrees of temperature, were very numerous; one or two were so very hot as to boil meat. In other parts, among the rocks, hot and cold springs might alternately be seen within a hundred yards of each other, differing in their temperature." McKenzie observed that the thermal waters tasted like gunpowder, while the mineral-laden ground around the hot pools he deemed salt deposits.[7]

Five years later in 1824 a French-Canadian trapper, Baptiste Ducharme, from the north followed the Yellowstone River into the present-day park, trapping along the way. To his amazement Ducharme saw water shooting skyward. Two years afterward he returned, again witnessing the phenomenon. Still later a reflective Ducharme spoke of his journeys on the Yellowstone plateau, expressing an inability to accurately describe the strange sights he had witnessed.[8]

Adventurous Americans, too, advanced into the Yellowstone region. Jim Bridger, perhaps the most famous of fur trappers, visited the region multiple times from the early 1820s to about 1850. His colorful oral accounts eventually found their way into various publications. J. W. Gunnison, an early historian of the American West, mentioned Bridger in his 1852 history of the Mormons in Salt Lake, Utah, a town roughly three hundred miles southwest of Yellowstone. By this time Bridger had gained a widespread reputation as both a frontiersman and—earned or not—a teller of tall tales. Many who heard his stories of Yellowstone found his words riveting but beyond credibility.

"He [Bridger] gives a picture, most romantic and enticing, of the headwaters of the Yellowstone," Gunnison remarked of Bridger's Yellowstone stories. "A lake, sixty miles long, cold and pellucid, lies embosomed among high precipitous mountains. On the west side is a sloping plain, several miles wide, with clumps of trees and groves of pine. The ground resounds with the tread of horses. Geysers spout up seventy feet high, with a terrific, hissing noise, at regular intervals. Waterfalls are sparkling, leaping and thundering down the precipices, and collect in the pool below. The river issues from this lake, and for fifteen miles roars through the perpendicular canyon at the outlet. In this section are the 'Great Springs,' so hot that meat is readily cooked in them, and as they descend on the successive terraces, afford at length delightful baths. On the other side is an acid spring, which gushes out in a river torrent." Although an apt description of Yellowstone, Bridger's travels in and descriptions of the otherworldly Yellowstone region defied even learned men's boundaries of earthly knowledge.[9]

Many other trappers from around 1830 to about 1850 also told their own otherworldly tales of the Yellowstone region. The first known published account of thermal activity within the present park appeared in the September 27, 1827, edition of the *Philadelphia Gazette and Literary Register*, in the form of a letter from American trapper Daniel Potts. Along the southern border of Yellowstone Lake Potts described "a number of hot and boiling springs some of water and others of most beautiful fine clay and resembles that of a mush pot and throws its particles to the immense height of from twenty to thirty feet in height." Describing the northern area of the West Thumb Geyser Basin (an area today known as Potts Hot Spring Basin), the fur trapper observed that "The clay is white and pink and water appear fathomless as it appears to be entirely hollow underneath. There is also a number of places where the pure sulphor is sent forth in abundance one of our men visited one of these whilst taking his recreation at an instan [*sic*] made his escape when an explosion took place resembling that of thunder. During our stay in that quarter I heard it every day."[10]

As these and other amazing stories circulated orally among trappers and sometimes appeared in letters, in 1834 a clerk for the American Fur Company visited Yellowstone. While mapping the Rocky Mountain region, native New Yorker and surveyor Warren Angus Ferris took time off from his duties and set out to see the "astonishing" sights of Yellowstone asserted by "the united testimony of more than twenty men." Although prepared to be amazed, upon his first sight of Yellowstone's thermal springs Ferris wrote that he "might have exclaimed with the Queen of Sheba, when their full reality of dimensions and novelty burst upon my view, 'The half was not told me.'"[11]

Keeping a journal, Ferris recorded the most detailed description to that point of the park's geysers. In a large clearing on a fork of the

Madison River (likely the Upper Geyser Basin), from the ground "burst forth columns of water, of various dimensions, projected high in the air, accompanied by loud explosions, and sulphurous vapors, which were highly disagreeable to the smell," he noted. "The rock from which these springs burst forth, was calcareous, and probably extends some distance from them, beneath the soil. The largest of these wonderful fountains, projects a column of boiling water several feet in diameter, to the height of more than one hundred and fifty feet—in my opinion," he observed, the "explosions and discharges" occurring "at intervals of about two hours."[12]

As would untold thousands of visitors in distant decades yet to come, Ferris also discovered that beneath the majesty and beauty lay danger. He approached "near enough to put my hand into the water of its basin, but withdrew it instantly, for the heat of the water in this immense cauldron, was altogether too great for comfort, and the agitation of the water, the disagreeable effluvium continually exuding, and the hollow unearthly rumbling under the rock on which I stood, so ill accorded with my notions of personal safety, that I retreated back precipitately to a respectful distance."[13]

From a safe location Ferris then observed that the "diameter of the basin into which the water of the largest jet principally falls, and from the centre of which, through a hole in the rock of about nine or ten feet in diameter, the water spouts up as above related, may be about thirty feet." He continued, putting into clearer wording a basic description of geyser activity that had eluded some less-educated trappers. Nearby were "other smaller fountains that did not throw their waters up so high, but occurred at shorter intervals. In some instances, the volumes were projected obliquely upwards, and fell into the neighboring fountains or on the rock or prairie. But their ascent was generally perpendicular, falling in and about their own basins or apertures."[14]

In addition to offering the first accurate description of Yellowstone's geysers, Ferris made a second major contribution in the ongoing discovery of Yellowstone by Euro-Americans. In 1836 upon returning home he produced the first map of the region. Despite a lack of modern instrumentation, his map dimensions were essentially correct. A few other maps followed over the next two decades, including one in 1851 likely drawn by

Jesuit missionary Pierre-Jean De Smet drew this 1851 map of Indian reservations designated by the 1851 Fort Laramie Treaty. The western reaches of the Crow Reservation included the "headwaters of the Yellowstone River," encompassing a significant portion of present-day Yellowstone National Park. LIBRARY OF CONGRESS, GEOGRAPHY AND MAP DIVISION WASHINGTON, DC, G4050 1851 .S6

Jesuit missionary Pierre-Jean De Smet based on descriptions personally provided by Jim Bridger.[15] Ferris has also been credited by Yellowstone historian Aubrey Haines as the first tourist to the region, because his visit was curiosity rather than business.[16]

Meanwhile, as fur trappers decimated the Yellowstone region's beaver population by the late 1840s and subsequently abandoned the area, enough information in the form of trapper stories and maps existed to potentially arouse the public's interest in the exotic high mountain redoubt. But unfortunately, Americans' attention lay elsewhere—namely, in gold rushes, an Oregon Trail, and a Civil War.

Being far from population centers of any size and away from the common routes of travel, the Yellowstone region failed to capture the imagination of the public, fantastic stories notwithstanding. More pressing issues consumed newsprint and journals, many pertaining to the escalating tension over the Southern states' intransigence over their "peculiar institution" of "African slavery." Politicians assembled in the nation's capital struggled to navigate the rapidly growing abolitionist movement in the North and the uncompromising pro-slavery ideology of the South. Making matters all the more complex, many Northern banks were complicit in making loans for the purchase of slaves, while Northern industrialists and consumers benefited from the processing of Southern cotton into clothing. Largely financed by Northern capitalists, Southern slave labor in cotton fields powered most of the economic output of the South.

Meanwhile, waves of newly arrived European immigrants in northern urban centers placed pressure on eastern labor markets. Unable to compete with cheap immigrant labor, many whites migrated westward in search of new opportunities. Simultaneously in the South many poor white men, their labor of little value in the Southern slave economy, also migrated outward in search of jobs. Some joined Northern fortune-seekers rushing to western mining sites during the California Gold Strike. Others staked claims to western homesteads. But whether panning for gold in the mountains or breaking sod on the American prairie, most western transplants struggled merely to survive.

Even so, land rather than industry yet remained the leading indicator of prosperity. Clustered in the South along the banks of the Mississippi River in the Louisiana Delta and in the temperate South Carolina coastal lowlands were the nation's wealthiest counties. In these fertile environs massive plantations, forced labor camps in reality, each deployed hundreds to more than one thousand enslaved Blacks to plant, tend, and harvest cotton and rice. Working in punishing conditions from sunup to sundown, routinely beaten, and living in hovels with but little to eat, slaves enriched their owners with their stolen labor, many of those owners counted among the nation's wealthiest men. But like poor Southern whites displaced by slave-driven wealth inequality, the South's planters, too, sought new opportunities in the American West. Their plantation lands drained of nutrients from decades of cotton planting, they pressed Congress to allow slavery in newly created western states rich in unbroken soil, their demands clashing with Northern visions of western lands for free white settlers.

In the late 1850s it all came to a head, the clash between slave and free ideologies leading to bloodshed in the halls of Congress and on the western plains of Kansas and Nebraska territories vying for statehood. Escalating all the more, abolitionists' surging activism contrasted with judicial pro-slavery court decisions in the nation's capital, the impending and titanic political clash giving birth to the antislavery Republican Party. With neither side willing to stand down, in the bitter presidential election of 1860 a nation divided by Black slavery elected Republican Abraham Lincoln as president. Defiant of Lincoln's promise to thwart slavery's westward expansion, Southern slaveholding elites and their supporters refused to recognize the legitimacy of the man they derided as the "Black President." Determined at all costs to hold onto ill-gotten riches, South Carolina seceded from the United States and, alongside ten other Southern states, formed the Confederate States of America. Raising a military, the Confederacy in 1861 declared war on the United States, an act of full-blown treason.

Four years of battlefield carnage later the War of the Rebellion, as the American Civil War was officially called, came to an end in 1865. The Southern Confederacy lay in smoldering ruins, hundreds of thousands dead in both South and North, the last remaining slaves freed by the victorious United States.[17]

During the war some white men, North and South and including restless civilians and discharged or deserting soldiers alike, had trickled westward in search of gold in the interior West. Throughout the Rocky Mountains gold strikes proliferated, prospectors moving from one to the next in search of riches. In 1862 a large strike at Bannack, deep in the Rockies and some one hundred miles west of the Yellowstone plateau, attracted many prospectors. The riches dug out of the ground in Bannack led Congress to create Montana Territory in 1864. Christened as the first territorial capital, Bannack's gold assisted the Union's war against the Confederacy. But only briefly did the spotlight shine on Bannack, its veins of gold quickly thinning. Soon attention shifted eastward to a strike at Virginia City, a mere fifty miles from the Yellowstone plateau. Mushrooming in population, in 1865 Virginia City seized the title of territorial capital from Bannack.

Surrounded by mountains, heavily forested, crisscrossed with rivers, and covered with snow much of the year, Yellowstone posed many challenges for early visitors in pre-park days. COPYRIGHT BRUCE GOURLEY

As more and more men traversed valleys and crossed mountains in the vicinity of Yellowstone, a few ventured upon the mysterious plateau nearby, including Virginia native Walter W. DeLacy, a surveyor and engineer. Following several years of prospecting in the Pacific Northwest, in 1863 DeLacy briefly tried his hand in Virginia City. Ever restless, that summer he led a group of prospectors from Jackson Hole northward into Yellowstone. In their travels the party saw a number of geysers, including on the shore of Shoshone Lake. The following year upon the establishment of Montana Territory the federal government hired DeLacy to create the territory's first map. Completed in 1865, his map included the Yellowstone region, albeit in limited detail like many other maps both before and after him.[18]

Meanwhile, some forty miles north of present-day Yellowstone in a wide and fertile valley surrounded by mountains, the community of Bozeman, Montana, sprang up in 1864 as an agricultural and supply town for the gold miners of Virginia City. During the following year, indicative of a growing interest in the Yellowstone region beyond prospecting, a young, curious Jesuit priest serving near present-day Great Falls, Montana, came calling. Guided by Piegan Indians, Father Francis Xavier Kuppens gazed upon the Grand Canyon of the Yellowstone and stood awestruck at geysers along the Firehole River. Months later the priest related his experience to Acting Territorial Governor Thomas Francis Meagher, who suggested that if such a place of wonders truly did exist, it should be preserved as some kind of national park.[19]

Meagher, however, was not the first to envision a national park. To Pennsylvania native George Catlin, a lawyer turned painter of Native Americans of the West, belongs that distinction. In the early 1830s and long before public knowledge of the Yellowstone region, Catlin steamed up the Missouri River in the company of fur traders to the plains of present-day North Dakota. There he painted Assiniboine, Blackfoot, Crow, Plains Ojibwa, and Cree peoples. A man of foresight, at that early date he feared westward expansion would harm Native Americans, wildlife, and wilderness alike. In an 1832 letter Catlin envisioned a government-protected "magnificent park" of "pristine beauty and wilderness" in the West, "A nation's park, containing man and beast, in all the wild and freshness of their nature's beauty!" In Catlin's mind such a park would preserve horse-mounted Indians' way of life "amid the fleeting herds of elk and buffaloes," a romanticized image of Native peoples' existence.[20]

More than three decades after Catlin's epiphany the post–Civil War gold rush in the Rocky Mountains brought a semblance of civilization dreaded by the artist to within a few days' horseback ride of Yellowstone. From gold prospectors to general opportunists and the merely curious, Virginia City and Bozeman pulsed with restless men, their desire for adventure tempered but not altogether restrained amid rising tensions with Native peoples unappreciative of white newcomers exploiting their lands.

But there would be no stemming the growing Euro-American tide. In 1868 brothers Frederick and Philip Bottler, sensing an opportunity to profit off growing interest in Yellowstone despite tensions with Native peoples, settled in the Paradise Valley near the Yellowstone River some twenty miles north of the present-day park. Their Bottler Ranch became a popular base camp for prospecting, exploring, and, especially, hunting in Yellowstone. At the Bottler ranch and in saloons and other gathering places throughout southwest Montana Territory, gun-toting men spun braggadocious tales about Yellowstone, the area quickly becoming known both as a place of natural wonders and a vast reservoir of large game animals.[21]

Wonders and game, on the other hand, were secondary for prospectors. Men who seldom found riches, they nonetheless spun memorable yarns, some far different from priest Kuppen's account a few years prior and, apparently, more compelling. A description of Yellowstone published by a correspondent of the *Cincinnati Commercial* and subsequently reprinted in a number of other periodicals as distant as the *Weekly Trinity Journal* of Weaverville, California, originated, allegedly, with prospectors. Headlining Yellowstone as "The Valley and Pass of Hell" and drawing on dark imagery, the account described "grotesque cliffs" surrounding foreboding plains upon which "jets of bluish white flame" sailed upward in "endless turbinated convolutions." "One cannot help thinking that fiercest fires rage somewhere below ground," powering "volcanic action," the article intoned. Even so, the correspondent deemed "the geysers of Iceland" more impressive than those of Yellowstone, the latter the domain of "fearful desolation" and "nameless dread . . . teeming with diabolism . . . gloomy . . . darksome . . . under the jurisdiction of the Evil One."[22]

This rather dark article might have evolved from an earlier, fanciful account of a late summer exploration of the upper Yellowstone River by prospectors from Montana Territory's Bear Gulch and published in the August 31, 1867, edition of Virginia City's *Montana Post*. Embedded within a larger story under the headline "The Upper Yellowstone," the article declared of the prospectors' adventure, a party including a Mr. Hubbel: "For eight days they traveled thro' a volcanic country, emitting blue flames, living streams of molten brimstone . . . steam and blaze . . . constantly discharging from . . . subterranean channels . . . As far as the eye could trace." Through a landscape of "blue flame and smoke" they carefully walked in an "atmosphere . . . intensely suffocating" and void of life. "The prospectors have given it the significant name—Hell!" Thanks to "Providence" their "souls" were "delivered ... during their sojourn on the Yellowstone," and "they will never go there again."[23]

Two weeks later the *New York Herald* published a one-paragraph summary of the *Montana Post* story. Sensationally headlined "Hell on the Yellowstone River," the New York piece highlighted the "blue flame" and "living stream of molten brimstone," concluding with the prospectors declaring Yellowstone to be "Hell."[24] From there the story further evolved into the more elaborate and widely hellish articles of late 1867 and early 1868 that doubtlessly did little to endear the name "Yellowstone" in the minds of readers.

A second story about Yellowstone likewise offered but little in the way of truth, albeit with less dark imagery. Published widely in newspapers across America in late 1867 under the headline of "Niagara Eclipsed," the brief article, its contents evolving over time, compared the mysterious Lower Falls of the Yellowstone River to the well-known Niagara Falls of the East. Columbia, South Carolina's *Daily Phoenix* published an early version of the story, devoting one paragraph to "the falls of the Yellowstone, where it is said the whole volume of the river is precipitated over a precipice 1,600 feet high, and loses itself in a lake twenty-five or thirty miles in circumference, which contains an island of several hundred acres area, covered with boiling springs."[25] By the end of the year many articles under the same headline ran several paragraphs long, proclaiming the region "curious" and "monstrous." Some accounts portrayed the falls of the Yellowstone as plunging from a mountain "thousands of feet" high into a canyon far below.[26]

Meanwhile, neither ghoulish and outlandish stories nor hostile Indians failed to dissuade the most curious of locals. Late in the summer of 1869 three men, remnants of a larger planned excursion that fell apart from fears, mounted their steeds in Diamond City, a mining town near Helena, Montana. With two pack horses in tow the trio departed for a six-week exploration of Yellowstone. Friends feared the three men would not come back alive.

Cautious but undeterred, the men, each with a unique skill set, would prove up to the adventure. Born in New Hampshire and raised in Maine, David E. Folsom was an expert woodsman and hunter as well as a trained surveyor. Migrating to Montana Territory in 1862, he tried his hand at mining and ranching, eventually moving to Diamond City to work with childhood friend Charles C. Cook. Also a Maine native, Cook upon arriving in Montana worked as a cattleman before becoming a business manager in Diamond City. Cook brought a businessman's eye, as well as enthusiasm and curiosity, to the expedition. Altogether different from friends Folsom and Cook, William Peterson, a native of Denmark and formerly a sailor, had traveled the farthest to reach Montana. Adaptable and strong, the sailor-turned-prospector was a veteran of frontier mining camps, an associate of both Folsom and Cook, and a master of horses and packing. Each with his own expertise, Folsom and Cook in particular were professionals in their own right, learned men of judgment and acumen in a land of few schools and books.[27]

From Diamond City on September 6 the three men passed through Bozeman and continued east to the Yellowstone River. Following the waterway southward into the present-day park, they encountered a friendly band of Sheepeaters, conversing "with them as well as their limited knowledge of English and ours of pantomime would permit." Slowly traversing the wilderness they visited Tower Fall, stood awestruck before the Grand Canyon, and marveled at the Lower Falls. A "masterpiece of nature's handiwork" they deemed the deep, colorful canyon and massive, plunging falls far less than thousands of feet high, but nonetheless impressive. Farther southward along the river above the falls, the distant thundering of a cave (known now as Dragon's Mouth Spring) drew their attention, the sound "like the discharge of a blast underground," the sight of mud raging to and fro amid veils of steam eliciting great wonder. Following the river upstream to Yellowstone Lake, "a beautiful sheet of water," they skirted the shoreline to present West Thumb Geyser Basin, exploring the thermals at length.[28]

Turning westward, the adventurers topped a rise and looked back at Yellowstone Lake, an "inland sea, its crystal waves dancing and sparkling in the sunlight, as if laughing with joy for their wild freedom." Rather than the dark themes emphasized by Mr. Hubbel's prospecting party two years earlier, Folsom and Cook perceived Yellowstone as attractive and enticing. "It is a scene of transcendent beauty, which has been viewed by but few white men; and we felt glad to have looked upon it before its primeval solitude should be broken by the crowds of pleasure-seekers which by no distant day will throng its shores," the men concluded.[29]

Continuing, they visited Shoshone Lake and, turning northward, came upon a place they recognized from descriptions of previous explorers. "Burnt Hole" and "Death Valley," they remembered hearing as descriptors of the thermal basins along the Firehole River, words they found misleading. Spending several days among the mesmerizing geysers and hot springs, they continued onward as the weather turned cooler. Returning home to Diamond City thirty-six days from their departure, to the relief of friends they were no worse for the wear. Having witnessed strange sights only a select few had previously seen, the trio came to understand why previous explorers' accounts had been dismissed as nothing but a "too-vivid imagination." But unlike some who earlier beheld Yellowstone's wonders, David Folsom and Charles Cook did not resort to outlandish imagery or hellish metaphors.[30]

Nor did they return to civilization eager to regale friends with tall tales over a pint of whiskey at the local saloon. More systematically than had prior explorers, Folsom and Cook journaled their experiences. Even so, fearing ridicule they remained reluctant to publicly discuss the strange things they had witnessed. Only upon persistent prodding did Folsom and Cook collaborate in producing a singular narrative for an inquisitive friend, "Mr. Clark." Recognizing the importance of the account, Clark suggested the two men submit the manuscript for publication. Rebuffed, Clark obtained permission to do so on their behalf. But reinforcing decades of disbelief about the Yellowstone region on the part of the eastern establishment, both *Scribner's Monthly* and *Harper's* magazines rejected the Folsom-Cook manuscript on the basis of having "a reputation that they could not risk with such unreliable material." Nonetheless, the following year in 1870 the Chicago-based *Western Monthly* magazine printed the article—albeit absent portions deemed too fantastical— the earliest published account of Yellowstone's wonders in a respectable journal.[31]

Meanwhile, lest he be branded a liar, Folsom shied from public speaking engagements. More comfortable in quiet conversation with learned men, he cautiously discussed his adventures with but few citizens of Helena, not the least of whom was Nathaniel P. Langford, a longtime friend and prominent man of some means. Folsom's level-headedness about the mysterious Yellowstone region, in turn, impressed Langford and led to a job in the surveyor's office in Helena. There Folsom worked with earlier Yellowstone explorer Walter W. DeLacy in updating and expanding the latter's 1865 map of the Yellowstone region. In addition, Folsom's account of Yellowstone and his suggestion that the region be set aside for public use intrigued Montana Territory's newly appointed surveyor general, General Henry D. Washburn, formerly a US congressman and a Union veteran of the Civil War.[32]

As David Folsom settled into his new job, America remained largely unaware of the incredible natural wonders yet hidden upon the high mountain plateau. But Langford—formerly a banker, then one of Montana's famed vigilantes, more recently the territorial collector of internal revenue, and now looking for a new opportunity to make money—and Washburn, two of Montana's most well-placed men, sensed opportunity. So, too, did friend and confidant Samuel T. Hauser, industrialist, developer, civil engineer, railroad man, president of the First National Bank of Helena, and future governor of Montana Territory. Together the three men mulled the undertaking of a more thorough, private exploration of Yellowstone in the summer of 1870. And together the three men also shared an interest in a new corporation with much promise: the Northern Pacific Railroad Company of St. Paul, Minnesota. Should the railroad be routed through Montana Territory, they stood to benefit.[33]

A previously moribund company, the Northern Pacific in 1870 received new life with financing from banking magnate Jay Cooke. Farmers, ranchers, and lumber mills on the Upper Plains and in the Northwest needed an efficient way to transport their produce, livestock, and timber to market. Cooke intended to profit from their needs. Selling government land grants along the route also promised good returns. And now, if some of Montana's leading men were to be believed, future tourist travel to the region promised yet another revenue stream.[34]

Seizing the initiative, Langford in the spring of 1870 ventured east to gin up support for a summer Yellowstone excursion. A visit to Jay Cooke's

Philadelphia home proved pivotal. Cooke was considering routing the Northern Pacific through Montana. Langford believed a reputable exploration of Yellowstone with attendant publicity could lay the foundation for a Northern Pacific monopoly of rail tourist traffic to the region. But it would be costly. Deeming the price well worth the opportunity, Cooke pulled out his checkbook. The two men shook hands and Langford returned to Montana to recruit a few more men of the right caliber.[35]

Intrigue. Capitalism. Politics. All swirled in the collective imagination of the large contingent of men who departed Helena, Montana, on August 17, 1870, on what became known as the Washburn-Langford-Doane Expedition. A proven leader, General Henry Washburn headed the party. Langford's deal with the Northern Pacific's Jay Cooke made the expedition possible. Lieutenant Gustavus C. Doane—a Civil War veteran assigned to Fort Ellis near Bozeman to deter Native Americans from resisting white encroachments—with a detachment of five soldiers, the contingent secured through Langford's political connections, was charged with protecting the explorers and making a report. Along with banker Samuel Hauser, other key figures included Cornelius Hedges, a Massachusetts-born and Harvard-schooled lawyer who would soon be named the territory's district attorney, and Truman C. Everts, until recently Montana Territory's assessor of internal revenue.[36]

Separated from his exploring party and lost deep in Yellowstone's wilderness for thirty-seven days, Truman C. Everts of the 1870 Washburn-Langford-Doane Expedition nearly starved to death prior to being rescued. He published the story of his dramatic ordeal in *Scribner's Monthly* and became famous. *DIARY OF THE WASHBURN EXPEDITION TO THE YELLOW-STONE AND FIREHOLE RIVERS IN THE YEAR 1870*, NATHANIEL PITT LANGFORD, 1905

Under Washburn's leadership and with Doane's protective military escort, the party systematically explored present-day Yellowstone National Park. They journeyed through the mysterious region not to gape in wonder—although that did happen on many occasions—but with the express purpose of analyzing the possibilities and crafting a public narrative advantageous to the Northern Pacific. With instruments in hand they scoured valleys, climbed mountains, measured waterfalls, and descended into the Grand Canyon. Among the Firehole's thermal basins they bestowed a fitting name upon a particular geyser that for decades had fascinated the few who witnessed it: Old Faithful Geyser, a name reflective of its consistent eruptions. Throughout their sojourn and amid an abundance of game they hunted at will, all the while fretting needlessly about hostile Indians who never materialized.

Numerous party members kept journals of varying extent. Foremost, Doane carefully chronicled the party's experiences in detail, including measurements and data of many of the park's wonders. A second diarist, Walter Trumbull, son of Senator Lyman Trumbull of Illinois and Montana Territory's assistant assessor of internal revenue, also chronicled his experiences. A man with an artistic bent, Trumbull supplemented his written account with sketches of select geysers and the Lower and Upper Falls of the Yellowstone River. Langford, among still others, kept a journal as well, an account that would not be published for another thirty-five years.[37]

Never had such a large, prominent, and politically connected group of men traversed the Yellowstone plateau, their party of learned men and soldiers equipped with plentiful provisions for safe passage through a dangerous region—albeit less hellish than some believed—of Earth. Unparalleled were their careful travels, observations, and analysis. Even so, weeks into their exploration something unexpected happened. As if the gods of fate had read the minds of the increasingly confident men, the wilderness swallowed one of their own.

One moment he was there, and then he was not.

Truman Everts simply disappeared.

Not that he nor his companions thought of it that way. In Yellowstone's forests the men had grown accustomed to occasional and momentary separation. For such instances they had contingencies in place, agreed-upon rendezvous locations. When night fell upon a lone Everts yet lost and fitfully sleeping apart from his companions, he and his separated companions anticipated a quick reunion.

But it was not to be. On the next day Everts's horse ran away, depriving him not only of transportation but also of blankets, guns, fishing tackle, and matches. With only the clothes on his back and several knives and a small opera glass in his pockets, he searched in vain for his companions, until dark arrived, a second night alone.

Days and nights passed, pine boughs serving as a crude bed. On the fourth day Everts, famished, discovered that thistle roots were edible, only to be treed by a mountain lion that seemed intent on eating him. The lion eventually left him alone, and the following day as he lay in hunger and despair he grabbed a small bird that wandered within his reach. Killing and plucking it, he ate it raw. One day he saw steam in the distance and made his way to a thermal basin. Lingering for days, he cooked roots in a small hot spring and slept amid the steam vents on thin, mineral-encrusted ground near hot springs, the warmth of his open shelter only partially deflecting a three-day snowstorm. Comfort remained elusive, his feet suffering frostbite and his hip scalded one night when the crust gave way to the hot water beneath.

Meanwhile, Everts's separated companions desperately searched for him, but to no avail. Eventually as the snows grew more frequent they continued on, but not before Henry Washburn fell sick from exposure, an illness from which he would die prematurely a few months thereafter. On to the Firehole thermal basins the somber party journeyed, examining the geysers, hot springs, and surrounding terrain prior to returning home to Helena in early October.

All alone, Everts eventually realized he could use his opera glass to start fire from sunlight, allowing for the welcome warmth of a campfire. Leaving the thermal basin he paced along the shore of Yellowstone Lake, finding an old camp left by his companions now long gone. There would be no rendezvous. Now the extent of his predicament fully realized, Everts from day to day wandered in the wilderness, subsisting on roots. Making matters worse, one windy night his campfire blew out of control, severely burning his left hand and starting a forest fire. Meanwhile, he broke his spectacles, his world now reduced to what little his poor vision could comprehend. Then the delusions set in, specters and voices traveling alongside him for weeks as he stumbled about, slowly starving and half frozen to death with winter setting in.[38]

Meanwhile, friends in Helena, saddened at Everts's death, offered a reward for his remains. "Yellowstone Jack" Baronett and George A. Pritchett, two hardy mountain men responding to the reward, on October 16 and deep in Yellowstone's wilderness encountered a delusional, frost-bitten, badly burned, incoherent fifty-pound shadow of a man. It was the thirty-seventh day of Everts's lostness.[39]

Rescued from what would have been sure death, Everts slowly recovered over a period of months. The following year he wrote an account of his harrowing survival. Published in *Scribner's Monthly*, "Thirty-Seven Days of Peril" chronicled Everts's truly hellish experience in Yellowstone. One newspaper reviewer, speaking in the plural, proclaimed Everts's story "the most intensely exciting narrative we have ever read."[40] Elkton, Maryland's *Cecil Whig* published a brief review on page one, praising Everts's narrative as "one of the most extraordinary bits of autobiography ever penned."[41] The *Chicago Tribune*, a bit more reserved but complimentary nonetheless, deemed the story "graphic . . . as a personal narrative and as a topographical and scientific record, it will richly repay perusal."[42]

Amazing though Everts's story was, in the public eye it was secondary to the headlines praising the successes of the Washburn Expedition. For this the *Helena Weekly Herald* claimed credit. In October 1870 the paper noted with approval "the extraordinary interest manifested throughout the country" of the "wonderful and awe-inspiring" region "located on the head-waters of the Yellowstone river. We have spared neither pains nor expense in giving the world descriptions of the great water falls, spouting geysers, mineral and boiling springs, sulphur mountains, mud volcanoes, and other great natural curiosities that numerously abound in the Yellowstone country." The *Herald*'s editor crowed that his paper's Washburn articles had "been largely copied by the press, and have furnished the basis of numerous and extensive leading editorials. Our drawer is full of these articles clipped from our exchanges."[43]

From his surveyor's office in Helena, David Folsom must have smiled. The doubters were no more.

Finally capturing the public's imagination, the mysterious Yellowstone region, minus hellish imagery, seemed pleasantly exotic, and real. But just as Folsom had learned months earlier, published words went but so far: Bending the ear of the right people mattered the most. Folsom's story had inspired Nathaniel Langford, who in turn secured the financial backing of Jay Cooke that made the Washburn Expedition possible, and following the excursion embarked on an influential lecture series in the East. Credit, too, belonged to two other members of the party: Lieutenant Gustavus Doane, his detailed and meticulous record of the expedition, the most authoritative written account of Yellowstone thus far, soon landing in the right hands; and Walter Trumbull and Private Charles Moore, their meticulous sketches, the first reliable visual representations of Yellowstone's marvels, lending further credence to the fantastic verbal accounts of the Hayden party.[44]

Doane, for his part, sensed what lay ahead. Near the close of his remarkable written report published by Congress in early 1871, the lieutenant gave voice to the impending struggle between capitalists and preservationists for control of Yellowstone. "We saw many strange and wonderful phenomena, many things which would require volumes for adequate description, and which in future geography will be classed among the wonders of the earth," he noted. Railroads bearing tourists were inevitable, observed Doane, singling out not the nascent Northern Pacific, but rather a famed rail line that had partnered in the completion of the first transcontinental rail the previous summer near the Great Salt Lake. "The district will be in easy reach of travel if the Union Pacific Railroad comes by way of the lower Yellowstone Valley," Doane reasoned. "As a country for sight-seers, it is without parallel; as a field for scientific research, it promises great results; in the branches of geology, mineralogy, botany, zoology, and ornithology it is probably the greatest laboratory that nature furnishes on the surface of the globe."[45]

Meanwhile, amid the excitement and superlatives garnered by the Washburn Expedition, a second, unpublicized 1870 foray into Yellowstone quietly brought closure to the prospecting era and opened the door

LOWER FALL OF THE YELLOWSTONE.

ORIGINAL SKETCH.

Private Charles Moore, an amateur artist, accompanied the 1870 Washburn-Langford-Doane Expedition as part of a military escort. Moore sketched this image of the Lower Falls of the Yellowstone River, one of the earliest depictions of the famed waterfall. *DIARY OF THE WASHBURN EXPEDITION TO THE YELLOWSTONE AND FIREHOLE RIVERS IN THE YEAR 1870*, NATHANIEL PITT LANGFORD, 1905

of yet another opportunity for capitalists. From near present-day Livingston five local men—A. Bart Henderson (who first explored Yellowstone in 1866), James Gourley, Ed Hibbard, Adam "Horn" Miller, and a fifth man known only as "Dad"—ventured into Yellowstone not to see the region's famed marvels, but rather in search of gold, the West's most prized commodity. Although they would return empty-handed, as fate would have it they left their mark upon the park's history in other ways.

Descending into north central Yellowstone, between present-day Mammoth Hot Springs and Tower Junction they encountered, in the words of Henderson, "thousands of buffalo quietly grazing" in a place the prospectors named "Buffalo Plateau." Henderson also noted many "elk, blacktail deer, bear & moose." Farther eastward across the northern reaches of the park the men again found "plentiful" buffalo, elk, and bear. In the Lamar Valley they observed "a very singular butte, some 40 feet high, which has been formed by soda water. We gave the cone the name of Soda butte, & the creek the name of Soda Butte Creek."[46]

Then it happened. Wandering just outside of the present-day northeast boundary of Yellowstone in Montana's Beartooth Mountains, they found the object of their dreams: gold. Twice. First near Lake Abundance, and again near present-day Cooke City. But rather than stake a claim at either site, they continued onward in search of better pickings. It was not a good decision. A violent encounter with hostile Indians in the Lamar Valley (Arapaho, according to James Gourley), left the party horseless and without supplies. Fleeing northward out of Yellowstone and across the Beartooths they fought off wolves and yet more hostile Indians. Empty-handed, they eventually reached the safety of Fort Parker near present-day Livingston, Montana.[47]

Although neither successful nor headline-making, the Henderson Party, on the eve of Yellowstone's unveiling to the world, left a lasting imprint. Their sightings of bison, while somewhat exaggerated, provided an eyewitness account of the abundance of the great beast of which the Washburn Expedition a few months later saw only tracks. Although some thirty to sixty million had once roamed across North America, the Plains Bison by 1870 stood on the brink of near extinction, a victim of relentless hunting on the part of white men. Soon the once ubiquitous wild animal would be gone except for a few lurking in the wilds of the Yellowstone plateau.[48]

But that was not all. In time the area of their gold strikes, to which they returned and staked a claim in 1872, would be coveted by railroads and politicians determined to run a rail line through Yellowstone's Lamar Valley to reach valuable ores nearby. And finally, the Henderson Party's encounters with hostile Indians, quite different from the Cook-Folsom's encounter the prior year with peaceful Sheepeaters, furthered a growing and false narrative among white settlers in which all Indians in the region harbored evil intentions.[49]

Amid the swirling currents Congress and capitalists alike sought definitive proof of Yellowstone's assets. Having attended Langford's January 1871 Yellowstone lecture in Washington, Ferdinand V. Hayden, head of the US Geological Survey of the Territories, petitioned Congress for the funding of an official government survey of Yellowstone. He defined the survey's purpose as examining and mapping "all the beds, veins and other deposits of ores, coals and clays, marls [carbonate-rich muds], peats and other such mineral substances as well as the fossil remains of the various formations" and compiling "ample collections in geology, mineralogy, and paleontology to illustrate notes taken in the field." Congress readily acquiesced.[50]

Following months of preparation and from their base camp in Ogden, Utah—the Union Pacific rail terminus closest to Yellowstone—a large party of thirty-two men, scientists mostly but also a few politically connected individuals, departed northward on June 1, 1871, traveling through Virginia City to Fort Ellis east of Bozeman. Accompanying the first government-sponsored Yellowstone party were photographer William Henry Jackson and Philadelphia artist Thomas Moran, the latter's expenses paid by Jay Cooke's Northern Pacific Railroad.

From Fort Ellis and following essentially the same route as had the Washburn Expedition the year before, Hayden's party pressed eastward to the Yellowstone River and proceeded upriver. Entering Yellowstone via the Gardner River, in great detail they examined Mammoth's terraces, Tower Fall, Yellowstone River's Grand Canyon, and the river's Lower and Upper Falls. Farther upriver they examined nearby thermal basins, of the latter preparing "charts of all the Hot Springs groups, which were very numerous." A "systematic survey of the [Yellowstone] lake and its surroundings" followed, the surveyors working from the shore and "from the water in boats." From soundings "the greatest depth" of the lake "was found to be three hundred feet." The party also "sketched the entire shoreline with care."[51]

Westward in the "Fire-Hole Valley" Hayden's team "made careful charts of the Lower and Upper Geyser Basin," locating all the principal springs and determining their temperatures. Throughout the duration of the exploration, meanwhile, the botanists in the party had "great success" in collecting specimens. Photographer William H. Jackson "obtained nearly 400 negatives of the remarkable scenery." Jackson's assistant, Joshua Crissman of Bozeman, composed stereo views. With pencils in hand, artist Thomas Moran studied the Grand Canyon's "exquisite variety of color," declaring its "beautiful tints . . . beyond the reach of human artistry." Upon the completion of the expedition Moran set to work transferring and coloring his sketches on canvas.[52]

David Folsom's and Charles Cook's persuasive journal account. Lieutenant Doane's meticulous report. Trumbull's visual sketches. Langford's popular speaking tour. And now, the fruits of the government-funded Hayden Expedition: topographical surveys; maps and charts; measurements of lakes, waterfalls, and geysers; an abundance of botanical specimens; Jackson's astonishing photographs (Crissman never achieving widespread recognition); Moran's stunning canvases. Remaining vestiges of skepticism of the legendary region fell away in the face of all this irrefutable evidence. Yellowstone truly was a land of astonishing and unique wonders. Enterprising locals, regional authorities, opportunistic politicians, moneyed capitalists, intrigued scientists, and newly emergent conservation advocates found themselves in agreement: No greater display of nature's grandeur existed in the United States than that atop the plateau of the headwaters of the Yellowstone River. Each interest group with its respective and sometimes overlapping visions for the remote wilderness's future pondered proposals for protecting or developing—or a measure of both—the suddenly valuable region as a public park.

Photographer William Henry Jackson, accompanying the 1871 US Geological Survey of Yellowstone led by Ferdinand V. Hayden, captured this image of Mammoth Hot Springs. The surveying expedition was the first federally funded exploration of Yellowstone. Jackson's photographs helped convince Congress to establish the region as a national park the following year. "MAMMOTH HOT SPRINGS FROM THE SUMMIT OF JUPITER TERRACE," WILLIAM HENRY JACKSON, 1871. LIBRARY OF CONGRESS, PRINTS & PHOTOGRAPHS DIVISION, LC-DIG-PPMSCA-68723.

But what did "public park" mean? Originating in Europe, public parks typically took the form of cultivated, sculpted gardens created and maintained by the wealthy and to varying degrees accessible to ordinary citizens. How might the remote wilderness of Yellowstone be managed as a public park? Opinions varied. Conservationist advocates argued for preservation for the public good of Yellowstone's natural marvels. On the other hand, many local boosters as well as politicians in the nation's

Renowned artist Thomas Moran, also accompanying the 1871 US Geological Survey of Yellowstone, made many sketches of the park's scenery,
thereafter turning his images into dramatic paintings. Alongside Jackson's
photographs, Moran's work inspired the setting aside of Yellowstone as
a national park. Moran returned to Yellowstone in 1874, further expanding his portfolio of the park. The pictured painting—Moran's *The Grand
Canon, Yellowstone*—was produced circa 1875 as a chromolithograph by
Louis Prang & Co. of Boston. LIBRARY OF CONGRESS, PRINTS & PHOTOGRAPHS
DIVISION, LC-USZC4-3245

capital and ever-opportunistic capitalists, including the Northern Pacific's
Jay Cooke, envisioned a first-class tourist resort alongside Yellowstone's
remote wonders and connected by rail to eastern cities.[53]

It would take some maneuvering to achieve Cooke's vision. The magnate feared that Congress would likely respond to Hayden's report by setting aside the Yellowstone region as "a park, similar to that of the Great
Trees and other reservations in California," a reference to the Yosemite
state park, a nature preserve created in 1864 and distant from railroads.
"Would this conflict with our land grant, or interfere with us in any way?"
Cooke wondered, mindful of monetizing Yellowstone. "It is important to
do something speedily," Cooke declared on October 30, 1871, "or squatters and claimants will go in there [Yellowstone], and we can probably deal

much better with the government in any improvements we may desire to make for the benefit of our pleasure travel than with individuals."[54]

Knowing that time was of the essence, Cooke seized the reins. On November 9, 1871, as Truman Everts basked in his newfound fame in the pages of *Scribner's Monthly*, the railroad financier summoned Nathaniel Langford to Northern Pacific Railroad headquarters in Minnesota. Working in tandem with allies in the nation's capital, Cooke and Langford played a role, the extent not fully known due to a lack of documentation, in crafting legislation for the establishment of Yellowstone as the nation's first national park.[55]

Cooke and Langford's intrigues signaled the dawning of a new chapter in the story of Yellowstone, a place newly minted as "Wonderland." Billions of years in the making, thousands of years in the discovery, more recently dismissed as hell on Earth but now esteemed: As if by magic Yellowstone transcended special interests, ideologues, politicians, and capitalists.

Meanwhile, for a few more months only and beneath a deep winter's snow, the most remote and most interesting place in America remained largely undisturbed.

CHAPTER FIVE

Wonderland Besieged

Intrigue and Exploitation of Yellowstone's Wilderness

Our Government, having adopted it, should foster it and render it accessible to the people of all lands, who in future times will come in crowds to visit it.
—NATHANIEL LANGFORD, YNP SUPERINTENDENT, 1872

AS THE DISCOVERY PERIOD OF YELLOWSTONE NATIONAL PARK CAME TO an end, a decades-long conservation movement in America reached a critical point. Some historians point to an 1847 speech by Vermont US congressman George Perkins Marsh as the beginning of an intentional effort to conserve natural lands. Eastern forests and wildlife, rapidly disappearing in the face of urban growth and agricultural practices, concerned Marsh, who advocated for conservation as a tool of managing forest lands.[1]

Two years later the federal government established the United States Department of the Interior, charged in part with oversight of federal lands, particularly in the West. Concurrently in the 1850s "nature essays," literature extolling the benefits of wilderness, wildlife, and clean air in an age of crowded, polluted cities, came into vogue. At the forefront of the literary movement, Henry David Thoreau in 1854 published *Walden; or, Life in the Woods*, a series of essays about nature and life penned during his semi-isolation near Walden Pond. For years thereafter Marsh and Thoreau both remained leading advocates for preserving natural lands.

In the late 1850s painter Albert Bierstadt visited the Rocky Mountains and painted magnificent images of western scenery that captured the public imagination. Simultaneously the first major natural park in an American city—Central Park in New York—took shape, profoundly influencing the future development of landscape architecture in the United States. Thousands of miles away on the West Coast, the Yosemite Valley was transferred by Congress and President Abraham Lincoln in 1864 to the state of California for "public use, resort and recreation." The following year Frederick Law Olmsted, one of America's earliest landscape architects, published a report about the Yosemite Valley and the region's ancient trees, articulating a systematic rationale for preserving public landscapes. Natural lands, Olmsted argued, contributed to the well-being of humanity by enhancing psychological, physical, and social health.[2]

Against this backdrop and following the 1871 Hayden Survey of Yellowstone, US representative William H. Clagett of Deer Lodge, Montana, and US senator Samuel Clarke Pomeroy of Kansas introduced respective and complementary congressional bills to establish Yellowstone Park. The legislation came at an opportune moment not only in American history, but for men of certain persuasions. Natural landscapes mattered most to conservationists, natural resources to scientists, public opinion to politicians, and profit margins to capitalists. Many prominent Americans, particularly westerners—collectively and even individually ranging across the disciplinary and ideological landscape—waxed enthusiastically about the Yellowstone legislation.

A news dispatch from Washington summarized the excitement: "The Hon. N. P. Langford, of Montana, the leader of the famous Yellowstone expedition of 1870 and several scientific and literary gentlemen are engaged in an effort to have the Yellowstone region declared a National Park. The district, of which some features have been described in *Scribner's Monthly*, is said to be unadapted for agricultural, mining, or manufacturing purposes, and it is proposed to have its magnificent scenery, hot springs, geysers, and cataracts forever dedicated to public use as a grand national reservation. Congress is to be petitioned to this effect."[3]

Nathaniel Langford was not the only Montanan lobbying in the nation's capital. Walter Trumbull, Truman Everts, and Samuel Hauser, Langford's companions on the 1870 Washburn Expedition, lent considerable weight to the legislation vaguely invoking the primacy of "public use." But with ambiguity came angst from some quarters, including a newspaperman in Montana who feared the bill would enshrine Yellowstone as wilderness "and shut out for many years the travel that would seek that curious region if good roads were opened through it and hotels built therein. We regard the passage of the act as a great blow struck at the prosperity of the towns of Bozeman and Virginia City which might normally look for considerable travel to this section if it were thrown open to a curious but comfort loving public."[4]

Nonetheless, there is little indication that anyone involved in the legislative conversations actually anticipated that Yellowstone would be set aside in its entirely natural state and devoid of human intrusion. Rather, the questionable assessment of the region as unsuitable for mining in particular served as a sleight of hand to steer the focus to a newly emerging market envisioned by railroads: tourism. So, too, a determination of the region as unsuitable for human habitation effectively framed a future of human visitation, rather than occupation.

In addition to crafting the future of the proposed national park as a place for public visitation—thereby implying the necessity of an accommodative infrastructure from which capitalists and the government alike stood to benefit—Congress turned to the matter of park boundaries. In this respect the Hayden Expedition's recommendation of the setting aside of some two million acres roughly centered around Yellowstone Lake carried the day. Finally, a legislative precedent, the 1864 Yosemite Land Grant, served as a basic blueprint for establishing Yellowstone as a public park, albeit with a twist: Rather than granting land to a state—in the case of Yosemite, to California—Congress now proposed carving the nation's first federal park from territorial land not yet transitioned to statehood. In rapid fashion the bill passed both houses of Congress, and on March 1, 1872, President Ulysses S. Grant signed "An Act to set apart a certain Tract of Land lying near the Head-waters of the Yellowstone River as a public Park," the legislation creating what soon became formally known as Yellowstone National Park. Thus was born the world's first national park.[5]

Prohibiting "settlement, occupancy, or sale" of the land, the bill mandated that anyone attempting to "locate or settle upon or occupy"

Yellowstone National Park "be considered trespassers and removed therefrom." At the same time the park was "dedicated and set apart as a public park or pleasuring-ground for the benefit and enjoyment of the people," broad language similar to that of the Yosemite legislation and evoking ornamented European parks landscaped for the pleasure and recreation of visitors. Federal regulation of the park would be necessary to prevent exploitation by unscrupulous persons, yet the legislation placed no timetable for establishing laws governing the park, nor did the language of the bill offer clear-cut mandates.[6]

Eventually, or "as soon as possible" in the wording of the Act, "rules and regulations" were to be published by the secretary of the interior as "deemed necessary or proper for the care and management" of the new park. "Such regulations shall provide for the preservation, from injury or spoliation, of all timber, mineral deposits, natural curiosities, or wonders within said park, and their retention in their natural condition." The "preservation" of flora and geological formations in "their natural condition" seemed straightforward enough at that moment, although in time interpretive complications would arise. Management of fauna, on the other hand, remained vague in nature, a product of compromise among congressmen of varying sentiments who could only agree that future regulations "provide against the wanton destruction of the fish and game found within said park, and against their capture or destruction for the purposes of merchandise or profit." But what exactly did "wanton destruction" mean? Whatever the definition, future regulation should require that "all persons trespassing upon the same [fish and game] . . . be removed therefrom." At the same time, the legislation did not require, as it did for flora and geological formations, preservation of fauna and fish in their natural condition.[7]

As did capitalists and local territorial officials, US congressmen understood that in order for the public to "benefit" from the park, internal infrastructure would be required, necessitating to some degree a modification of the natural-wilderness landscape. Accordingly, the Act placed certain restrictions on the development of the park for tourism, empowering the interior secretary to "grant leases for building purposes for terms not exceeding ten years, of small parcels of ground . . . for the accommodation of visitors." All proceeds from the leases, in turn, were required to be used by Interior for oversight of the facilities "and the construction of roads and bridle-paths therein," language reflecting both a pre-automobile era and a general lack of interest in hiking on foot in a horse-centric transportation world.[8]

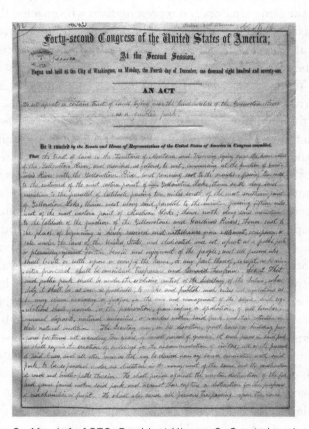

On March 1, 1872, President Ulysses S. Grant signed "An Act to set apart a certain tract of land lying near the headwaters of the Yellowstone River as a public park," thereby establishing the world's first national park. Today this act is referred to by the National Park Service as the "Yellowstone National Park Protection Act." US NATIONAL ARCHIVES

Although creating a rudimentary management framework, the Yellowstone Act failed to provide financial support for the park. At this point comparisons to the 1864 Yosemite Act diverged. Having deeded the Yosemite Valley and Mariposa Grove of redwoods to the state of California, Congress went about its business, requiring no federal funding for the state park. Eight years later in 1872 and with a Congress comprised of some of the same senators and representatives who enacted the Yosemite bill, legislators took a similar tack in declining to appropriate federal funding. But whereas California had assumed financial responsibility for Yosemite, neither federal nor territorial governments took fiscal responsibility for Yellowstone, thereby setting the stage for jurisdictional confusion and private exploitation of the nation's first federal "public park."[9]

Amid the funding vacuum many assumed that the Northern Pacific would soon follow through on plans to extend the company's rails through Montana and, presumably, develop a spur to Yellowstone, thereby stimulating tourist infrastructure within the park. Ironically, however, the timing could not have been worse. Jay Cooke & Company, the major financier of the railroad, leading corporate advocate of the Yellowstone Act, and already deep in debt from westward rail-expansion, ran into the stiff headwinds of a national economic depression in 1873 that would last for five years. Struggling to stay afloat, the railroad's expansion stalled at the Missouri River at Bismarck, Dakota Territory. Sinking into bankruptcy in September 1873, Jay Cooke & Company lost control of the railroad. Matters grew yet worse as the Northern Pacific succumbed to bankruptcy two years later. Not until late 1882 would the Northern Pacific under new ownership reach the town of Livingston, Montana Territory, some fifty miles north of the park's border.[10]

Meanwhile, upon setting aside the Yellowstone region as a national park in March 1872, the US government selected none other than Nathaniel Langford as the park's first superintendent, sans a salary. Neither park nor superintendent benefited from federal coffers. Nevertheless, the government provided funding for a second and much expanded Hayden Expedition in the summer of 1872.

Dividing the new survey into two parties, from the north one party traveled southward along a nearly completed private toll road between

Livingston and the park boundary. At Mammoth Hot Springs the expedition encountered a crude log hotel constructed the year before without federal permission, along with dozens of ailing visitors seeking healing in the mineral-laden hot water. Hotel and visitors alike attested to early interest in, and the capitalist possibilities of, the alleged therapeutic powers of Wonderland's thermal springs. Generally continuing southward the Hayden Expedition's northern party scaled mountains and trekked through forests, upon the former bestowing names of politicians helpful in the establishment of the park.[11]

Attaching himself to the southern Hayden party traveling along the Snake River northward into the park, Superintendent Langford set out for a personal inspection of the wonders of which he was now in charge. Along the way he climbed the imposing Grand Teton—perhaps reaching the pinnacle, perhaps not—prior to continuing on into Yellowstone, where the two survey groups converged at the Lower Geyser Basin. There the surveying began in earnest while Langford, gathering a collection of specimens, bade farewell to the scientists and other learned men. Angling northeastward, Langford and two companions visited the Falls of the Yellowstone prior to turning in a more northward direction and following an established trail over the Washburn Range before exiting the park.[12]

Nathaniel Langford's official report following his first of two visits to Yellowstone in his capacity as superintendent evidenced the challenges and opportunities inherent in administering a wild and remote Wonderland, a task he essentially left derelict after the 1872 inspection. The park remained "accessible only by means of saddle and pack trains, a mode of travel attended with many privations and inconveniences," he informed Congress. Expressing misplaced confidence that the railroads would reach the park within a "few years," he concluded that "until then it must be accommodated with good wagon-roads, or remain unvisited except by the few who are willing to endure the privation and exposure incident to horseback travel."[13]

Offering suggestions for road routes amid mountains and heavy timber, he noted his denial of road permits to private parties and his belief that it was of "the highest importance" that government construct roads "at an early day for the accommodation of tourists." Applications for hotel leases "at the leading points of interest" in the park were also piling up, he reported. Rejecting all petitions until the government appropriated funding for roads, Langford anticipated that the hotel leases would effectively reimburse the government's road expenditures. With disapproval the superintendent noted that squatters had settled within park boundaries prior to the March 1, 1872, congressional legislation, in some cases "making improvements for the convenience of visitors." The government should not extend leases to the enterprising individuals, but rather "acquire" their infrastructure when funding materialized, the superintendent recommended.[14]

As for the abundant wild game within federal boundaries, Langford declared that all "hunting, trapping and fishing ... except for purposes of recreation by visitors and tourists, or for use by actual residents of the park, should be prohibited under severe penalties," as should "cutting of timber ... except as prescribed by the superintendent." All too soon his vague pronouncements would be exploited by schemers stretching the recreational exemption for taking game and fish and testing the actual powers of early superintendents. In addition Langford "especially recommended" a strict law against "unextinguished" fires in the wilderness refuge, noting even then the problem of wildfires in the heavy forests ignited by campfires. Prescient, too, was his conclusion that harsh winters would effectively prescribe visitation from late April to early November, with the months of July, August, and September holding the most potential.[15]

Then at some length expounding in detail upon many of the marvels of the park, he concluded: "Nothing has been, nothing can be said, to magnify the wonders of this national pleasuring ground. It is all and more than all that it has been represented. In the catalogue of earthly wonders, it is the greatest, and must ever remain so ... here, the grandest, most wonderful, and most unique elements of nature are combined, seemingly to produce upon the most stupendous scale an exhibition unlike any other upon the globe. It should be sustained. Our Government, having adopted it, should foster it and render it accessible to the people of all lands, who in future times will come in crowds to visit it."[16]

Having placed into Congress's hands the initiative of developing Yellowstone, Langford essentially sat idly by in his personal office in Helena, seemingly content to give time for his favored railroad, the Northern Pacific, to reach the park. His only other visit to Yellowstone, a quick trip in 1874 to evict a contentious squatter doing business near Mammoth Hot Springs, comprised the sum of his direct involvement as superintendent.[17]

As Yellowstone's first superintendent largely ignored the park, however, the railroads he counted on staggered under debt and bankruptcies. In the absence of nearby rails, tourists in small numbers braved difficult travel conditions. From the west, tourists bound for Wonderland could ride the Union Pacific Railway only as far as Corinne, Utah, some fifty miles north of Salt Lake City. That was the easy part. Next came a four-day, dusty, bone-jarring, and uncomfortable stagecoach ride of more than four hundred miles to Virginia City, Montana. There the line ended for coaches, requiring tourists to secure horses or some other personal means to reach Wonderland, from the west along the Madison River. From the east, visitors disembarked the Northern Pacific Railroad at Bismarck in Dakota Territory, traveled more or less smoothly, if slowly, by steamboat for 834 miles up the Missouri River to Fort Benton, Montana, then boarded stagecoaches for the jarring journey south to either Bozeman (250 miles distant) or Virginia City (390 miles). By 1874 Bozeman became more attractive due to the option of securing a seat on the weekly Monday morning passenger-and-mail stagecoach to Mammoth Hot Springs.[18]

An estimated three hundred to five hundred hearty souls braved the journey each year during Nathaniel Langford's distant superintendency. Some lodged at "Horr and McCartney's Hotel" in Mammoth Hot Springs, a small, shabby, sod-covered log building of some thirty-five by twenty-five feet dimensionally. Ferdinand Hayden described the accommodations as "very primitive" with floor space only and no beds, while the British Lord Dunraven, venturing to Yellowstone in 1874 to hunt elk, deemed the lone hotel at Mammoth "the last outpost of civilization—that is, the last place where whiskey is sold." Near the hotel several enterprising individuals offered guide services to the geyser basins and sold simple souvenirs, immersing various objects, from horseshoe nails to baskets, in the mineral waters for several days to produce mineral-coated specimens. Many visitors came not to venture into the depths of the park, but rather to soak in the mineral waters. McCartney initially provided a "bath house" for such visitors in the form of a hole in the ground filled with diverted spring waters and enclosed within a tent, later a primitive log-structure.[19]

Apart from local dignitaries, government officials, military personnel, scientists, naturalists, and the occasional aristocratic visitor such as Lord Dunraven, many tourists in the park's earliest years exhibited few if any principles. Without inhibition visitors often shot animals and birds en masse, while souvenir hunters bit by bit dismembered the mineral casings of hot springs and geysers.

In 1875 Captain William Ludlow, Civil War veteran, accompanied by young scientists George Bird Grinnell and E. S. Dana, arrived in Mammoth via the Missouri River route to see the park's thermal wonders. With alarm Ludlow witnessed visitors armed "with shovel and axe, chopping and hacking and prying up great pieces" of mineral deposits in the thermal basins. Following his visit the officer wrote a forward-thinking report to Congress. A military presence was needed to put an end to the rampant lawlessness, he insisted. Yellowstone should be placed under the control of the War Department for the tasks of policing, "keeping meteorological and geyser records," marking park boundaries, improving roads and horse paths, and building bridges and other necessary improvements. Only upon satisfactorily establishing law, order, and sufficient infrastructure under War Department management would the park be ready for a return to civilian rule. Ludlow's pleas, however, fell on deaf ears. Not until eleven more years had passed would Ludlow's suggestions be heeded.[20]

Captain Ludlow's companion, George Bird Grinnell, the 1875 trip his second visit to Yellowstone (the first in 1870 prior to the creation of the park), departed Wonderland equally disturbed at the lawlessness he witnessed in the park. Emerging as a leading conservationist in America, in the 1880s Grinnell's voice as the newly christened editor of the popular outdoor magazine *Forest and Stream* would soon prove pivotal to Yellowstone's future.[21]

As Ludlow and Grinnell's Yellowstone experience weighed heavily upon those two conscientious men, Colonel Philetus W. Norris, Civil

Yellowstone's second superintendent (1877–1882), Philetus W. Norris inherited a park under siege. Despite minimal funding and lacking legal means to adequately protect Yellowstone from vandals and poachers, Norris served with distinction. His successes included early efforts to protect the park's wildlife, the beginnings of Yellowstone's double-loop road system, and detailed, official annual reports. Norris Geyser Basin is named in his honor. NPS PHOTO

War veteran and entrepreneur, visited Yellowstone the same year. Packing some one hundred empty specimen boxes, he journeyed through Bozeman into the park via Mammoth Hot Springs. Norris, like Grinnell, from curiosity had previously visited Yellowstone in 1870. This time Norris came representing the Smithsonian Museum, founded in 1846 "for the increase and diffusion of knowledge." Setting up camp in the park's geyser basins and filling his specimen boxes, Norris observed the frequent earthquake activity in Yellowstone and theorized (correctly) a relationship between earthquakes and geyser behavior. Departing the Upper Geyser Basin for the return to Mammoth, Norris opted to take a newly established and direct route northward to Norris Geyser Basin and Mammoth, a trail soon to be developed as a road.[22]

Evidencing the lasting pull that Yellowstone exercised on many who visited in the years prior to its establishment, a third 1870 visitor, Lieutenant Gustavus C. Doane, also returned in 1875. With a party of fellow Army officers, including US secretary of war General William W. Belknap, and enlisted men, his contingent of several dozen men came to hunt and fish. This time around Doane, absent the responsibilities of chronicling his travels and protecting civilians, visited the park in the more relaxed manner of a tourist. First-timer General W. E. Strong from Chicago, on the other hand, took it upon himself to chronicle the visit, his tourist journal among the earliest of thousands of written tourist accounts over the next half-century.[23]

Some men in the military party approached Yellowstone from the west via the Union Pacific, disembarking at Corrine, Utah. Thereupon the officers switched to a Concord stagecoach commanded by a "very drunk" and talkative "Jehu," as drivers were sometimes called. Riding next to the driver, Strong, with his companions "afloat on the great plains of Idaho" at "a killing pace," when not choking in "great clouds of dust" marveled at the natural beauty of the landscape. But later in the day following several changes of horses and on a high and narrow mountain pass, Strong glanced over and to his astonishment "saw the driver nodding, and the reins hanging loosely in his hands." The general "grasped the reins, and at the same time shook the fellow gently." Upon waking, the driver, expressing no concern, took back the reins. At the next stop another driver—sober—took the reins and steered his passengers safely through the night. Four hard days of riding passed before the party reached Virginia City. Following a brief visit in the mining town, they continued on to Bozeman and Fort Ellis prior to turning, with escorts from the fort and wary of Indians, south toward Yellowstone.[24]

A noon stop at the Bottler ranch introduced Strong to the brothers' mother, "a garrulous old woman," and their rough and tumble enterprise from which they eked out a living by servicing travelers and hunting game. A "mighty hunter," Strong said of Fred, the elder of the brothers and whose trophy heads and skins of "mountain sheep, elk, deer, bear and mountain lions" were "abundant." Continuing, the party joined Lieutenant Doane and his pack train later that day, and on the following day reached "Soda Mountain Springs," a common name at the time for Mammoth Hot Springs, "a great white mountain of soda." For nearly two weeks the men wandered in Yellowstone, Strong marveling at the geysers, waterfalls, and the Grand Canyon of the Yellowstone, the party collectively bagging adequate game for meals. Following their adventure, Strong turned his pen to a treatise of his observations concerning "The Game and Fish of the National Park."[25]

Five years earlier, "when Lieutenant Doane first entered the Yellowstone Basin, it was without doubt a country unsurpassed on this continent for big game," Strong noted. Elk, mountain sheep, deer, and grizzly and black bears "were numerous." But "since the fall of 1871" (following the Hayden Expedition) professional hunters—shameless, "merciless human vultures"—had indiscriminately "slaughtered" defenseless animals during the winter months "for their hides alone." Now, from Fort Ellis to Yellowstone Lake, Strong observed, few "elk, deer or mountain sheep" were visible "along the regular trail." Instead, "carcasses and branching antlers can be seen on every hillside and in every valley." Soon, "every elk, deer and mountain sheep will have been killed, or driven from the mountains and valleys of the National Park." If the government did not make efforts to prevent the "wanton destruction of the game and fish" within the park as mandated by the 1872 Yellowstone Act, soon "there would be none left to protect." The egregious offenders were well known, so,

Strong wondered, "How is it that the Commissioner of the Park allows this unlawful killing?"[26]

Nathaniel Langford, to be certain, had his reasons. Busy with his paying job, waiting for the financially strapped railroads to reach park boundaries, and with his entreaties for government funding ignored by Congress, a largely passive Superintendent Langford did little, his inaction leading to his removal in 1877. In Langford's place the Department of the Interior installed Philetus W. Norris, who two years earlier had collected Yellowstone specimens for the Smithsonian. Mere months into Norris's tenure and one year after the victory of Lakota, Northern Cheyenne, and Arapaho warriors over Lieutenant George Armstrong Custer's ill-equipped 7th Cavalry at the Little Big Horn in eastern Montana Territory, the new superintendent faced a unique crisis.

Angered by the devastating loss at Little Big Horn, the US Army determined to force remaining Native peoples onto reservations. The Nez Perce people, led by several chiefs, including Chief Joseph, resisted the Army's efforts. Fleeing toward freedom in Canada, en route they traveled through Yellowstone. From the west entering the park along the Madison River north of the present-day town of West Yellowstone, their presence in Yellowstone Park created no small sensation. Traversing through Yellowstone the Nez Perce, pursued by the Army, encountered some twenty-five tourists, taking several hostage and killing two.[27]

Outfoxing the Army for thirteen days in August 1877, the Nez Perce left the park by crossing over the Absaroka Mountains, passing by the present-day town of Red Lodge, Montana, and continuing northward. In far north-central Montana Territory, the Nez Perce approached the Canadian border with the Army close behind. Almost within sight of Canada and freedom they made a futile last stand, the exhausted braves no match for their heavily armed pursuers. Overpowered in the Battle of Bear Paw Mountain, most of the tribe surrendered, a few escaping to Canada. Chief Joseph, sensing the end of freedom for his people, made a decision. "From where the sun now stands, I will fight no more forever," he reportedly declared with resignation. Afterward survivors were relocated to Indian Territory in Oklahoma, a place the Nez Perce hated, which they called "the hot country." A singular and storied drama in the

HARPER'S WEEKLY.

DESECRATION OF OUR NATIONAL PARKS.
A scene that may be witnessed if the Yellowstone Park is leased to speculators.—[See Page 46.]

Following a decade of detached oversight on the part of Congress, Yellowstone National Park, exploited by commercial interests, teetered on the brink of collapse. Conservationists raised their voices in protest. This illustration by W. A. Rogers in the January 20, 1883, edition of *Harper's Weekly*—titled *Desecration of our national parks—A scene that may be witnessed if the Yellowstone Park is leased to speculators*—warned Americans of the park's problems. Note the stagecoaches, the closed gate to Yellowstone, and the sign over the gate. *HARPER'S WEEKLY*, VOL. 27 (1883 JAN. 20), P. 47. LIBRARY OF CONGRESS, PRINTS & PHOTOGRAPHS DIVISION, LC-USZ62-122812.

history of Yellowstone, the tragic flight and plight of the Nez Perce signaled a bitter future for all Plains Indians.[28]

Indian issues aside, Superintendent Norris struggled daily with a vexing problem: wanton vandalism in thermal areas and slaughtering of wildlife by visitors of little if any scruples. From a reluctant Congress in 1878 Norris secured $10,000 to fund his salary and for other expenses, a rather meager figure relative to managing such a vast domain, but a much-needed start nonetheless. Having opened the spigot of funding ever so slightly, thereafter Congress's financial commitment to the nation's first federal park would grow dramatically, if slowly, over time.

More immediately, however, the challenge of policing the park remained. In hopes of curtailing the worse of offenders, Norris in 1880 hired Harry Yount as Yellowstone's first gamekeeper. Previously a guide and hunter for multiple Hayden geological surveys and a savvy frontiersman, Yount would be a precursor to later park rangers. Even so, the veteran woodsman gave up a mere fourteen months into the job, declaring that no one man could adequately protect the park's wildlife. Instead Yount suggested that a "police force of men" be employed to better fulfill the task.[29]

While Norris tried to bring law and order to Yellowstone, a post office, the formal imprint and indicator of civilization, opened in the gateway town of Gardiner some five miles to the north of Mammoth Hot Springs. In tandem with the nearby post office came yet more signs of civilization: expanding wagon roads, the number of miles doubling more than twice over to some 150 miles during Norris's tenure. In similar fashion, horse trails doubled from some one hundred miles to two hundred. Alongside a post office and improved roads, too, came renewed attention from the long-sidelined and still distant Northern Pacific Railroad, of late having clawed its way back to solid financial footing and building west across Dakota and into Montana by 1881.

Few marvels apart from impressively frigid winters characterized eastern Montana, but the ambitious Northern Pacific from afar remained fixated on the wonders of Yellowstone. Accustomed to getting its way by greasing the palms of politicians, the powerful and well-connected corporation envisioned reaching deep into the heart of the park with a rail line delivering tourists directly to the geyser basins along Yellowstone's Firehole River. For this purpose the Northern Pacific quietly created a paper corporation, the Bozeman and National Park Railway. It was an audacious undertaking, and that was only the beginning. In addition to collecting fares from rail passengers, plans included the construction of hotels at strategic points in the park for lodging these passengers.

Made aware of the veiled plans, Superintendent Norris, perceived by some to favor the Union Pacific Railway slowly approaching Yellowstone from the west, criticized the Northern Pacific's attempted land grab, in turn angering Bozeman backers of the NPRR's scheme. Whether from his opposition to the railroad's plan or otherwise, Norris's tenure as park superintendent soon came to an end, whereupon he returned home (Michigan) to write a book and to spend much time investigating the prehistoric mounds of Ohio for the Smithsonian.[30]

Its clandestine Yellowstone plan exposed, the Northern Pacific Railroad did not give up easily. Political engineering secured the appointment of a new park superintendent presumably supportive of the corporation's ambitions: Patrick Conger, brother of US senator Omar D. Conger of Michigan, a supporter of the railroad.[31]

This was, after all, the Gilded Age, an era of corrupt industrialists, none more so than railroad barons and brazen politicians who from their seats of power raked in riches to the detriment of the working classes. Not even Wonderland could escape their greedy reach, it seemed. As the riches rolled in and the rails rolled ever westward, in the summer of 1882 the Northern Pacific's line reached Livingston, Montana, a town hastily founded in anticipation of the railroad's arrival. At the same time, Conger settled into his new office in Yellowstone some fifty-five miles to the south.

Recognizing the public and political impropriety of openly monopolizing Yellowstone, the Northern Pacific worked through yet another paper corporation, the innocent-sounding Yellowstone National Park Improvement Company (YNPIC). Principally owned by Carroll Hobart, a superintendent with the Northern Pacific Railroad, the YNPIC stood ready to help carry out the railroad's schemes within the park. So, too, did Secretary of the Interior Henry M. Teller, head of the government department overseeing Yellowstone. Dispensing with any pretense of impartiality or propriety, Teller the same year granted Hobart's YNPIC expansive rights to develop an astonishing forty-four hundred acres within Yellowstone to serve the needs of tourists. At Upper Geyser Basin (home of Old Faithful Geyser), Yellowstone Lake, the Grand Canyon of the Yellowstone, Mammoth Hot Springs, and other prime locations the YNPIC received exclusive permission without limits to construct buildings, provide tourist transportation, cut timber, and mine coal.[32]

Breathtaking in scope and clearly in violation of the spirit of the Yellowstone Act, the capitalistic land grab in Yellowstone opened a new and sordid era in the story of Yellowstone. For his part, Superintendent Conger upon his appointment found himself riding a whirlwind. Assessing the situation, he rightly perceived that Yellowstone remained unprepared for the large-scale tourist traffic envisioned by capitalists and politicians alike. Devoid of enforceable rules and regulations, lacking good roads, and served only by the crudest of visitor facilities, the park's visitor infrastructure remained far beneath that which discerning tourists expected. Under pressure to improve the situation, Conger set about further improving yet-rough wagon roads, constructing bridges, and trying to enforce the lax regulations under which the park was allegedly governed.[33]

Carroll Hobart and his Yellowstone National Park Improvement Company approved of Conger's efforts, the superintendent in turn praising Hobart's, and hence the Northern Pacific's, hasty construction of a hotel at Mammoth, the National Hotel. More troublesome to Conger, but initially unhindered, were the YNPIC's heavy logging of timber and indiscriminate slaughtering of wild game for tourists' meals. Amid the flurry of questionable activity in Yellowstone, the Northern Pacific in 1883 completed a spur from Livingston to three miles north of the park, constructing a depot at the small community of Cinnabar. The Northern Pacific's plan, it seemed, was well on track.[34]

Opposition, however, was mounting. It began when Senator George Vest from Missouri learned of the forty-four-hundred-acre monopoly of the Northern Pacific's Yellowstone National Park Improvement Company and alerted conservationists. Lieutenant General Philip Sheridan and George Bird Grinnell's *Forest and Stream* magazine responded, adding their considerable voices to a growing chorus of discontent echoing in the hallways of the nation's capital. Appealing to the White House for support, Sheridan persuaded President Chester A. Arthur to join him for a visit through Yellowstone during the summer of 1883, thereby impressing upon the president the necessity of preserving the park's wonders.[35]

Buttressed by a growing outcry public and political, key lawmakers demanding reform in Yellowstone convinced Congress to revoke YNPIC's overly generous lease and restrict future leases to a mere ten acres total for any one company, mandating construction of buildings at least a quarter of a mile distant from geysers or the Lower and Upper Falls of the Yellowstone. Park Superintendent Conger, noting the shifting winds, by late 1883 likewise positioned himself against Carroll Hobart's monopolistic practices, timber-cutting violations, and illegal harvesting of game.

Undaunted, the Yellowstone National Park Improvement Company continued building hotels and other tourist infrastructure and logging at will, much to the chagrin of Vest and his allies. A furious war of letters ensued, Conger and Hobart each pointing their fingers at the other's perceived infractions and petitioning their respective political allies in Washington. Momentarily, the Northern Pacific's Hobart prevailed when the secretary of the interior removed Conger in 1884, citing the superintendent's failure to properly manage the park. But quickly the tide turned. Training its attention on Hobart's shoddy business practices, Congress, led by Vest and influenced by conservationists' voices, soon terminated YNPIC's reduced lease, driving the company into bankruptcy in 1886.[36]

And so it happened that far from the nation's capital, America's first national park—vandalized by scavenging tourists, abused by scheming capitalists, contested by distant politicians, and lacking firm leadership—by 1884 stood upon the precipice of collapse due to human greed. An angry Congress in quick succession appointed two more superintendents—one incompetent and one too late with competence—both lasting for only a short time. Upon the subsequent collapse of the ill-fated Yellowstone National Park Improvement Company, a despairing Congress finally turned to the solution proposed by Captain William Ludlow a decade earlier: the appointment of the US Army as the guardian of Yellowstone.

But was it now too late? Could Wonderland yet be saved?

CHAPTER SIX

Wonderland Rescued

Establishing Law, Order, and Infrastructure in Yellowstone—the US Army Years

All sorts of worthless and disreputable characters are attracted here by the impunity afforded by the absence of law and courts of justice.
—CAPTAIN MOSES HARRIS, YNP ACTING
SUPERINTENDENT, 1886[1]

"WHEN I TOOK CONTROL I FOUND EVERYTHING IN CONFUSION," DAVID W. Wear, Yellowstone's last civilian superintendent of the nineteenth century, wrote of his arrival in the park in July 1885. His predecessor, Robert Carpenter, had held the office less than a year. Allied with the Northern Pacific Railroad's Yellowstone National Park Improvement Company (YNPIC), Carpenter had treated Wonderland as merely another place for capitalists to exploit, leading to his firing. In his wake dozens of crudely constructed commercial buildings sprawled across Wonderland, unsightly stains on the canvas of nature's masterpiece.[2]

It began innocently enough in Mammoth Hot Springs, the first of the park villages greeting most visitors. Here the park's singular hotel of stature, the National Hotel, welcomed tourists, a massive wooden structure 414 feet in length and fifty-four feet wide. From the outside it seemed inviting, an imposing edifice planted at the edge of a vast wilderness. Tended to by cooks, waiters, dish washers, chambermaids, launderers, porters, bell boys, scrub girls, a barkeeper, and an electrician collectively serving guests and maintaining the hotel's lobby, rooms, and restaurant, the National remained a work in progress on the inside, the interior in constant need of repair and far less than elegant. Worse still, danger lurked for unsuspecting guests tucked away in their beds, the ever-present combination of electricity, furnaces, and wood a combustible mixture. One night in July 1885 the laundry room caught fire and likely would have burned the National Hotel to the ground if a passing hunter had not spotted the flames.[3]

One visitor surely spoke for many in portraying park accommodations as "insufficient, unsuitable, and managed in such a way as to make it unfit for any but very strong persons to subject themselves to the discomfort and possible danger of occupying them." Behind the scenes, YNPIC conflicts with park management and Congress over leases dragged down prospects for facility improvements and led to the company's bankruptcy in early 1886. Yet ever resourceful, the Northern Pacific simply created yet another straw man corporation, the Yellowstone Park Association (YPA), to manage the National Hotel and a newly constructed, prefab hotel at Norris, the latter, according to Superintendent Wear, a "splendid new hotel building" one day's stagecoach ride from Mammoth.[4]

A new corporate title, however, meant but little functionally, the YPA like its predecessor taking liberties with its lease. A Department of the Interior inspector, following up on public complaints about park concessionaire facilities, criticized the YPA for constructing buildings over some forty acres in the Mammoth area—far more than the ten acres total legally allowed throughout the entire park—and for having built a crude "undressed pine slab" hotel in the Upper Geyser Basin too close to Old Faithful Geyser. Freely disregarding legal boundaries, the Northern Pacific remained as determined as ever to construct hotels at will and build rails to the geyser basins of the Firehole Valley.[5]

Yet this was but part of the corporation's planned monopoly of Wonderland. As the Interior inspector discovered, the Northern Pacific wanted much more than tourist revenue alone. Mesmerized by the lure of gold, that most valuable of commodities, the railroad was quietly working Washington's political levers for permission to lay rails not only to the geyser basins of the Firehole, but also across the Lamar Valley in the park's northern tier to Cooke City's gold mines first discovered by the Henderson party in 1870. A master stroke it would be for the Northern

Pacific, but a crushing blow for the people's park. "A railroad through the park would go far to destroy the beauty and besides it is not demanded by the public," the troubled Interior inspector lamented in his report.[6]

Nonetheless, amid the dark capitalistic intrigue Superintendent Wear reported favorably upon the expanding wagon road system—"no complaints having been made to me by anyone"—and offered a sunny assessment of wildlife, reporting "more game in the park now of every kind than was ever known before." In his mind Wear had managed the park well, his accomplishments greatly exceeding those of his predecessors. Among his many achievements, the superintendent also touted the prevention of "the wholesale slaughter of game that existed theretofore." Even so, partisan wrangling in Washington and a lack of funding for the care-taking of Yellowstone worked to his disfavor.[7]

Forced out of his position in only thirteen months, the superintendent offered a glowing assessment of his brief tenure: "I have endeavored to do my duty, and my whole duty, without favor or affection toward anyone. In my official capacity I have done nothing that I would not under similar circumstances, and have no apologies or excuses to offer for anything I have done." According to his defenders, Wear had reason to boast: He had taken his position seriously and been more effective than his two immediate predecessors. And he had accosted YPA manager Carroll Hobart over lease violations and sought to enforce campfire violations committed by tourists of high and low stature alike, even if his efforts had little teeth under the unwieldy and confusing laws in place within the park.[8]

To be fair, Wear's brief tenure fell during a time when federal law yet remained absent in the nation's first national park, by default necessitating the imposition of Wyoming territorial law within Yellowstone. Wear considered the arrangement "of very questionable validity," further enabling rampant lawlessness within the park. He implored Congress to immediately create "a [federal] court within and for Yellowstone Park" enforced by proper "officers" to protect and keep "the Park in a state of preservation beautiful to look upon."[9]

David W. Wear did not speak in a vacuum. A lawyer by profession and a two-term Missouri state senator, he had been chosen for the Yellowstone's superintendency by US senator George G. Vest of Missouri.

For years a major advocate of protecting the national park, Vest was among a growing cadre of prominent politicians allied with conservationists demanding change in Yellowstone's administrative structure. Yellowstone's notable friends spoke loudly and forcefully on behalf of the park, their campaign reinforced by Wear's inability to convince Congress to appropriate adequate funding for the park.[10]

Also frustrated, the Department of Interior turned a corner. Under the leadership of Lucius Q. C. Lamar—soon-to-be namesake of Yellowstone's Lamar Valley—the department on August 6, 1886, requested that the US Army assume control of Yellowstone, as first recommended by Captain William Ludlow following his 1875 visit to the park with conservationist George Bird Grinnell. The Army agreed, and to US commanding general Philip Sheridan fell the task of appointing Wonderland's new guardian. Slowly the news traveled from the nation's capital to the wilds of Yellowstone, eight days passing before Superintendent Wear received word. He did not seem at all disappointed.

As the shadows stretched long on the evening of August 17, Captain Moses Harris rode into Mammoth, Troop M of the First US Cavalry trailing behind him, officers and men dispatched from Montana's Fort Custer by order of Sheridan. Neither Harris nor Wear wasted time. Three days later, having quickly acclimated the captain to his new post, Wear resigned. Harris, commander of a fifty-man contingent, assumed "control of affairs in the Park" in the capacity of acting superintendent. Wear's last act followed as he, also a Civil War veteran and a colonel in rank, accompanied Captain Harris through the park as the new acting superintendent stationed soldiers at key tourist areas: Norris Geyser Basin, Lower Geyser Basin, Upper Geyser Basin, the Grand Canyon, along the Madison River on the park's western boundary, and at Soda Butte in the Lamar Valley. Finally, on August 20, 1886, and more than a decade after first proposed, the US Army at Mammoth's Camp Sheridan (so named in honor of the general) now commanded the nation's besieged and despoiled national park.[11]

No mere tourists as had been visiting military men of the past, a highly visible, uniformed, armed, and stationed Troop M commanded immediate respect in Wonderland. On August 21 Captain Harris issued his first order, announcing the "practice of turning stock loose to graze in

In 1886 Congress, pressed by conservationists, turned Yellowstone's administration over to the US Army. Establishing law and order in Wonderland, as the
park was also known by that time, proved challenging even for the Army. Initially
named Camp Sheridan, in 1891 and with the Army's status deemed permanent, park headquarters became known as Fort Yellowstone. In this 1893 image
captured by pioneering woman photographer Frances Benjamin Johnston, a
soldier in Yellowstone holds the reins of a woman's horse. An African-American
soldier stands nearby. A number of African-American soldiers served as "Buffalo Soldiers" in the 25th Infantry Regiment stationed at Fort Yellowstone. The
US Army remained in Yellowstone through 1918. LIBRARY OF CONGRESS, PRINTS &
PHOTOGRAPHS DIVISION, LC-USZ62-38275

the vicinity of the various objects of interest [i.e., hot springs and geysers]
in the National Park … will, from this date be discontinued." Next he
turned his attention to squatters in violation of previously unenforced
park regulations, serving two persons unlawfully squatting in Yellowstone
a notice to vacate. The order "promptly obeyed in both instances," Harris
ordered their illegal buildings "demolished and removed." For the "preservation of good order and property," the captain quickly expelled "a number of disreputable characters from the Park."[12]

A rash of fires, too, demanded the soldiers' attention. In the heavily timbered park, Harris believed, many fires had been intentionally set by "old frontiersmen, hunters and trappers" intent on driving game from within the park to waiting marksmen just outside the park's boundaries. Numerous Indians, too, frequented the area, Harris observed, "not particular whether they cross the line of the Park or not." That Yellowstone was a traditional hunting ground for Native peoples Harris may or may not have known, but he did convey suspicions that "unscrupulous white men" were inciting Indians to "hunt in the Park" by furnishing them with whiskey, thereby giving credence to a common and prejudiced troupe of white scoundrels taking advantage of gullible Native peoples, both groups being wandering ne'er-do-wells in a West yet in need of proper law, order, and decency.[13]

Far more detailed and precise in his initial report than had been former superintendent Wear mere months earlier, Harris echoed Wear in noting "an abundance of game." But unlike his predecessor, the captain explained the causation: Hunting pressures outside of park boundaries had driven wildlife in the region to seek shelter in Yellowstone, especially in remote areas "not frequented by ordinary tourists." While the movement of wildlife into the park may have happened, left unsaid was the reality, likely unknown by Harris, that Yellowstone had historically harbored much wildlife. Regardless, in Harris's assessment the national park, in the early years often described as a killing field for the illegal slaughtering of game, due to its remoteness had more recently become, despite inadequate oversight and enforcement of park laws, a sanctuary for wildlife wary of hunters.[14]

But no words of encouragement did Moses Harris offer about conditions in the geyser basins. "It may be said without exaggeration," he reported, "that not one of the notable geyser formations in the Park has escaped mutilation or defacement in some form." In addition, "efforts are constantly being made [by visitors] to destroy the geysers themselves by throwing into them sticks, logs of wood, and all sorts of obstructions." As a result, Harris bemoaned, some geysers no longer erupted, and in many instances heavy foot traffic upon "the silicious deposits ... surrounding the geysers will present the appearance of the worn pavement of a city street." If the park's "beautiful" thermal "objects" were to remain even partially intact, "watchful supervision, supported by the rigid enforcement of lawful penalties" would be necessary.[15]

Of the park's crude and limited road system, which at that point traversed southward to Norris Geyser Basin and continued to the geyser basins along the Firehole River, Harris envisioned the completion over time—should Congress appropriate enough funding—of what would become the park's iconic figure-eight layout, consisting of an upper and lower loop. For the moment, Harris deemed transportation within the park "adequate," although the "large number of irresponsible persons" illegally engaged in guiding tourists evidenced the need for enforcement of concessions laws. Hotel accommodations at large Harris pronounced "excellent," offering a counter-narrative to some visitor complaints. Among the numerous "operative"—and hence legitimate—tourist-service leases, the captain singled out the troublesome Yellowstone Park Association company, now steward of large hotels at Mammoth and Norris Geyser Basin, as well as smaller and cruder structures at the Lower Geyser Basin, Upper Geyser Basin, and the Grand Canyon of the Yellowstone River. Yet in each instance, the hotel structures and/or support buildings sprawled outside the company's leased land boundaries, a situation Harris determined to rectify through site surveys and forced compliance.[16]

Concluding his report of October 1886, Yellowstone's newly installed Army acting superintendent noted the uneven enforcement of laws in the park's past, as well as a lack of "applicable" regulations in the present. Implementation of "certain rules and regulations ... proper and necessary" and administered by federal law, he perceived as an immediate need. The task of compiling regulations he took upon himself. Clearly identifying Wonderland's peril and promise, Captain Moses Harris, having at his command enough manpower for law enforcement, pointed Yellowstone toward a more structured future. Little did he or anyone else realize how long the Army's presence would be needed to accomplish his vision.[17]

Hastily assembling simple wooden barracks offering but little protection from the cold, Troop M settled in for their first winter in Wonderland. The season's first snowstorm transformed the human presence on the Yellowstone plateau, driving tourists away but drawing hunters to the park's borders, where they camped out in wait for game migrating downward from the park's higher elevation. A game of cat and mouse ensued, soldiers shadowing hunters along vague borders not yet learned or even formally surveyed, arresting some offenders, chasing others off, and in disputable cases exercising caution. Upon the arrival of spring, the soldiers' attention shifted to policing infractions by the Yellowstone Park Association, demolishing unapproved buildings within park boundaries, repairing roads, and distributing copies of park rules and regulations to arriving tourists.[18]

They had their work cut out for them. In July 1887, Yellowstone's soldier-guardians investigated a stagecoach holdup and ejected a "large number of professional tramps and hard cases." During the same month the Norris hotel burned to the ground, the fire caused by a "defective chimney flue." Fortunately, no human injuries were sustained. At their strongest, three commissioned and sixty-four enlisted men, Troop M could do nothing to prevent the wooden hotel's rapid destruction by fire, but they did successfully extinguish a number of small forest fires during the summer season. Summer months consisted of many responsibilities: sorting out lease disputes; protecting wildlife from poachers (at a time when North America's wild bison teetered on the brink of extinction due to mass slaughter by hunters, Harris estimated no more than one hundred of the animals remained within the sanctuary of the park, although it was but a guess); guarding the geyser basins from vandals and picking up discarded trash, the latter "a labor of love on the park of the soldiers"; removing unregistered businessmen from the park; granting permits to approved new enterprises; and generally monitoring an evolving landscape of hotels, tourist shops, and guide services eagerly capitalizing on Wonderland's tourist traffic. Only when the snows of autumn arrived did the tourist season come to an end and the seasonal rhythm of policing Yellowstone begin anew.[19]

Near the end of the Army's first real summer season in 1887, eight buildings in total comprised a temporary encampment at Mammoth. Although Harris believed his time in Wonderland to be limited, in work and thought he nonetheless tended to the park's long-term interest. Ever perceptive, he offered insightful observations about the human-wildlife dynamic of Yellowstone. On the one hand, evolving rules and regulations based on the 1872 Yellowstone Act mandated protection of all wildlife in the park. Nonetheless, Harris observed that many "who profess interest in the Park" desired containment or eradication of "carnivorous animals" (although not named specifically by Harris, the roster of undesirable predators included wolves, coyotes, and mountain lions) for the protection of game animals such as elk and deer. The forward-thinking, acting superintendent also noted with approval a US Geological Society mapping project of the geyser basins with the goal of affixing permanent names to thermal features; advocated for "no extensive improvements" in the park beyond necessary roads, bridges, and bridle paths; and opined, of the park's geology, that "this 'wonderland' should for all time be kept as nearly as possible in its natural and primitive condition."[20]

If Harris's reasonable suggestions for protecting all of the park's fauna (with the possible exception of skunks, by the captain's own admission) and strictly preserving the park's geological wonders would have in fact been implemented, Yellowstone's history might well have unfolded differently. Instead, anti-predator sentiment within the Department of Interior soon ushered in a decades-long extermination program against wolves, coyotes, and mountain lions. In addition, visions of preserving intact the park's thermal wonders proved hard to implement and maintain as visitors insisted upon, and park personnel acquiesced to, the right to approach the very edges of hot springs and geysers. Imprudent tourists, when not under watchful eyes, frequently damaged the delicate thermals by tossing various objects into their waters and cavities, and by ripping pieces from the formations.

Nonetheless, from the time of the US Army's arrival in Yellowstone in 1886 to its departure in 1918, the soldier-guardians of Wonderland succeeded in protecting the park from the worst impulses of human greed and curiosity. In 1890, with the Army's assignment still open-ended, Congress provided funding for a permanent military outpost at Mammoth Hot Springs. During the following year Fort Yellowstone took shape in the form of four rows of buildings: headquarters and officers' quarters on the front row facing the parade ground and Mammoth Terrace beyond, barracks behind, stables in a third row, and non-commissioned officers' quarters in the rear and lower on the hill. In 1897, additional buildings were added to accommodate a second troop. A dozen years later beginning in 1909, seven large sandstone buildings, whose rock was quarried between Mammoth and the Gardner River, essentially put the finishing touches on a then-elegant wilderness military installation that remains in form, albeit not purpose, to the present day. At its height more than three hundred persons resided in Fort Yellowstone, including soldiers' families and some civilians. Currently utilized by the National Park Service, Fort Yellowstone's nearly three dozen remaining buildings comprise many of the edifices at today's Mammoth Hot Springs Village.[21]

Alongside ski patrols in the winter and summer's intense and diverse oversight responsibilities, life at Fort Yellowstone in time came to resemble that of a small, isolated mountain village. Families entertained guests in their homes. Children received education in a small schoolhouse from private tutors. Holidays featured parties and dancing. A gym and bowling alley provided entertainment all year long, and card games were common. Recreation in the form of skiing, sleighing, and ice skating marked the long winter season. Warm summer months welcomed by all featured many social events among families, most inevitably including food. While the Commissary provided a variety of basic food staples, horse-drawn wagons delivered fresh foods from a grocery store and meat market in nearby Gardiner. A village store sold a few novelties, while clothing and household supplies often arrived by mail order at the village post office.[22]

Fort Yellowstone's early years, however, were shadowed by an unrelenting battle in the nation's capital over the future of Wonderland. Year after year capitalist-minded US congressmen allied with railroad interests concocted variations of a thinly veiled scheme to lay rails into Wonderland to carry tourists to the geyser basins and transport gold from the Cooke City mines. And year after year equally powerful conservationist interests represented in Congress by US senator George Vest blocked those capitalists' efforts. Conversely, Vest routinely offered bills designed to better protect Wonderland from those who would do it harm, only to be sometimes thwarted by railroad lobbyists and their congressional allies. Through the prolonged stalemate, Grinnell's *Forest and Stream* magazine covered the ideological warfare between capitalists and preservationists, the latter ever so slowly winning the public's sentiment.[23]

Although the Army's presence in Yellowstone helped tip the balance toward preservation over exploitation, the political battle waged unabated. In 1887 railroad interests amended a protectionist bill by Vest to shrink Yellowstone's northern border and thus allow rails to be laid on the resulting private land in the Lamar Valley. Following several more years of railroad boosters' failing efforts to secure congressional approval to lay track in the park, in 1892 one rails-allied congressman called for the repeal of the 1872 Yellowstone Act. If passed, Yellowstone National Park would have been dissolved. Against the backdrop of such a scandalous prospect, the president of the Northern Pacific Railroad—the corporation that for years had funded efforts to lay tracks within Yellowstone—disavowed any further interest in freighting gold from the Cooke City mines across the Lamar Valley. Nevertheless, during the following year one last effort by the Northern Pacific, a proposal to run less-polluting electric trains into the park, fell short.[24]

While the conservationist community and other preservationist interests rallied Congress and slowly checked railroad monopolies in Yellowstone, the US Army began waging battle against capitalists of another kind: poachers. Acting Superintendent Harris had ratcheted up pressure on hunters in 1888, forbidding a common practice of transporting game killed near Yellowstone into the park, allegedly for use as meat in hotel dining rooms. During the same year, the Army approved Harris's request for additional manpower for poacher patrols. Although the captain was reassigned the following year, he established practices carried on by his successors, including vigilance against illegal harvesting of game animals despite a lack of congressional enforcement legislation.[25]

As had Harris, Captain George S. Anderson, appointed in 1891 as Yellowstone's third acting superintendent, struggled to prevent tourists from behaving badly. He expelled visitors found responsible for leaving burning campfires unattended, but many more went unidentified, and wildfires remained a problem. To prevent tourists from breaking off pieces of, or writing upon, thermal formations, he stationed soldiers at each main geyser basin, men charged with arresting persons caught in the act. Anderson personally tongue-lashed many offenders, ordered others to publicly scrub off their graffiti, and mandated expulsion for second offenses. But still tourists could not resist adding their names to the growing rosters of scribbled notes throughout the geyser basins. Exasperated, in 1892 Anderson ordered soldiers to remove all graffiti by chisel and hammer, thus lessening the temptation of future tourists to deface the thermal formations. It also allowed the park to start anew and somewhat virginal.

While policing careless and unscrupulous tourists perplexed the acting superintendent, poachers presented a far more maddening problem. By the early 1890s and following decades of massive slaughtering of wildlife in the West, the few remaining bison in America sheltered in Yellowstone, as did many other wildlife valued by hunters, including deer, beaver, and elk. No laws yet existed in Yellowstone for punishing poachers. Many taxidermists in towns within the vicinity of the park openly offered large sums of money for the heads of trophy animals, especially the nearly extinct bison, whose mounted head was worth a small fortune to certain wealthy collectors. For opportunistic locals disdainful of game preservation and in need of cash, poaching Yellowstone's wildlife offered great rewards with little downside.

To turn the tide Anderson beefed up his contingent of patrolling soldiers and hired as a scout a local civilian knowledgeable of poachers and their habits. In winter and summer alike soldiers patrolled throughout the park, paying particular attention to remote areas where poachers might be hiding. Upon catching an offender, however, the park's soldiers lacked jurisdiction to punish the perpetrator. On one occasion Anderson took it upon himself to imprison a repeat offender and add time by referring the matter to the Department of Interior. A month passed before orders were handed down to release the offender, Interior lacking any legal recourse otherwise. More commonly Anderson ordered patrolling soldiers to expel poachers from the park by marching them on foot over rough terrain for long distances, with the hope of generating a lasting impression. At the same time and evidencing inconsistencies in regard to game preservation, the Smithsonian was permitted to trap animals in the park for shipment to zoos, while stocking of lakes with fish, originating with Anderson's immediate predecessor, continued.[26]

A turning point in Yellowstone's history came with the capture of notorious poacher Ed Howell in the winter of 1894. At a time when American wild bison, numbering very few and sheltered in the park, were on the brink of extinction, Howell had been poaching the iconic beasts within park boundaries. The dramatic story of Howell's capture by Yellowstone's soldier guardians, published nationwide and accompanied by photographs, outraged Americans. Captured by Charles M. Gandy, this image—*Men Who Captured Poacher Ed Howell, Posed with 8 of the Confiscated Bison Heads*—helped galvanize Congress to quickly pass the Lacey Act, providing federal protections for Yellowstone's wildlife. Pictured left to right, in uniform, are: Dr. Charles M. Gandy (standing), Lieutenant John T. Nance, Captain George Lawson Scott, and Lieutenant Forsythe.
YELLOWSTONE NATIONAL PARK ARCHIVES, YELL 36953. PHOTOGRAPHER CHARLES M. GANDY.

Ever vigilant, America's conservationists, upon defeating the railroad lobby, turned more of their attention to the problem of poaching. Led by Senator Vest and *Forest and Stream* editor Grinnell, they publicly advocated for laws protecting Yellowstone's wildlife. And again, they set their crosshairs on Cooke City—or, more properly, poachers operating out of Cooke City. Park administration singled out a local citizen, E. E. Van Dyck, for having bison heads mounted by a Livingston taxidermist. Apprehended in the park, Dyck also had beaver pelts in his possession. Making an example of Dyck, Anderson temporarily confiscated the poacher's property and imprisoned him in the Fort Yellowstone guardhouse. But lacking the legal means to maintain his confinement, Anderson soon released Dyck. Several catches and releases of poachers thereafter, in March 1894 a soldier ski patrol under Captain G. L. Scott tracked suspected poacher Ed Howell, also of Cooke City. East of the Yellowstone River near Yellowstone Lake they observed Howell kill and remove the scalps of several bison. Daringly and unobserved by an armed and usually diligent Howell, the soldiers skied across open terrain and successfully arrested the poacher.

Resigned to the knowledge that Howell would merely be temporarily imprisoned and then released, the soldiers en route to Mammoth stumbled upon another winter game party of an entirely different composition.

Ever pressing to educate the public about Wonderland's endangered state, *Forest and Stream* magazine had funded a Yellowstone National Park Game Expedition in hopes of capturing poachers in the act. Among the party members were magazine correspondent Emerson Hough and photographer F. Jay Haynes, the "official park photographer" according to the Northern Pacific. T. E. "Billy" Hofer, backcountry expert and accomplished skier, guided the group. Journalist Hough got the story of a lifetime. Accompanied by Haynes's photographs, the resulting article in *Forest and Stream* inflamed conservationists, who demanded a resolution to Yellowstone's poaching problem. Amid the outrage editor Grinnell personally leaned on high-placed friends to make a compelling case to Congress for the passage of legislation protecting Yellowstone's wildlife. Two months after Howell's capture and under immense public pressure, Congress relented and passed the requested legislation. Deemed the Lacey Act, the legislation extended federal law with applicable penalties over all offenses within Yellowstone, including poaching.

Acting Superintendent Anderson called the Lacey Act "the most fortunate thing that ever happened to the Park." Even so, the legislation occurred too late to punish Ed Howell who, following a month of imprisonment in the guardhouse at Mammoth, was released, escorted out of the park, and warned never to return. But Howell, not taking his banishment seriously, returned to the park a few months later, where he was spotted in Mammoth by Anderson and arrested a second time. Initially the impetus for the Lacey Act, Howell fittingly became the first perpetrator prosecuted and convicted under the Act, serving a month in prison and paying a fine of $50.[27]

Now managing Yellowstone with the long arm of the law, Captain George S. Anderson in the years ahead slowly but steadily reduced the park's poaching problem. Arriving at a critical time, these federal regulations helped wildlife advocates—park personnel, conservationists, and politicians—with the important task of saving once numerous wild bison from extinction. So few were the great beasts by 1894 that the park, their last redoubt, became a laboratory in the years thereafter for not merely keeping the animals alive, but also expanding their gene pool to ensure long-term viability. By 1902, bison corrals were constructed near Fort Yellowstone and in the Pelican Valley, their presence believed necessary to better protect the animals from human poachers as well as harsh winters.

In time the artificial management of Yellowstone's bison, which continued for many decades, proved to be a great success story, as evidenced by the abundance of free-roaming wild bison in Yellowstone today. Nonetheless, the artificial management of the rest of Yellowstone's wildlife during the park's Army years generated additional long-term problems, including the feeding of bears at hotel garbage dumps and by tourists, the feeding of hay to elk, and extermination campaigns against cougars, wolves, and coyotes. Minus bison, Yellowstone's artificial management efforts into the 1960s focused not on preservation, but rather for the purpose of helping tourists view the animals they preferred to see.[28]

Rather than prioritizing preservation of the park's natural ecosystem, a concept not fully understood in the early twentieth century, the Army years witnessed the shaping of Yellowstone's wilderness into a suitable "pleasuring ground" for primarily wealthy tourists. Although heralded as the people's park, most Americans did not have the financial means to travel to Yellowstone. Nevertheless, travel within the park by stagecoach (the only wheeled mode of transportation, except for bicycles, until 1915) remained primitive compared to city life, a problem the Army, finally provided with adequate funding, tackled with gusto.

Originally envisioned by Nathaniel P. Langford, the park's first superintendent, the Grand Loop Road took true shape during Captain Anderson's tenure and under the direction of engineer Lieutenant Hiram Chittenden. In 1891 the road from Old Faithful to Yellowstone Lake opened, which completed a lower loop, the Lake-to-Canyon and Canyon-to-Norris stretches having been completed earlier. Spur roads near the Canyon's Lower and Upper Falls followed in the next several years. Major bridges, including over the Yellowstone River, and ongoing improvements to roads took much time and effort. By 1905 the final segment of the upper loop, the mountainous stretch between Canyon and Tower Junction over Mount Washburn, was in place but remained primitive. So rocky was the road over the top of Washburn that a park report in 1917, in which motorized vehicles completely replaced stagecoaches on the park's roads, declared it "very difficult for a large car to go up there at the present time and extremely hard on tires, as the road is practically covered for miles at a time with sharp stones."[29]

Nevertheless, the officers and soldiers who served in Wonderland from 1886 to 1918 effectively transformed an endangered, exploited park into a place of order, shaping the contours of modern-day Yellowstone. Under the Army's guardianship, the park's public ethos, modes of transportation, and unique lodging accommodations emerged and captured the imagination of America and the world, dramatically transforming the trajectory not only of Yellowstone, but other western national parks as well.

CHAPTER SEVEN

Nature's Greatest Show

Heavenly Marvels and Hungry Bears

Old Faithful is sprinkling star dust in the highways of heaven!
—A VISITOR TO YNP, 1884

FOR ALL THE NORTHERN PACIFIC RAILROAD'S CLANDESTINE AND ULTI-
mately failed efforts to exploit Yellowstone for monetary gain by plotting
to build rails to geyser basins and across the Lamar Valley, the corporation's creative marketing only succeeded in raising public awareness of the
park's natural marvels. Touting Yellowstone as "Wonderland," the Northern Pacific from the 1870s through the turn of the century envisioned
thousands of moneyed travelers experiencing Yellowstone's natural grandeur and mystical marvels. But with construction stalled at Bismarck in
Dakota Territory due to financial problems, the challenges of laying rails
to Wonderland were formidable.

Between Bismarck and Yellowstone National Park, a vast prairie
loomed, home to Indigenous peoples resistant to the land grabs and violence of white civilization. Predatory wildlife, too, frightened early settlers
and visitors. But with Euro-Americans holding the upper hand, changes
came fast. By the end of the decade remaining Native resistance in the
Upper Plains fell away under the withering and year-after-year fire of the
US Army, while hordes of hunters, whether for sport or profit, indiscriminately mowed down predators and ungulates alike.

In dire straits, the Northern Pacific turned to its last remaining asset:
the immense land holdings granted to the railway by the federal government. Unfortunately, buyers were few. Only by setting up a successful

model homestead and wheat farm on choice land and subsequently targeting wealthy American and European investors did the railway manage to procure sales of their best land holdings. Now gathering steam by cheerful, albeit deceptive marketing, the Northern Pacific touted all prairie lands as fertile, failing to adequately explain that remaining tracts—some owned by the railroad, others public lands upon which anyone could freely file a claim—were of much less quality.[1]

Again the sound of sledgehammers on spikes rang across the prairie. Mile after mile of new westward rails appeared, accompanied by renewed efforts to entice destitute American families and impoverished European immigrants to settle in those lonely hinterlands. Claim your fertile prairie land and start your life over, the missives enthused. It was simple. Sink your plow into the ground, work hard, and reap riches from a land of abundance. Here are the photographs to prove it.

And there they were, black and white images of an alleged, promising new world. The potential buyers saw docile Indians staring into the camera and settlers breaking the prairie with plows pulled by teams of horses. Ultimately, they saw a bountiful harvest of wheat with nary a sight of dangerous beasts.

Through the camera lens of Northern Pacific photographer F. Jay Haynes, Dakota shimmered with promise. This is what your new life could look like. Purchase land or file a claim for free acreage, compliments of Uncle Sam. For a fee the Northern Pacific would transport your family and belongings to your new home, and for a fee the railway would transport your future wheat crops to market in Minnesota.

And come they did, European immigrants especially, with many momentarily harvesting wheat in abundance. But soon the unusually wet springs and summers evaporated, mono-cultural farm practices drained the prairie soil of nutrients, and brutal winters year after year wore down the hardiest of souls. Root cellars and kitchens grew ever barer of food. Wheat shipments waned. Realizing the folly of their plight, many settlers quietly packed up and moved away.[2]

While transporting settlers westward and wheat eastward across Dakota Territory, the Northern Pacific dusted off Jay Cooke's decade-old vision of additional profits ripe for the picking in the nation's first national park. With Yellowstone again in its sight as the railway reached Montana Territory, the Northern Pacific reassigned Haynes to photograph the park in 1881, the photographer now charged with producing compelling images to captivate moneyed travelers. Marketed heavily by the railroad, Haynes's photographs of Yellowstone's geysers, waterfalls, and wildlife expanded public awareness of the park, heralding the beginning of a golden age of railroad advertising.

Serving railroad corporations' coffers well for decades thereafter, publicized photography, as well as artistic renderings of Wonderland's major attractions, lured many to the remote, strange place. Appropriating a popular novel—Lewis Carroll's *Alice in Wonderland*—the Northern Pacific distributed an illustrated brochure titled "Alice's Adventures in the New Wonderland." Fictionalized depictions of Yellowstone's bears, on the other hand, would much later characterize a major theme of the competing Union Pacific's marketing efforts, the renderings in time morphing into humanized, cartoonish images of friendly, playful creatures cute and cuddly. From the late nineteenth century until World War II and beyond, railroad posters, tour brochures, and other items portrayed Yellowstone through an evolving lens of public desires, moods, tastes, and trends.[3]

Having left the dry plains for the verdant sanctuary of Yellowstone, F. Jay Haynes soon settled in for the long haul, in 1883 successfully petitioning the Northern Pacific Railroad to designate him as "Yellowstone's official photographer," even though the railroad had no power to do so and could only designate him its own official photographer. A remarkable career of photographing Wonderland followed for Haynes, spanning nearly four decades until his death in 1921. Prolific and creative, Haynes composed and produced thousands of photographs of the park, selling his images in various formats to tourists through his popular and namesake Haynes Photo Shops. He also published numerous editions of the *Haynes Guide to Yellowstone*, books illustrated with beautiful photographs and popular with tourists.[4]

Hyped by the railroads, captured by Haynes's cameras, creatively rendered by artists, and gradually carving out a literary niche in newspapers and magazines throughout America and in England, images and stories of Yellowstone conveyed a Wonderland grander even than Europe's great cities and cathedrals. For travelers with disposable time and deep pockets, a new adventure awaited, nature's greatest show. Like moths lured by a flame, many could not resist! Well-heeled tourists by the thousands scrambled each year to make a once-in-a-lifetime pilgrimage to a shrine of nature unparalleled.

From America's eastern cities and Europe they came, tourists heading west and transferring to the Northern Pacific in St. Paul. In posh comfort, they rolled past Dakota wheat fields worked by weather-beaten settlers, the undulating and treeless landscape eventually giving way to much the same in eastern Montana Territory. After seeing mountains distantly first and then nearby, passengers switched trains at Livingston in breathless anticipation for the final leg. Following the Yellowstone River southward and disembarking near the park's northern border, weary but excited they boarded stagecoaches for the short ride into the park and a relaxing evening at Mammoth Hot Springs.

In Wonderland, they gawked at Mammoth's thermal terraces, stood speechless on the rim of the Grand Canyon of the Yellowstone at the Lower Falls, marveled at geysers, and gazed into rainbow-colored hot springs along the Firehole River. In America's first national park, they found that rarest of gems in a modern marketplace of overblown promises: a reality even better than depicted in promotional material. Seasoned travelers not easily impressed often experienced in Yellowstone wonders unique, marvelous, breathtaking, and forever memorable. Upon concluding their days-long adventure, satiated tourists re-boarded the train for the return trip eastward, many savoring a repertoire of stories to last a lifetime, and hundreds if not thousands choosing to write their stories for their local newspapers.

From 1883 to 1903, the Northern Pacific Railroad enjoyed a monopoly on transporting tourists to Wonderland's doorstep. But bit by bit other rails drew closer to Yellowstone, in 1901 the Burlington Railroad reaching Cody, Wyoming, some fifty miles east of the park. Two years later a stage-road connected Cody to the park's eastern entrance, servicing the Burlington's tourist passengers.[5]

From the west the Union Pacific Railroad, in the 1870s seemingly having the upper hand in the race to Yellowstone but unable to

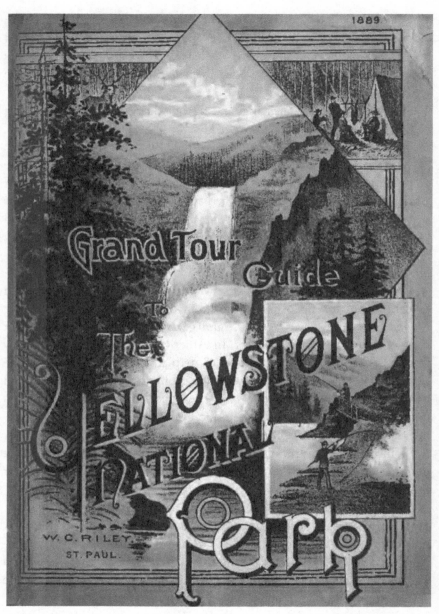

Stagecoach tours of Yellowstone grew in popularity during the 1880s, an era in which park tour guides proliferated. This is the cover of an 1889 tour book. *GRAND TOUR GUIDE TO THE YELLOWSTONE NATIONAL PARK*, ST. PAUL, MINN.: W. C. RILEY, 1889

completely follow through at the time, renewed its efforts. From Idaho the Union Pacific's Oregon Short Line in late 1907 reached the park's western boundary in Montana near the Madison River, the stopping point almost instantly known as Yellowstone, which ten years later would become "West Yellowstone." There the Union Pacific constructed a beautiful depot of native rock, later adding a dining lodge of similar style. From the depot stagecoaches carried eager visitors into nearby Wonderland.[6]

When not gazing at geysers shooting hot water high into the sky, staring into brilliantly colored hot springs, or marveling at the vast Grand Canyon and plunging Lower Falls, early travelers in Yellowstone longed for glimpses of animals once common throughout the North American continent, and still often seen in the park. No longer lords of vast reaches, many mammals far reduced in numbers nevertheless still inhabited the park's remote and rugged wilderness. Protected by law from hunters, Yellowstone's bears, elk, moose, bighorn sheep, wolves, and bison—the latter very few in number—represented the hopes of a young conservationist community increasingly concerned with humankind's wanton destruction of wildlife.

In Yellowstone, visitors from cities experienced wildlife anew. Compared to what their forebears once feared as terrors lurking in dense eastern forests, the bears of Yellowstone appeared harmless. Once prized for their meat, elk and deer grazed peacefully in spring and early summer meadows to the stares and delight of tourists. More elusive and lofty of height, moose elicited awe. To the amazement of onlookers, bighorns scaled sheer cliffs.

But rarely sighted were mountain lions and wolves, frightening animals in the minds of urban easterners and ranching westerners, and predators of the park's elk and deer as well as occasional domestic cattle in proximity to the park. Targeted for eradication by park officials bent on pleasing tourists and ranchers both, large carnivorous canids and cats by the 1930s largely disappeared from the park, victims of lingering human fears and prejudices, as well as the agricultural marketplace.

In an ecologically fractured Yellowstone, human visitors beheld but learned little of the workings of nature. But enamored with the park's geysers, canyons, waterfalls, and favored wildlife they established enduring patterns. Experiencing an astonishing place ancient yet modern and wild yet docile, they marveled, gasped, and journaled. Throughout America from the 1880s into the 1920s and prior to the proliferation of consumer cameras, newspapers large and small routinely published travel accounts. Brimming with superlatives and straining to remotely approximate the sheer joy of experiencing extraordinary natural beauty and mystique, many accounts of Wonderland pulsed with enthusiasm.

In 1883 as the Northern Pacific's rails arrived near the park's borders, a correspondent of Britain's *London Daily Telegraph* captured the tone for decades to come. For Englishmen tired of "the Alps ... Switzerland and the Pyrenees ... Hamburg ... the cathedrals and picture galleries of Europe, we strongly recommend a trip across the Atlantic and a trip to that marvelously beautiful National Park on the Yellowstone, which is commonly spoken of by our enthusiastic kinsmen as 'Wonderland.'" Offering effusive words of praise for the Northern Pacific's lead in opening Yellowstone to the world, the writer continued: "The scenery along the Northern Pacific [en route to Yellowstone] never ceases to be interesting, and the traveler has the advantage of occupying the finest palace [rail] cars in the world, which are equally comfortable by day or by night ... It can no longer be pretended that the journey involves anything approaching hardship." From Europe "well-fitted English vessels" bridged the Atlantic Ocean, and on land the rail "journey is rendered easy by the drawing-room and sleeping cars."[7]

Of wonders yet seen by few, the English correspondent noted the mighty falls of the Yellowstone, the incomparable geysers—in particular "The Beehive," "Old Faithful," and "The Giant"—and the wildlife. Adequate for the moment were the hotels, "neither better nor worse than those generally found in the far west, and as the district becomes more popular and frequented it cannot be doubted that the accommodations for travelers in this respect will be vastly improved." Offering a tip of his hat to her majesty's former colonies, the British writer noted that with "good reason" Americans were "congratulating themselves on the fact that this magnificent country is now opened up; nor are they over-sanguine in the expectation that when the charms of the beautiful region are fully known the Yellowstone Park will be among the most popular of the holiday resorts visited by the most enterprising class of European tourists."[8]

Surely Americans reading such glowing words from the Old World must have swelled with national pride. For generations they had lived in the shadow of Mother England. They could not boast of stately old cities like London or Hamburg, nor soaring stone cathedrals devoted to God. But lo and behold, Providence had long secreted away the most glorious of edifices, a natural cathedral unsurpassed in splendor, a beautiful garden of Eden guarded by mountains, an unparalleled place deserving of praise far and wide.

Yet national pride could only go so far. With little fanfare and indicative, perhaps, of a lesser imagination than they fancied themselves to have, the stewards of Yellowstone proceeded to shape the magnificent Wonderland into the mold of an upper-class resort. Appeasing the visual expectations and meeting the anticipated desires of discerning Americans and Europeans required charming viewscapes, nice hotels, fine dining, leisure activities, and courtly services. Gradually within the wilderness of Yellowstone a cultivated getaway emerged. Offering amenities expected by society's finest citizens, Wonderland serviced well-heeled tourists in comfortable lodging from which they leisurely ventured forth to experience the park's most dramatic sights.

Just such an esteemed assembly of "ladies and gentlemen from all parts of the habitable globe" assembled before Old Faithful Geyser the evening of September 17, 1884. From the cities of the American East and far away London, Liverpool, and Scotland—apparently the limit of the "habitable globe"—they had come to behold the famous spouter, accompanied by one of Yellowstone's assistant superintendents, W. C. Cannon. In "a semi-circle on the south and east side of Old Faithful" they stood in great expectation, "a million stars of a clouded heaven" above, "not a leaf" stirring nearby. Two minutes, five minutes passed, but there was "only one spurt of ten feet. 'Is that all,' said a voice in a deprecatory tone." Five more minutes still, but only another small jet of water "puffing and blowing." "Old Faithful has failed for once," a disappointed voice bemoaned into the night air. "Faithful is becoming old and forgetful," another lamented. "Old Faithful never fails!" the knowing assistant superintendent replied. "If she is behind time she will make it up by a grander display."[9]

Proving the doubters wrong yet again, as always the mighty geyser blew when the time was right, the sudden gush of water climbing "higher and higher," heads turning upward in amazement at "the liquid tower." "See! See!" shouted one. "She has reached the great dipper, filled it and is still climbing toward the North Star," exclaimed another, Miss E. L. Drexel of Philadelphia. "Yes, and will mop the floor of heaven," responded another. "Its waters are now poured into the milky way!" "Old Faithful is sprinkling star dust in the highways of heaven!" And "'Glorious old geyser! I am well paid for crossing the ocean to see thee,' cried more than one" of the visitors from the mother land. "Grey headed savants clapped their hands with all a schoolboy's fervor and shouted their applause" as "the steeple-shaped stream arose gradually, jet after jet, to the height of over 220 feet," proclaimed the newspaper article, as Old Faithful Geyser, the crown of nature's glory in the young American nation, seemingly elicited sheer marvel and joy.[10]

Old Faithful Geyser always impressed finely tailored visitors, but other wonders were known to steal the spotlight. "More impressive than Niagara, more mighty than the sea, more beautiful than the alps" one visitor wrote of his experience in 1895. "There are many wonders within the limits of the Yellowstone park, but of them all there is nothing so wonderful as the Grand Canyon of the Yellowstone river." In words enthusiastic and exalted, the writer declared, "no American looks upon it without a sense of absolute humility and insignificance. The thought, the meaning, the expression of the Grand canyon is something the human mind is unable at first to grasp." Days of study were required to experience the "many mountain lights" of the brilliant yellow, orange, and red hues of the massive canyon walls that "give a thousand different expressions to the face of nature," an experience one chronicler deemed "worshipful."[11]

But awe sometimes gave way to something else entirely. Whether gazing at the Grand Canyon of the Yellowstone or upon one of thousands of thermal marvels, the specter of death remained ever present, mere feet or even inches away, no barrier intervening. A foolish moment or careless misstep upon the canyon rim could send one tumbling or falling, often while screaming, hundreds of feet below to a mortal end. Perching on the precipice of a dazzling hot cauldron put one but a singular stumble from plunging into water capable of cooking human flesh. Although death sometimes befell an ill-fated soul, more commonly injury, possible hospitalization, and embarrassment followed the wayward visitor on his or her way home from Yellowstone.[12]

The latter characterized the August 24, 1897, encounter of George E. Earnshaw of Philadelphia with an unidentified "geyser pool," his misfortune immediately published in newspapers near and far. The hapless man "came near losing his life yesterday," read the stories, dispatched from Yellowstone's Lake Hotel. The *Alexandria Gazette* of Virginia declared that Earnshaw "walking backward, beckoning to some friends . . . tripped and fell backwards into one of the boiling bottomless geysers."[13]

On the plains of Kansas halfway from the East Coast to Yellowstone, Topeka's *State Journal* offered more details. Earnshaw had been at the Fountain Hotel, in the Lower Geyser Basin. Tripping over a stick, he "fell into one of the geyser pools in the rear of the hotel." Both accounts agreed that he landed "upon a ledge under five feet of water and was rapidly slipping off its cone to certain death when he grasped a pole overarching the edge of the pool and by the assistance of those nearby was rescued," albeit "badly burned." The Topeka paper added more, ending with the sobering words, "Post Surgeon Godfrey dressed his wounds, which are not believed to be fatal." George E. Earnshaw was likely not that summer's only hot springs–burned victim that First Lieutenant Guy C. M. Godfrey, Army surgeon and temporarily stationed at Fort Yellowstone during the summer months, treated over the course of the season.[14]

Apart from sobering stories of injuries, newspaper accounts of Yellowstone's glories glowed so brightly as to seemingly stretch credibility. But lofty oratory, too, often characterized the massive trove of personal travel journals, letters, and postcard inscriptions penned in the late nineteenth century and first few decades of the twentieth century. Even the most educated of tourists fumbled for words to adequately describe Wonderland, including Harvard-educated attorney John Harrison Atwood.

That Atwood from his academic perch in Massachusetts did not know until 1883 of the national park called Yellowstone attests to the difficulty

In addition to protecting Yellowstone's wildlife, the soldiers of Fort Yellowstone improved park roads, policed visitor behavior, engaged in early interpretive efforts, and provided for the safety of tourists, among other duties. This image shows Fort Yellowstone at Mammoth Hot Springs circa 1900; construction of the buildings of Fort Yellowstone continued until 1913. Many of the fort's buildings remain to the present day, now utilized by the National Park Service. NPS PHOTO

that early park promoters faced in telling the story of Wonderland in a nation compartmentalized East and West and saturated with newspaper headlines. Rather than reading about Yellowstone, Atwood learned of the park from a fellow academic, Yale professor F. A. Gooch, who had done field studies of Yellowstone's geological composition alongside renowned geologist Arnold Hague.

In 1898, the Harvard man finally visited the park, of which by then he had heard much. But nothing could adequately prepare him for the experience. In Wonderland he fell speechless before nature's majesty, deeming the wonders "wider than words, mightier than metaphors, sublime beyond similitudes, and too marvelous to be told of withal." Nonetheless, he tried, publishing a pamphlet of his experiences in Wonderland.[15]

As with so many lesser mortals, Atwood upon arriving in Yellowstone's Lower Geyser Basin transformed into a state of haplessness and stupor before nature unfathomable. It began at an erupting Fountain Geyser, the sight "simply indescribable." Of "surpassing beauty," the massive eruption of steaming water disintegrated "into drops . . . a multitude of brilliants." Mesmerizing, too, he found the paint pots. Grasping for household metaphors, he described the bubbling mud as "constantly leaping . . . little flecks of paint" falling back earthward and creating "the most remarkable shapes—roses, lilies, lacework, but more often the shape identical with that of an egg when broken in the skillet for frying." And, oh, the colors, beyond "ordinary imagination . . . that were a Raphael to here paint the diluvian sunset, with the bow of promise in the sky, he would never find his palette lacking of a single tint."[16]

In the Upper Geyser Basin, Atwood's rhetoric soared with the skyward geysers and crashed back earthward, victim of "a poverty of language" to describe the wonders. Roaring "like a thousand steam engines," Beehive Geyser exhibited "a power too tremendous for possible calculation." Rushing toward the geyser, he touched the water, feeling the "overwhelming, unconquerable force" of "upward moving liquid, a crystal tree two hundred feet high."[17] And yet like so many others, the Harvard lawyer reserved his greatest praise for Old Faithful Geyser, "the most marvelous of all." He watched it repeatedly, transfixed especially by "gleaming . . . columns of crystal and gems" at sunset. As he departed the geyser basin, the world traveler observed that the famed fountains of Versailles "sink into insignificance when compared with the aqueous wonders of the Yellowstone."[18]

But to Atwood, "the crowning glory of the Park, aye, of the natural world. . . . The most stupendous sight that was ever mirrored on human retina!" was the Grand Canyon of the Yellowstone, the lower falls "a mass of foam three hundred and sixty feet high, as white as hammered platinum, while from its foot, like incense before an altar of silver, rises the mist eternally." The cavernous canyon he described as a "gorge piled with tower and dome and minaret," the walls "as golden as the temples of the Incas . . . crimson as an Aztec stone of sacrifice reeking with human blood . . . a perfected harmony of color that God alone can call into being . . . an altar to the Infinite."[19]

While Old Faithful and the Grand Canyon elicited awe, wading in thermal pools—a dangerous and damaging practice long since prohibited—brought smiles to the faces of many early visitors, as depicted in this image, *Tourists Wading in the Great Fountain, 1908.* NPS PHOTO

And so, the story went. Year after year and into the twentieth century as visitation rose to ten thousand annually and beyond, first-time experiences in Wonderland left tourists awed at splendor greater than anything humanity had ever created, with dozens of enraptured visitors comparing the Grand Canyon to heaven.[20]

For many visitors Yellowstone's geological marvels, readily available to behold, outshone the park's wildlife, whom some visitors deemed aloof. Magazine writer Myra Emmons put her finger on the pulse of the void during her visit in July 1901. "The only animals we were fortunate to see in the Park were bears and chipmunks," the very two animals, one large and one small, most commonly begging tourists for morsels. Her companion insisted "she caught a glimpse of a cottonwood rabbit," but Myra remained doubtful. And where were "the 50,000 elk and many deer in the Park"? Perhaps "with unappreciated modesty they kept" out of sight, Emmons mused.[21]

Within Myra Emmons's clever rejoinder lurked a sliver of truth. Yellowstone acting superintendent Captain John Pitcher, summarizing a dynamic true to the present day, observed that "Late in the summer, when the tourist traffic becomes heavy and the flies and mosquitoes become troublesome, nearly all the elk and deer move back into the high mountains and are seldom seem by the tourists who travel through the park by stage or wagon." By July, Emmons and other visitors would have had to "take a horse and ride out into the mountains" to see the elusive animals.[22]

Some tourist accounts failed even to acknowledge the park's animals. A year following Emmons's visit, the Rev. Cornelius H. Patton of Boston, a Yale graduate, spent six weeks in Yellowstone, much of the time in the backcountry, where he most certainly encountered wildlife. Although extolling the geysers and the Grand Canyon—"The Yellowstone Falls are the most beautiful single object I have seen in nature"—the reverend made no mention of wildlife of any kind, save "abundant" fish too easy to catch.[23]

Patton's seeming dismissal of animals aside and ungulates' aversion to human crowds notwithstanding, one species of wildlife grew ever more attached to humans. Increasingly migrating from the backcountry into tourist areas in search of human food, many of the park's bears through time abandoned their natural diets. In 1902, park officials fretted about the growing number of bears feeding at garbage piles near lodging facilities in the park, their presence attracting gawking tourists. Tensions mounted as bruins and humans alike became acclimated to the presence of the other. When scraps in the park's garbage piles proved too meager to satisfy, some bears took to begging tourists for morsels. Park visitors, in turn, perceived the bears as harmless. Trouble brewed.

"It is a difficult matter to make some of tourists realize that the bear in the park are wild, and that it is dangerous to trifle with them," lamented Acting Superintendent Pitcher. On August 8, 1902, "a circular was issued and posted at all of the hotels and permanent camps, absolutely prohibiting the interference with or molestation of bear or any other wild game in the park, etc." By Pitcher's orders the feeding of bears was prohibited apart from the garbage dumps.[24]

In this circa 1924 image a tourist feeds a bear, a common sight along roads in the park's early days. Each year, some visitors sustained injuries from aggressive bears. YELLOWSTONE NATIONAL PARK ARCHIVES, YELL185 328-214. OPEN PARK NETWORK, YELLOWSTONE PHOTO ALBUM 25, PAGE 75.

The new rules had been posted but for a little more than a month when R. E. Southwick of Michigan, lodging with his wife at the Lake Hotel, decided otherwise. On September 11, 1902, Southwick took an evening stroll with his wife. "Not far from the hotel" the couple encountered a bear cub. Stopping to pet the cub, Southwick was attacked by the angry mother bear. Heroically, his wife "seized a club and wielded it upon the bear with such force that the animal was driven off."[25]

Following the Southwick incident Acting Superintendent Pitcher "recommended that the gist of the circular relative to the bear be made a part of the regulations governing the park" and violators be charged. He expressed confidence that "strict compliance" on the part of tourists would "render the bear in the park perfectly harmless," vowing to take "timely measures" in the years following to enforce the new regulations.[26]

Pitcher's optimism, however, would prove woefully overblown. Glorious Old Faithful, the majestic Grand Canyon with its spectacular Lower Falls, and human-acclimated bears headlined for many generations nature's greatest show. Each encounter being both thrilling and potentially lethal, some visitors for venturing too close came away nursing injuries, a few succumbing to death.

But above all the bears in their popularity proved troubling, with park officials unable and soon unwilling to entirely distance humans from bruins. As annual visitation to Yellowstone soared into the hundreds of thousands in the 1920s and 1930s, hotel garbage dumps grew in size accordingly, huge nightly buffets for dozens of bears and drawing thousands of eager onlookers. From behind fences, the spectators watched, mesmerized as the hungry bears, having forsaken their more nutritious natural diet, rummaged for chicken, vegetables, eggs, and other scraps discarded from tourists' dining tables. Nearby and silently arrayed, park rangers with high-powered rifles dutifully stood watch, ready at a moment's notice to put down a threatening bruin. And as customary by then, Yellowstone's bears frequently plied the roadways, begging from car to car, often rewarded with a tasty morsel, and not infrequently biting the hand that either fed or refused to feed them.

Not until there was a dramatic decrease of visitation during World War II did park officials close public bear-feeding grounds, for decades thereafter confining garbage dumps to a few locales far removed from tourists' sight. But panhandling bears remained, ubiquitous as ever, impervious to the angst of park rangers. Only after scientific studies proved the detrimental effects of human food in bears' diets did park officials in the 1970s begin separating humans and bruins, thus breaking the longstanding and unnatural relationship between the two species.

Even so, as annual visitation topped two million during the 1970s, the trinity of nature's greatest show remained the same. Young and old alike, first or second or even third-generation visitors watched Old Faithful Geyser in wonder, stared in awe into the Grand Canyon of the Yellowstone River at the Lower Falls, and hoped to see a bear.

CHAPTER EIGHT

Traveling in Yellowstone

Horses, Stagecoaches, and Automobiles

"Are the horses afraid of bears?"
—UNNAMED TOURISTS OF THE STAGECOACH ERA

IN THE LATE EIGHTEENTH CENTURY THROUGH THE CIVIL WAR ERA AND astride hardy steeds, western explorers, fur trappers, and gold seekers first approached and then wandered into Yellowstone. Equines carried rider and supplies alike, saddle bags often bulging, pack animals in tow. On horseback the hunter of hides or gold, as well as the merely inquisitive, navigated thick forests, climbed steep mountains, and forded rivers and streams of varying depth and current. Horses, too, in the early years provided some degree of protection in encounters with often unfriendly Native peoples and predatory wildlife. A man without a horse in the pre-park days of Yellowstone was a man in danger of death, a circumstance the aforementioned Truman Everts learned in an instant.

On the ninth day of September 1870, and with winter fast closing in, Everts astride his horse became separated from his Washburn Expedition companions. Even so, he remained confident of reunion until "in the dense growth of the pine forest" near the south shore of Yellowstone Lake he watched his horse disappear "at full speed among the trees," never to be seen again. Left alone with no supplies and no transportation other than his own two feet, Truman Everts, and later his remarkable survival story, became legendary.[1]

Not so fortunate were a handful of mounted soldiers during Yellowstone's Army years, at least four of whom were thrown from their mounts and died from injuries between 1891 and 1912, according to Yellowstone historian Lee Whittlesey.[2] Typically, however, horses were a benign if interesting and lively presence in early Yellowstone as the necessary, ever-present, and sometimes cantankerous means of transportation.

Before soldiers galloped into Yellowstone in August 1886 to replace civilian administrators, Thomas E. Sherman, son of renowned Civil War general William T. Sherman and a law student, visited the park late in the summer of 1877 astride a horse. By coach, having traversed "over eighty miles of passable wagon road" to the entrance of Yellowstone at Gardiner—the Northern Pacific's rails yet floundering in Bismarck, Dakota Territory—Sherman dismounted from his vehicle, noting "there is no highway into Wonderland." Visiting the national park required "the fatigues of rough riding" on horseback and trusting one's "baggage to the mercy of a pack animal," declared the young man who, unlike his father, was no expert horseman.[3]

In a letter recounting his adventures, Sherman gave ample ink to the actions of the horses that bore his party. In the first few hours of his tour of Wonderland, Sherman wrote of his eyes being "cheered by rich wild-flowers" while his party's horses "find delight in tall waving grasses, at which they nibble eagerly, as we pause to rest from time to time." Passing Tower Fall the next day, they continued, up "one long hill after another," their climb to Mount Washburn so "gradual and gentle" that "the traveler is not fully conscious of its character or elevation until the summit is fairly reached." That which would have been laborious on foot even without a pack "can readily be made on horseback," Sherman aptly concluded.[4]

Thomas Sherman's party counted among several touring the park at that time, all on horseback. Also simultaneously on horses—many stolen from tourists—and noted by Sherman as he rested atop Washburn, hundreds of Nez Perce Indians, probably looking at their possible escape routes to the northeast, were fleeing through the park. Pursued by horse-mounted soldiers, equines played a starring role in one of the most storied events in Yellowstone's early history. Within days the Nez Perce and their pursuers raced out of the park and northward toward the United States' northern border, most of the desperate Natives finally surrendering to Army forces less than fifty miles shy of freedom in Canada.[5]

Most early Yellowstone tourists entered the park from the north via Gardiner, Montana. Beginning in 1903 they passed through the Roosevelt Arch, a massive structure inscribed with the words "For the Benefit and Enjoyment of the People," from the 1872 Yellowstone Act. In this 1912 image a "Tally-Ho" stagecoach with passengers and driver Frances James "Happy Jack" Kelly has just passed through the Arch. NPS PHOTO

Unaffected by the unfolding Nez Perce tragedy, Thomas Sherman observed that his party's "trail skirts the heavily-wooded sides of Mt. Washburn . . . and gradually descends to the valley of Cascade Creek."[6] Continuing south from Washburn, Sherman's party rode along the west bank of the Yellowstone River to the Mud Volcano alongside the "Devil's Den" (now Dragon's Mouth Spring), both of which fascinated the young man. In the Hayden Valley men and horses then turned westward, first traveling through "meadows thickly clad in waving grasses" and encountering occasional "somber woods." Soon, however, they encountered "considerable difficulty," "ugly, steep ditches" forcing a pause. Jumping the chasms "tested our horsemanship," declared Sherman, "and the agility of our animals, as little accustomed as their riders to such exercise." This was merely the beginning of "toilsome" terrain including "standing timber dark and dense" and a myriad of fallen trees, wherein "the pack mules wriggling to and fro" against the trees sought to shed their loads.[7]

Emerging at last from the rough going, in the days following, Thomas Sherman's party visited the Upper Geyser Basin along the Firehole River, a place of spectacular sights according to the young man. Eventually turning back eastward, the party returned to the banks of the Yellowstone River and rode along the rim of the river's Grand Canyon, marveling at canyon and falls alike before retracing their route back to Mammoth.[8]

For a mere moment in time only did travel of the manner undertaken by Thomas Sherman characterize the experience of tourists in Yellowstone. The same year of Sherman's adventure Yellowstone's second superintendent, Philetus W. Norris, assumed the reins of Wonderland and quickly set about surveying and constructing a road system for visitors. Well within a decade, horse-drawn stagecoaches and wagons in the summer months plied much of the same route and beyond on rough roads replete with wooden bridges spanning rivers and streams. By the early

An early tourist scene at the Mammoth Hot Springs Hotel. J. Frank Haynes, photographer. NPS PHOTO

twentieth century today's familiar Grand Loop was functional throughout for horse-drawn vehicles, albeit the ride far from comfortable.[9]

A world of its own catering to a certain clientele, stagecoaching
in remote Yellowstone added a layer of mystique to the world's first
national park. By the turn of the century two main stagecoach companies served park visitors: the Yellowstone National Park Transportation Company affiliated with the Northern Pacific by way of the park's
North Entrance, and the Monida and Yellowstone Stage Company
aligned with the Union Pacific and accessing the park via the West
Entrance. Both companies typically transported moneyed travelers
from afar. "They were people accustomed to ease and luxury, experiencing a wilderness where very little luxury had been created," Yellowstone
historian Aubrey Haines wrote of these early travelers.[10] Two other in-
park transportation companies—the Wylie Camping Company and the
Shaw & Powell Camping Company—operated on smaller scales, catering to more frugal visitors.

Well-attired and emerging from the luxurious passenger and dining cars of the Northern Pacific at Cinnabar (or Gardiner after 1902),
the Union Pacific's Oregon Short Line at Monida (1895–1907) or at the
park's western entrance thereafter, or the Burlington's terminus in Cody
beginning in 1901, America's and Europe's elites thrilled to the experience of a unique world. These visitors witnessed the once dangerous Old
West giving way to an emerging New West, a world of western romance
supposedly subdued and safe.

Or was the West either new or safe in Yellowstone? Soon the newer
tourists would find out.

Into the early twentieth century most tourists arrived in the New
West via the Northern Pacific Railroad. But mere steps away from their
luxurious passenger rail cars at the Gardiner depot, travelers encountered
a lingering Old West far from refined, albeit colorful. At the depot Yellowstone Coaches awaited, specially built vehicles painted bright yellow
and unique to the national park. Pulled by six horses, the larger "Tally-
Ho" coaches, capable of holding more than twenty passengers, transported
both travelers and luggage from the train to Mammoth Hot Springs.
During these summer seasons, travelers climbed upward and onto their

carriages after donning dusters over their fine clothing as protection from road dust.

Aboard these wooden vessels tourists experienced a rugged Old West fading a bit but still very much alive, a world accompanied by bewildering but amusing language. Driven by "knights of reins" and yoked to a team of four-hoofed "tackies," coaches lurched and swayed and bounced into the park, passengers literally in the hands of veteran cowboys or ranchers with colorful "handles" such as Society Red, Scattering Jesus, and Geyser Bob.[11]

Riding to Mammoth Hot Springs in the "Tally-Ho" coaches, travelers disembarked at the National Hotel, also known as the Mammoth Hot Springs Hotel. Clearly visible from the hotel's entryway were the dazzling, bubbling, mineral-laden terraces to the south and the orderly buildings of Fort Yellowstone to the east, a groomed grassy area in between. The view took in the extent of the Mammoth village, a hub of human activity surrounded by wilderness. Long summer days allowed ample time for exploration of the hot springs. In an environment unique and intriguing, newly arrived visitors of the national park experienced a kaleidoscope of wilderness, otherworldliness, civilization, and military orderliness.

The next morning a procession of stagecoaches, most pulled by four horses and each typically seating eight or eleven passengers, lined up in front of the hotel, waiting for their charges to finish breakfast. Passengers and luggage aboard and with the crack of a whip or verbal signal each reinsman steered his harnessed team away from the hotel.

Unlike other stagecoaches, Yellowstone's coaches seated all passengers facing forward in order to allow for better viewing. Maneuvering along muddy roads in the spring and in the dry season maintaining enough distance between coaches to allow some settling of the dust, drivers tried to make the journey as pleasant as possible. Traveling in a place unlike any other, year after year ever-inquisitive tourists inevitably asked the same questions: "Driver, how far will we go today?" "When will we see a geyser?" "Are the horses afraid of bears?" "Do the geysers freeze up in the winter?" And on and on.[12]

Bantering with their captive audiences, drivers with reins in hand provided answers sometimes truthful, but often more playful or entertaining than factual. In response to the question "Where is the best place to catch fish?", drivers were sometimes known to answer, "Well, I think in either the lake or the river. You see, the only fish that are caught on land are the suckers, and I don't think you will find them in the park." But no animal garnered more interest than bears. Asked if bears were dangerous, drivers sometimes replied with something along the lines of: "Well, I guess so. Last summer one got ugly and they had to kill it, and when they cut it up they found it had eaten three hotel help, two barn dogs and seven tourists." Taken aback, some travelers were known to ask if the driver was telling the truth.[13]

From Mammoth the coaches ascended above the terraces and crossed Swan Lake Flat, passed Willow Park, and stopped at Apollinaris Spring, where passengers slaked their dusty throats with naturally sparkling cold mineral water. At "Devil's Frying Pan" (today's Frying Pan Springs), the next stop, drivers were sometimes asked if they had any eggs for frying, to which one once replied, "I don't know, I've got three old hens on the back seat," referring to three older, unmarried women, surely a sexist and ageist comment today but one that often "slid by" in nineteenth-century America. Passing by Roaring Mountain a bit farther along and asked how the hill received its name, drivers sometimes told a story of how a landslide long ago covered mountain lion dens, "and the lions have been roaring ever since, waiting to get out."[14]

Their drivers often having set a tone of tall tales and joviality sometimes tinged with a touch of good-natured rudeness, tourists (until 1902) arrived at Norris Lunch Station for their noon-day meal. Housed in a tent and operated (1893–1901) by Lawrence Francis Mathews, the lunch stop provided its own laughs. Known simply as Larry, the "funny Irishman," Mathews's gift for gab and wit, paired with his penchant for lighthearted sarcasm or even brusqueness, made the lunch hour memorable for all. A guided tour of Norris Geyser Basin followed, visitors' first encounter with the spouting wonders. Then back aboard the coaches they came, often clutching bottled beverages purchased from the ever-enterprising Mathews.[15]

In early afternoon Elk Park and Gibbon Meadows came into view, open areas frequented by wildlife early in the season. Then loomed a brief

Open from 1891 to 1916, the Fountain Hotel in the Lower Geyser Basin did not survive in the post-stagecoach era. The hotel was razed in 1927. Image: JP Clum, undated. NPS PHOTO

stop at Gibbon Falls, the first major waterfall on the tour. Soon the nearby Gibbon River gave way to the tumbling Firehole River. Farther upriver another meadow emerged, steaming geysers and hot springs of the Lower Geyser Basin visible in the distance, a sight long anticipated by many. A short ride farther and closer to the steam, the stagecoaches came to a stop for the night at the upscale Fountain Hotel (1891–1902) or the Old Faithful Inn thereafter.[16]

Two exciting days followed, visitors' hours spent wandering among the thermal marvels of the "Firehole Basin," as it was then called. Favorites included the Fountain Paint Pot and Great Fountain Geyser in the Lower Geyser Basin, as well as Excelsior Geyser and Grand Prismatic Spring at Midway Geyser Basin, then often called "Hell's Half Acre." But anticipated most of all was the granddaddy of thermal basins, the Upper Geyser Basin. Home to Old Faithful Geyser as well as dozens of other famed spouters and hot springs seemingly too many to count, the Upper Basin merited the most time and usually elicited the highest praise.

Having beheld superheated waters wildly shooting skyward and when at rest brilliant and seemingly serene, travelers boarded their coaches again for a long and nerve-wracking ride eastward through dense forest, across the continental divide twice, including the treacherous Craig Pass (after 1891), to (West) Thumb on the west end of Yellowstone Lake. There at dock lay the steamboat *Zillah*, or after 1904, the *E. C. Waters*. Tempting travelers tired and sore, each of these vessels offered the opportunity to briefly abandon the rough and dusty road for an adventure across the beautiful, mountain-ringed inland sea to the Lake Hotel, their destination for the night. Stagecoach drivers encouraged their charges to ply the waters, quietly receiving a kickback for each boat passenger while also lightening their stagecoach load for the last nineteen miles of the day along the western and northern shores of the lake.[17]

Luxurious by early Yellowstone standards, the Lake Hotel offered much-needed respite from a long day's travel. Whether having remained in the stagecoach the entire route, or having opted for the *Zillah* or *E.C. Waters* for the last leg, weary travelers at the Lake Hotel partook of a nice meal. A relaxing evening followed, visitors enjoying a stunning view of the lake and, after sunset on a clear night, a sky awash with a blaze of stars, unfettered by city lights.[18]

On the morning of their fifth day in Wonderland tourists, now veterans of rough stagecoach travel and refreshed from a quiet evening and night, re-boarded for a leisurely morning ride. Alongside the Yellowstone River they rolled, stopping at the Mud Volcano for a brief visit, then on through the expansive, grass-filled Hayden Valley often teeming with wildlife. Next came lunch at the Canyon tent hotel (1883–1885), the rustic one-story hotel (1886–1888), the barn-like second Canyon Hotel (1889–1909), or the cavernous third Canyon Hotel (after 1910), followed by afternoon sightseeing. Some settled for a horseback ride along the Canyon rim, others for a stroll, in either instance the magnificence of the great chasm and plunging falls readily visible.

Not content to merely stare downward, at the turn of the twentieth century a few fit visitors opted for a strenuous hike, requiring rope ladders, to the canyon floor in those halcyon days when it was legal. Guided by "Uncle Tom" Richardson, they descended far below to a close-up and breathtaking view of the Lower Falls. A strenuous steep climb upward to the rim followed Depending on the time of day, hikers picnicked at the base of the Lower Falls or enjoyed a campfire supper following their adventure. (Today's Uncle Tom's Trail, a safe if still-strenuous 328-step staired hike, takes visitors about three-fourths of the way down the canyon wall to a platform near the Lower Falls.) Later, as the day waned, canyon hikers and rim strollers alike enjoyed an evening of entertainment and merriment before retiring for the night.[19]

But with the next morning's dawn, the inevitable arrived, the sixth and final day of the tourists' adventure in Wonderland. For most it would be their last day ever in Yellowstone, that realization momentarily laced with sadness amid the beauty of their surroundings. A last look at their hotel room, a final breakfast in the park, and then it was back aboard their coaches. Eastward they rode through thick forest, stopping at the lovely Virginia Cascades. Then it was on toward Norris and the indomitable Larry Mathews, their second lunch with the Irishman often being as entertaining as the first. The final leg of the return trip to Mammoth Hot Springs followed. If not spending another night at Mammoth, travelers transferred to the "Tally-Ho" coaches. Descending downward from Mammoth toward their waiting train outside park boundaries, visitors viewed Wonderland for only a few minutes more. Back aboard the train and with their days in Wonderland suddenly over, the happy but weary travelers, flush with stories of a lifetime and many with ample souvenirs, settled in for the long and mostly comfortable ride home.[20]

Or at least that was the way it was supposed to happen, and most often the days-long stint in Wonderland went off without problems or "vexations," as a word of the era called them. But that was not always the case. In some instances, tourists experienced a dark side of the lingering Old West, which seemed largely confined to remote locales.

On five occasions from 1887 to 1915, tourists—frightened or thrilled or both—fell victim to stagecoach holdups. For the bandits, elite tourists traveling Yellowstone's isolated roads in slow-moving stagecoaches spaced far apart offered the possibility of a nice haul at little risk. One of the most brazen holdups took place in 1914 between Old Faithful and Yellowstone Lake in the park's remote southern wilderness. In a single

In a land of waterfalls, some Yellowstone tours in the early twentieth century added Virginia Cascades, between Canyon and Norris, to the itinerary, as depicted in this image: *The magnificent new Virginia Canyon Road and Virginia Falls, Yellowstone National Park*, by T. W. Ingersoll, circa 1905. LIBRARY OF CONGRESS, PRINTS & PHOTOGRAPHS DIVISION, LC-USZ62-97312

day, a gunman held up fifteen coaches carrying 165 passengers, afterward disappearing into the vast forest with some $1,000 in cash and jewelry, a small fortune at the time. In time the Yellowstone bandit was identified as Edward B. Trafton, an area resident and career criminal. Convicted, Trafton served almost five years in prison.[21]

Stagecoach holdups, albeit galling and even humiliating, in all cases did not end in lives lost. But death struck often in Wonderland, in ways unique to the park. Numerous employees—soldiers, concessionaire workers, wagon drivers, and contractors included—died from various causes during the stagecoach era. Fatalities frequently took the form of drowning, freezing, and freight wagon or stagecoach accidents, collectively reflective of the park's many natural bodies of water, extreme winters, and the challenges of horse-powered transportation on rough roads in the wilderness. Visitors most commonly fell victim, whether merely injurious or frighteningly fatal, to scalding thermal pools, a close encounter with a bear, or, again, stagecoach accidents.

Of transportation-related incidents, in most years from 1880 through 1916, coach companies reported "up to four stage wrecks" annually, according to park historian Lee Whittlesey. Many more accidents went unreported, the uninsured companies often settling directly with injured passengers. "Causes of accidents tended to be inept drivers, sudden wild flights of teams, mechanical failures of equipment, or intoxication" (of the driver, not the horses), according to Whittlesey.[22]

Regardless of the cause, by the second decade of the twentieth century stagecoach accidents in Yellowstone became increasingly troublesome as second-generation automobiles transformed the transportation market throughout America. If not for railways' financial investments in the park's stagecoach operations, the end of an era in Wonderland would have come all the sooner. But Yellowstone stagecoaches lingered, a charming anomaly, a fading vestige of the Old West, and even a symbol of defiance.

Nonetheless, pressure to allow automobiles in the park grew all the more with the advent of regional and national highways. Debuting in 1911, the "Yellowstone Trail" initially stretched from Minneapolis to the park's northern entrance at Gardiner, Montana, an endeavor undertaken by the "Yellowstone Trail" motor club that was formed the same year. Two years later the nation's first coast-to-coast automobile route, the Lincoln Highway, carried motorists through southern Wyoming. Petitions from automobile interests grew all the louder, the drumbeat growing with the approach of the 1915 Panama-Pacific International Exposition in San Francisco, the western terminus of the Lincoln Highway. From East to West, motorists demanded access to Wonderland, refusing to take no for an answer.[23]

It began in late summer 1915, a crack in the chink of the concessionaires' armor, a peek into the future of Yellowstone. On July 31 a motor procession including park acting superintendent Colonel Lloyd M. Brett, concessions operator Harry Child, and eager tourists drove through the stone archway at the park's North Entrance and into Yellowstone, the first permitted motorists to do so. The following day the first auto tour of Yellowstone commenced, departing from Mammoth Hot Springs. Also on August 1, many other permitted motoring tourists in larger numbers rolled into the park, some cross-country travelers en route or returning from the San Francisco Exposition at which, fittingly, the Union Pacific Railroad was hosting a Yellowstone exhibit. All told, between August 1 and September 15, 1915, a total of 958 automobiles motored through the North, East, and West Entrances of Wonderland.[24]

Having finally arrived, drivers of automobiles felt that they could no longer be held at bay. But still the park's transportation operators hedged, leading to an uneasy compromise in 1916 as horse-drawn stagecoaches *and* wheeled gasoline motorcars in choreographed fashion shared Yellowstone's roads. In an effort to avoid spooking horses and causing yet more accidents, awkward regulations confined automobiles to certain times of the day on a one-way route governed by low speed limits. Pleasing no one, the experiment ended badly, flighty horses failing to harmoniously share the road with big, noisy, wheeled, mechanical contraptions.

Whittlesey identified one particular incident in 1916 that more than others brought an end to Wonderland's stagecoaches. Bolting in fright at the unexpected sight of a stalled automobile, an out-of-control team of horses feverishly pitched and lurched along the park's narrow roadway, dragging behind it a wildly careening stagecoach, the vehicle ultimately crashing onto its side. All nine passengers sustained injuries, three suffering fractures. The unusual number of injuries in a single accident made front page news in the local *Livingston Herald* newspaper, cementing pro-automobile sentiment. Park officials at the end of the season formally announced the inevitable: Henceforth only motorized vehicles (excepting bicycles) would be allowed on the park's roadways.[25]

With the passing of stagecoaches, a major era of Yellowstone's history came to a close: Horse-powered transportation on the park's roadways would never return. In an interesting twist, horseback tours of Yellowstone experienced an upsurge in the 1920s. By then Yellowstone "dudes" found horseback riding a novelty rather than the necessity it was during the early days of park tourism. Yet nostalgia for the past remains today, and park visitors can still experience a glimpse of days long gone by boarding a refurbished stagecoach at Roosevelt Lodge for a short, off-road ride to a western cookout.

Symbols of the New West, automobiles claimed Yellowstone's roads for themselves in 1917 and never looked back in the rear-view mirror (although many did not have a rear-view mirror at the time). Transportation operators adjusted by purchasing open-air touring cars to transport railroad visitors around the park, some stage drivers trading reins

Beginning in 1917 motorized autos ruled Yellowstone's roads. In the years following more and more tourists drove to the park and camped out. This circa 1923 Jack E. Haynes photograph of the Mammoth auto camp depicts the freewheeling atmosphere of early automobile park camping. LIBRARY OF CONGRESS, PRINTS & PHOTOGRAPHS DIVISION, LC-USZ62-66079

Titled *Yellowstone Canyon and Great Fall, Wyoming* and captured circa 1931/32, this image depicts multiple dimensions of park tourism of that time. Near a parked automobile a group of tourists stands in awe of the Lower Falls of the park's Grand Canyon. Other tourists, pausing during a horseback trail ride, also marvel at a sight some equated to heaven. LIBRARY OF CONGRESS, PRINTS & PHOTO-GRAPHS DIVISION, LC-USZ62-126295

for steering wheels. But while professionally-driven and maintained touring cars largely proved up to the task, personal automobiles created new problems.

Clunky, unreliable, prone to breaking down, and under-powered for the park's rough roads and steep mountain grades, cars proved no less prone to accidents than stagecoaches, a problem that low speed limits failed to mitigate. Nor did time resolve the problem. In 1923, despite low speed limits, "the tremendous pounding of heavy traffic" from record visitation "severely damaged" park roads, then unpaved. That year signaled the arrival of the supremacy of private automobiles over rail passengers traveling in yellow-painted touring buses—introduced in 1917—as part of a tour package. Some two-thirds of park visitors consisted of "motorists in their own cars, most of whom camped out and carried their own [lodging] equipment."[26]

Despite more reliable automobiles and paved roads by the late 1930s, dangers proliferated alongside an even more dramatic growth in visitation, and hence automobile traffic. Thousands of cars, daily traveling at higher speeds on narrow, two-lane roads shared with wildlife, it turned out, posed no shortage of accident scenarios. Annual park reports chronicled incidents so numerous that in his bestselling book *Death in Yellowstone*, Lee Whittlesey declined to include deaths by automobile accident.

Dethroned by far faster automobiles, equines in Yellowstone were relegated to ranger patrols and slow-paced tourist rides. By the hundreds horses in a recreational capacity carried greenhorn visitors along a thousand or so miles of bridle paths. Yet this arrangement, too, would not last. Following World War II, the demand for physical exercise in Yellowstone grew, hikers increasingly hoofing along bridle paths on their own two feet, and the demand for horses shrank all the more. A legacy of the past, present-day scenic horse rides are available to park visitors at select locations.

Minus horses, automobiles dramatically changed tourist patterns in Wonderland. No longer confined to formal tours of the park tightly scheduled by concessionaires, travelers driving into Yellowstone could set their own itinerary and move about at their own pace. Even so, the railroads remained an attractive means of traveling to the park from far-away eastern cities. Railway tour packages included fine dining and comfortable traveling en route, and guided automobile tours, lodging, meals, and ranger-led talks and walks within the park. But during the Great Depression and World War II railways experienced a dramatic drop in passenger traffic to Yellowstone, signaling the beginning of the end of rail-passenger travel to the park. One by one the depots in the Montana towns of Gardiner, Gallatin Gateway (outside of Bozeman), and West Yellowstone, as well as Cody, Wyoming, shuttered, the end of passenger-service arriving by the 1960s.[27]

Corresponding with the gradual decline of rail service to Yellowstone, the socioeconomic dynamics of park visitation shifted. During Franklin Delano Roosevelt's first term (1933–1937) as US president hope returned to a destitute America even amid the Great Depression. As jobs again grew, courtesy of Roosevelt's New Deal federal employment programs, the government sought to further stimulate the economy by promoting domestic travel and tourism. Soon, cheaper and more reliable cars, paired with excellent national and state highways and encouraged by marketing campaigns, public and corporate, led to greater American mobility than ever before, including among budget-conscious Americans. As the modern age of American tourism emerged from the 1920s to the 1940s, Yellowstone increasingly attracted a previously marginalized class of travelers: campers.

Early tourists of moderate means, "sagebrushers" as they were called in the stagecoach days, were a minority of park visitors, often locals from nearby Montana, Wyoming, and Idaho. Upon their own horses or in modest horse-drawn wagons, they carried their own food and nightly shelter. Along the way to the park as well as inside the park, they often camped among the sagebrush plants, hence the label. More casual in dress and manners than wealthier visitors and looked down upon by some concession operators, sagebrushers often supplemented their meals with freely caught fish and purchased little in the way of souvenirs. Deemed by some as vagabonds in a Wonderland many then envisioned as a playground for the wealthy, sagebrushers represented a reality not yet fully realized: Yellowstone as the "pleasuring-ground for the benefit and enjoyment of the people" as worded in the 1872 Yellowstone Act. For decades sagebrushers were effectively "others."[28]

Upon the arrival of automobiles, however, the democratization of Yellowstone National Park took a step forward. Cheap and common, Model Ts (introduced in 1908) were abundantly available, new and used, while the inexpensive Model A debuted in 1927. By the end of the 1920s, large numbers of Yellowstone visitors were neither wealthy nor elite, but rather ordinary folks—albeit almost all white, as many states' segregated laws greatly discouraged travel by Black Americans—who carefully saved money for an inexpensive vacation in America's first national park. Many picnicked and camped for free, both en route and in the park. Outdoor camping in tents or simple trailers, in turn, corresponded with a growing movement among middle-class urbanites to reconnect with nature. In Yellowstone some visitors experienced for the first time the wonder of dark, star-filled skies.

Responding to a cascade of democratizing currents, Yellowstone's concessionaires during the 1920s, '30s, and '40s offered cheaper accommodations, luring some budget-conscious travelers to opt for inexpensive, wooden cabins situated in the shadows of the iconic Old Faithful Inn, the luxurious Lake Hotel, or the modernized Mammoth Hot Springs Hotel. In 1936 new and stylish yellow-painted touring buses, manufactured by the White Motor Company and capable of carrying fourteen passengers, replaced many of the older models that had been in service since 1925. By 1939, a total of ninety-eight passenger buses carried railroad tourists of various means on a tour of the park, taking in all the points of interest and providing transportation to hotels and cabins. Today, a few old, but refurbished yellow buses still ply park roads, providing tourists with an experience reminiscent of days gone by.[29]

The democratization of Yellowstone was vividly on display along park roads during the 1930s as more than five hundred thousand tourists visited the park annually immediately prior to World War II, most traveling in personal cars. During daylight hours in the people's park, visitors from all walks of life encircled Old Faithful Geyser elbow to elbow, jostled for the best views of the Grand Canyon and the Lower Falls, and leaned out of car windows to see and sometimes feed roadside bears. And as the

11300-1   11299-5
August 5, 1936 - Front view of Mammoth Hotel before start of remodeling and demolition for proposed
hotel-lodge development.

11306-9   11300-5
September 2, 1936 - Front view of Mammoth Hotel during demolition of hotel for proposed hotel-

Several Yellowstone hotels closed for a few years during the Great Depression, including the Lake Hotel and, pictured here, the Mammoth Hot Springs Hotel. Closure of Mammoth's hotel allowed for the near-complete demolition of the aging structure. Top: The Mammoth Hotel on August 5, 1936, prior to the beginning of demolition. Bottom: The Mammoth Hotel on September 2, 1936, with most of the left-hand side torn down. This little-known image was included in the August 1936 monthly park superintendent's report. NPS PHOTO

sun sank low each evening, happy tourists of a variety of means sorted themselves out among Yellowstone's comfortable hotels, simply furnished cabins, and free open-air campsites.

CHAPTER NINE

Civilizing the Wilderness

Yellowstone's Iconic Hotels, Tent Camps, Lodges, and Stores

The Old Faithful Inn. . . . is enhanced by an immense fireplace in which gleams a cheerful fire. . . . In the evening one is entertained by a Hungarian orchestra.

—A YNP VISITOR, 1904

For all Yellowstone's beauty and wonders, and beyond the hardships of travel, one problem above others dampened wealthy visitors' early experiences in Wonderland: the absence of a truly comfortable place in which to dine and lounge in the evenings, and afterward enjoy a restful night's sleep.

It seemed simple enough, the concept of building first-class hotels. But in Yellowstone's remote wilderness, nothing was simple.

From local entrepreneurs on a shoestring budget to railroad conglomerates, visionary businessmen dreamed of reaching into the pockets of elite American and European travelers. Ever shimmering in the distance, abundant profits beckoned like a siren song, a mirage always seemingly within reach, and always hoped for, but never quite touched.

As Congress debated the Yellowstone Act in the winter of 1871–72, the quest to civilize Wonderland began, enterprising Montanans and others descending upon Mammoth Hot Springs and staking their claims to tourist dollars. Lesions upon the once-pristine landscape, namely shanties providing basic services, popped up: tents and rudely constructed buildings offering floor space for sleeping, slabs and logs masquerading as tables and chairs, and crude shelves of simple souvenirs.

Although the first to throw up rude accommodations at Mammoth Hot Springs and other points of interest, local operators lived on borrowed time. For a decade the powers in Washington, DC, paid but scant attention to the nation's first federal park, allowing squatters to build cheaply and charge exorbitantly for services unbefitting of the surroundings and far beneath the expectations of refined travelers.

But this was just fine with the railroad companies, for it bought them more time. For decades their advocates in the nation's capital had refined the art of extracting government money and vast land grants, assets collectively needed for the financing of miles of their rails and support structures. With congressmen and government officials properly bribed by rail corporations, a side business of building hotels in the national park to serve their rail passengers would be simple enough. Even so, patience was in order. Unlike the shanty businesses in the park, the railways played a long game, their strategy necessitated by corporate financial difficulties throughout the 1870s that left their rails stalled far from Yellowstone. Allied politicians and early park superintendents delayed the issuing of official park leases, paving the way for the eventual monopolization of Wonderland.

Better positioned than its competitors, the Northern Pacific Railroad recovered and resumed westward expansion in the early 1880s, their powerful allies putting the squeeze on Yellowstone's non-leased entrepreneurs. At the same time, a government contract awarded for the development of lodging accommodations benefited the Northern Pacific, the locations of the leases corresponding to tourists' primary interests, including: Mammoth Hot Springs, the point of entrance and park headquarters; the Upper Geyser Basin, home to Old Faithful; the north shore of vast Yellowstone Lake; and the Grand Canyon and Lower Falls of the Yellowstone River.

Nonetheless, constructing buildings in Yellowstone's wilderness proved challenging for the Northern Pacific and other railroad interests. Among numerous structures from the park's early years only a few iconic hotels emerged and for many decades passed the test of time, fewer still standing in the present day. No ordinary structures were these magnificent buildings, but rather diverse edifices from majestically rustic to formal and stately, unique accommodations each suitable for the entertainment of wealthy tourist clientele of yesteryear, one eventually falling but rising again, another burned to ashes never to rise, and two still intact since their beginnings and accessible to all park visitors today.

MAMMOTH HOT SPRINGS HOTEL

August 1883 marked the beginning of a new chapter in the story of Yellowstone. Simultaneously the Northern Pacific Railroad reached Cinnabar, Montana, three miles from the park's northern border and eight from Mammoth Hot Springs, while in Mammoth the first significant hotel in the park opened. No small building, Mammoth's National Hotel boasted 141 rooms, a spacious lobby, and electricity. Amenities included private baths, room service, billiards, a pool table, boot blacking, and newspapers—not bad for 1883.[1]

The National Hotel in 1883, also known as Hatch's Hotel, Mammoth Springs Hotel, and Mammoth Hot Springs Hotel. This was the first major hotel in Yellowstone. NPS PHOTO

Beyond accommodations and amenities, the hotel stood at the confluence of competing ideological currents involving some of America's most prominent men, and it was destined to play a critical role in shaping Yellowstone's future.

It began with a celebration. "With the possible exception of Gould and Vanderbilt none of the New York millionaires is more widely known by reputation than Rufus Hatch," enthused a *Livingston Enterprise* story about the arrival of the prominent financier and president of the transparently named Yellowstone National Park Improvement Company (YNPIC). Hatch's Hotel, as locals sometimes referred to the National, represented the first major commercial step toward taming the park's wilderness. Seeking additional business partners to further develop Wonderland, Hatch hosted at "his leasehold property, the Yellowstone Park" an influential entourage of potential American and British investors capable of putting "money in his purse." As did much of the knowledgeable public, the newspaper equated the park itself with Hatch, and Hatch with a mission of enriching himself and the Northern Pacific Railroad.[2]

The financier's skills of persuasion, however, were quickly put to the test. "At dinner every day they run huge wine bills against him," one correspondent observed of Hatch's British guests. One wealthy gentleman "visited the only store in the Park, purchased a pair of drawers and told the proprietor to charge the same to Uncle Rufus." Of the proliferate spending "Uncle Rufus tears his hair, gnashes his teeth, and has actually offered Ashley Cole, his secretary, the Park privileges for ten years to bring down a few cowboys and Indians to kill off a few of his imported sight-seers."[3]

Perhaps his guests sensed Hatch's frustration. In jest some in the party played a "great joke" on the magnate, preying upon his anger and competitiveness. While touring the park, Hatch and his guests "stopped over night with the only rival hotelkeeper in the park, up at Fire Hole, and for this and a lunch the man charged him $97. Rufus was so mad that he ordered his men to erect a tent hotel to-day right at a point near by, which shall cut off travel from his rival. He says he will bust that hotel if he has to provide free accommodations."[4]

F. Jay Haynes captured this image of *Old Faithful in Action* during President Chester A. Arthur's 1883 Yellowstone Expedition. LIBRARY OF CONGRESS, PRINTS & PHOTOGRAPHS DIVISION, LC-USZ62-137257

Not to be outdone, Rufus Hatch went on the offensive. As the party camped on the shore of Yellowstone Lake, the financier arranged a snipe hunt, targeting the English "young bloods—mighty hunters if you heard them talk." With "rare patience" the unsuspecting hunters "held gunny sacks to bag snipe for the best part of the long, dark night. They straggled back, one after another, toward day break, weary and crestfallen, and swearing 'there wasn't a bloody snipe on the whole blawsted shore, you know.'"[5]

But the grinning host did not stop there, now arranging for gunmen to hold up four boastful Brits on an alleged elk hunt. Relieved of guns and pocket possessions by the bandits, the subdued quartet "made their way back to camp with exaggerated stories of their robbery," of which they had "barely escaped with their lives." After they finished their tale, "Uncle Rufus threw up the flap of a tent and on a camp table exposed every piece and parcel of their property."[6]

While financier Rufus Hatch alternatively whined about and made fun of his troublesome charges, a man of grander note slowly made his way northward through Yellowstone on horseback. President Chester Arthur had fishing on his mind, and he caught ample trout in the park. But the president's hosts—Lieutenant General Philip Sheridan, US senator George Vest of Missouri, and conservationist George Bird Grinnell, editor of *Forest and Stream* magazine—had their own agenda: advocating for the protection of Wonderland from speculative capitalists like Hatch.

Arthur's enormous party of nearly one hundred men included a cavalry escort of seventy-five men, numerous government officials and dignitaries, and park photographer F. Jay Haynes, and was accompanied by 175 pack animals. In addition to fishing, the party visited Yellowstone's most stunning sights, locations where Rufus Hatch's YNPIC planned on constructing scores of buildings, with little to no oversight. Should Hatch succeed, conservationists feared Old Faithful Geyser and the Lower Falls of the Yellowstone River's Grand Canyon would become scenes of crass commercialization.[7]

A novelist could not have penned a more fitting description of what happened next, nor a playwright a more vivid script.

Converging serendipitously at the National Hotel, these titans of government, capitalism, and conservation held within their wills and might the future of the nation's solitary federal park. Three powerful forces, two competing visions, and one wild card, the president of the United States of America: Whoever successfully courted President Arthur would claim victory for their cause, and the conservationists arrived with the upper hand.

Desperate to save Yellowstone National Park from exploitation, in 1883 conservationists convinced US president Chester A. Arthur to visit the park and see the damage for himself. Accompanying the group, early Yellowstone photographer F. Jay Haynes captured this portrait of the *Presidential Party, Upper Geyser Basin*. Left to right, members of the party are: John Schuyler Crosby, Lieutenant Colonel Michael V. Sheridan, Lieutenant General Philip H. Sheridan, Anson Stager, unidentified, President Arthur, unidentified, unidentified, Robert Todd Lincoln, and George G. Vest. Unidentified men may be Daniel G. Rollins, James F. Gregory, W. P. Clark, W. H. Forwood, and/or George G. Vest Jr. *PRESIDENTIAL PARTY, UPPER GEYSER BASIN*, F. JAY HAYNES, 1883. LIBRARY OF CONGRESS, PRINTS & PHOTOGRAPHS DIVISION, LC-USZ62-137259.

Having surveyed Yellowstone's wonders with his own eyes—the first US president to do so—Chester Arthur encountered at Mammoth Hot Springs the workings of a corporate monopoly in the people's park. Even as the president made himself as comfortable as possible in the National Hotel, under the same roof and behind closed doors, Rufus Hatch made his move.

Pitching his bold plan to the wealthy Americans and Brits he had endured for days in the park, Hatch sounded as if Wonderland were his personal playground. With the help of well-connected and palm-greased allies in Washington, the Northern Pacific planned to lay rails in the park and commercialize Old Faithful and the Grand Canyon of the Yellowstone River through the YNPIC, by monopolizing hotels, transportation, cattle ranching, and logging and mining interests within the park. Even as he spoke Hatch's employees were cutting forests for lumber needed to enlarge the National Hotel, and poaching elk to feed laborers.[8]

But there the intrigue was only beginning. Aware of Hatch's presence and in Shakespearean fashion if newspaper accounts are to be believed, President Arthur "tried to hide from [Hatch] in an undiscovered region"—in the hotel, presumably—albeit to no avail. Ever wily, the capitalist in devilish fashion sized up his prey, visiting "the president in the disguise of a cowboy." Hatch having had his fun and with Arthur's presence discovered by journalists, the two men apparently met face to face without further pretext. Afterward, and "happy because the president had to send and purchase supplies" from Hatch's operations at Mammoth, the capitalist smiled at Arthur's observation of the "abominable" road conditions in the park. Pledging to request substantial federal funding for road improvements, President Arthur effectively promised to smooth the way for Hatch's business interests in the park.[9]

Not merely content to triumph, Rufus Hatch seems to have planted bad publicity about President Arthur. Following the showdown at the National Hotel, a newspaper article in the *Daily Globe* newspaper of St. Paul, Minnesota—home of the Northern Pacific Railroad—offered a decidedly negative view of the president's party. President Arthur, widely known to enjoy intoxicating spirits, had been "too full for utterance"—slang for drunk—along with many of his party, including General Sheridan who "was too drunk to walk or talk with anything like ease of regularity." "What a spectacle!" the writer proclaimed. "A president of the United States, and the general of the army, occupying the places which should belong solely to the ordinary specimen of the genus loafer or bum. The idea is to condemn them forever in the minds of all reputable and respectable people."[10]

Capitalist Rufus Hatch seemed to have won the day, but in an instant a fate of epic proportions snatched defeat from the jaws of victory. Even as the railroad speculator wooed Yellowstone investors and manipulated

President Arthur at the National Hotel, Northern Pacific Railroad stock crashed, financially ruining the heavily invested Hatch.[11] With the railway in disarray, conservationists suddenly gained the upper hand. Yellowstone's dangers now being known in the White House, three years distant and amid continued lax congressional oversight of commercial activity and poaching in Yellowstone, Vest and Grinnell finally succeeded in maneuvering Congress to abandon ineffective civilian oversight of Yellowstone in favor of military administration.

As if on cue, alongside the arrival of law and order in Yellowstone in 1886 in the form of the US Army, the Yellowstone National Park Improvement Company declared bankruptcy. But ever resourceful, the Northern Pacific Railroad in a sleight of hand retained control of defunct YNPIC interests through a new corporate-controlled company, the Yellowstone Park Association, thereby effectively maintaining a near-monopoly on park hotels. Not until a decade later did the schemes of the Northern Pacific and other railroads fall apart.

Concessions contracts increasingly being scrutinized and the Northern Pacific being less influentially positioned following the end of the Gilded Age, by the close of the nineteenth century a fruitful relationship developed among railroad interests, conservationist advocates, and the Interior Department, who together perceived Yellowstone as a playground for the elite, the language of the "people's park" notwithstanding. For their part and through time, rail corporations adopted a less odorous and more subtle model of partnership with, rather than ownership of, park businesses. By the turn of the twentieth century the Northern Pacific Railway (until 1896 the Northern Pacific Railroad) developed a working relationship with Montana businessman Harry W. Child. An early Yellowstone concessionaire, Child became a major owner of park transportation and lodging enterprises. Struggling to maintain profitability, Child for decades relied upon the financial backing of the Northern Pacific. Not until the arrival of the Great Depression and attendant waning of rail travel to the park did their relationship fall by the wayside. In 1936 various Child Yellowstone operations were consolidated into the Yellowstone Park Company (YPC), which retained family ownership until 1980.[12]

Evolving during the park's early years, the National Hotel, the first of Yellowstone's iconic hotels, changed names and shape. No longer the sole grandiose hotel in Yellowstone by the early twentieth century, the National was but one of five premier lodging accommodations in Wonderland, in addition to other, smaller accommodations. Although located at park headquarters and the entry point for most park visitors in early decades, the magnificent hotel, renamed the Mammoth Hot Springs Hotel as early as 1883, soon faded in desirability. Compared to better-located hotels at Old Faithful Geyser, on the shore of Yellowstone Lake, at Lower Geyser Basin, and at the Grand Canyon of the Yellowstone River, the hotel at Mammoth Hot Springs failed to compete for the best scenery.

In addition, between 1913 and 1915, the structure was downsized by the removal of the fourth floor, flattening of the roof, and the addition of a North Wing. Increasingly the bulk of tourist activity in the park shifted to the geyser basins, as more visitors entered Yellowstone via the West Entrance. When the early years of the Great Depression brought a dramatic decline in visitation and the closure of several hotels and lodges throughout the park, Harry W. Child's YPC seized the opportunity to tear down the original Mammoth hotel structure, leaving the more recently built North Wing to anchor a new facility. The addition of cabins, designed by architect Robert Reamer, followed over the next two years and resulted in an old name being expanded: Mammoth Hot Springs Hotel and Cottages.[13]

Even so, the revolving door of names continued. Known as the Mammoth Motor Inn from 1966 to 1977, thereafter the present-day name, Mammoth Hot Springs Hotel & Cabins, has graced the oldest of Yellowstone's iconic hotels. Despite various renovations, updates, and structural work since the 1930s, the hotel's appearance has remained essentially unchanged since World War II.

Today's visitors enter the front doors of the hotel under a portico similar to that which stagecoaches and early automobiles used. To the right of the lobby is the unique Map Room, an elaborate 1930s-era, wall-sized map of the United States comprised of a variety of woods, designed by architect Robert Reamer. Behind the hotel are the Depression-era cabins, since that time significantly updated. To the left of the hotel is the nearby and stand-alone dining room, constructed during the 1930s. Throughout the lodging complex the interior of today's Mammoth Hot Springs Hotel is far more modernized and comfortable than in the past, and no longer do politicians, capitalists, and conservationists, in the modern era of wilderness preservation, lock horns for control of Wonderland.

GRAND CANYON HOTEL

In the early years of the Army's superintendency of Yellowstone and the existence of the Yellowstone Park Association, however, the government's park headquarters and the corporation remained at odds. Three years into his tenure, Acting Superintendent Moses Harris had removed a number of illegal operations in the park, and he was continuing to voice frustration at the Northern Pacific's veiled ownership of the Association and its violations of park policies. Finally resolving the matter in 1889, the Association voluntarily relinquished its folio of questionable contracts in return for six new leases of one to three acres each at popular locations in the park: Mammoth Hot Springs, Norris Geyser Basin, Lower Geyser Basin, Grand Canyon, Yellowstone Lake, and either Thumb or Shoshone Lake. Only three of these locations would eventually endure as lodging sites: Mammoth, Grand Canyon, and Lake. Shoshone Lake was never developed, while early hotels at Norris Geyser Basin and the expansive Fountain Hotel at Lower Geyser Basin (opened in 1891), as well as a tent camp at West Thumb, failed to survive in the park's post-stagecoach era.[14]

In June 1891, the Canyon Hotel (at the time referred to as the "Cañon Hotel") fully opened to the public (it had first opened in the summer of 1890, before it was complete), followed by the Lake Hotel one month later. A newspaper account that summer described both structures as "first-class hotels," whereas most facilities under the management of the Yellowstone Park Association stretched the definition of "first class" and "hotel" both. As for the actual hotels, "colored waiters" served guests at the Mammoth Hotel, and "white girls at the others."[15]

Imposing if not altogether stately, the Canyon Hotel, a wooden building three stories tall and boasting 250 rooms, sat on a hillside meadow above Lower Falls and overlooking the road. Nonetheless, the structure

Embodying luxury in the wilderness of Yellowstone, the Grand Canyon Hotel lodged and entertained visitors from 1911 to 1960. F. Jay Haynes Junior Photo #14056. IMAGE COURTESY OF THE LANCASTER YELLOWSTONE COLLECTION

received mixed reviews. In 1891, a visitor referring to the Grand Canyon and the Lower Falls "as the grandest sight of all" in Wonderland, lodged at the hotel "for a night's rest" but offered no words about the building.[16] An observer the following year spoke of the hotel as "the largest and best appointed in the Park."[17] A 1909 Yellowstone guidebook declared that the hotel "can make no claim to architectural beauty" but praised the views from its windows and veranda of "mountains and meadows with only a white fleck of the foaming water of the Upper Falls dotted in."[18] Park Acting Superintendent Harris spoke more frankly, deeming the structure "a most unsightly edifice."[19]

In addition to uninspiring reviews, the Canyon Hotel suffered from an unstable foundation, requiring repairs of cracked interior walls in 1896. Five years after this, twenty-four additional rooms were added, and repairs made to the foundation. Even so, the unsteady ground remained

The spacious lounge of the Grand Canyon Hotel. F. Jay Haynes Junior Photo #10174. IMAGE COURTESY OF THE LANCASTER YELLOWSTONE COLLECTION

problematic, in 1911 necessitating a major overhaul of the structure. Utilizing stable portions of the troubled Canyon Hotel, architect Robert Reamer designed a new hotel on the same hillside. Christened the Grand Canyon Hotel, at five stories high and 700 feet in length, the hotel lived up to its name The formal August 3, 1911, opening was celebrated "by a ball, in which the guests of the hotel, campers in the park, fisherman, hotel employees and everybody else within a radius of 50 miles joined in."[20]

A massive open lobby graced the interior, its floor of polished oak, walls of red birch, and French plate-glass windows impressing tourists. A spiral staircase led to guest rooms upstairs, and a grand stairway to the lounge and dining room. Both the Northern Pacific and Union Pacific railways touted the magnificent structure in promotional literature and through glowing accounts in popular, industry, and architectural magazines.[21]

From romantic strolls along the canyon rim to exquisite dining, evening dances, and an orchestra, fitting leisure activities and entertainment matched the hotel's splendor. Guest services included a hydraulic elevator, a telegraph office, a livery office, ample writing desks, and a cigar and newsstand for men, amenities in the backwoods setting reflective of a determination by Harry W. Child to build a refined resort in rugged and remote wilderness. It was, in the words of historian Tamsen Hert, "Luxury in the Wilderness."[22]

For decades the Grand Canyon Hotel remained a destination in and of itself, a glamorous seasonal resort for socializing, relaxing, dining, and sleeping in comfort while leisurely admiring the splendor of nature's greater glory nearby. Although the hotel entertained fewer guests in the early years of the Great Depression, visitation recovered nicely in the second half of the decade, the dancing and orchestra carrying on throughout, wealthy guests seemingly impervious to economic troubles beyond the park's boundaries.

But the glamour came at a cost, facility maintenance and upkeep for decades making profitability elusive. Making matters worse, in the 1950s two major problems confronted the now-aging Grand Canyon Hotel: foundation issues resurfaced yet again, even as the National Park Service formulated a major overhaul of Canyon visitor facilities that called for the dismantling of the hotel.

Beneath the umbrella of Mission 66, an architectural modernization of selective visitor infrastructure within Yellowstone and other parks, an NPS-mandated redesign of Canyon Village required Harry W. Child's Yellowstone Park Company to construct modern cabins while keeping the Grand Canyon Hotel open, thus further straining company finances. At the same time, a January 1959 architectural assessment of the Canyon Hotel revealed new structural issues so severe "that it was not economically feasible to rehabilitate the building and that it should be abandoned." YPC made the decision to raze, in the words of the *Cody Enterprise*, "the world-renowned Grand Canyon Hotel." Prior to tearing down the hotel, YPC dispensed with many of the hotel's stately furnishings, some reallocated to other company properties, and others purchased by a myriad of people with fond memories of the once magnificent structure. But in an ironic twist before the hotel had been completely demolished, a fire of unknown cause on August 8, 1960, destroyed the remainder of the building, in timely but tragic fashion burning to the ground the famed, luxurious resort.[23]

In many ways fortuitous, the passing of the iconic but flawed Grand Canyon Hotel paved the way in the 1960s for modern cabin facilities anchoring a redeveloped Mission 66 Canyon Village—a new complex that was low-slung, utilitarian, and located farther from the crowded canyon rim. Today much of Canyon Village retains vestiges of the Mission 66 redesign, accompanied by a new lodging facility opened in 2016. East of the village shops and cafeteria and projecting stately grandeur, a modern luxurious lodge is comprised of a series of free-standing buildings, each featuring contemporary rustic architecture, multiple units, and state-of-the-art conveniences.

Lake Hotel

The second lasting and iconic Yellowstone hotel to open in 1891, Lake Hotel on the north shore of Yellowstone Lake stood out starkly against the wilderness landscape. Vividly yellow in color from its earliest days, it could be seen from many miles away at certain points along the lake shore drive to the south. Lake-facing windows in the hotel offered sweeping views, the distant Absaroka Mountains in plain sight. But despite its spectacular setting, the plain-looking Lake Hotel failed to impress, garnering but little notice in newspapers in the months following its opening.

Rectangular in shape, three stories tall, and featuring a simple, front porch with wooden chairs upon which stagecoach and wagon passengers stepped upon arrival, the Lake Hotel held a mere fifty-one rooms. Although comfortable enough and featuring electric lights, hotel rooms lacked many modern conveniences. From the main floor a Queen Anne staircase took guests to rooms on the second and third floors. As in other park hotels, porters carried guests' bags. Rooms featured the basics: a bed beneath which lay a chamber pot, a marble washstand with a white porcelain washbasin and pitcher, a mirror mounted above, and towel bars on each side. All guests shared hall communal bathrooms. For most visitors,

Opened in 1891 and enlarged thereafter, Lake Hotel on the shore of Yellowstone Lake included a presidential suite that hosted President Calvin Coolidge. Pictured is the front entrance, facing the lake. F. Jay Haynes Junior Photo #20090. IMAGE COURTESY OF THE LANCASTER YELLOWSTONE COLLECTION

it was nothing to write home about, even after the interior was rearranged in 1901 to allow the addition of seventeen more rooms.[24]

In fashion similar to some other hotels in the park, the simplicity of accommodations belied excellent guest services that befitted city hotels in the East. For an additional fee, cleaning services kept ladies' dresses and men's suits nicely pressed. Haircuts, shaves, and baths cost extra and were popular. Dining included fine wines, white linen tablecloths, china, silverware, and fresh wildflower arrangements, the latter a touch of the West.[25]

Though the environs of the Lake Hotel lacked a major natural tourist attraction aside from Yellowstone Lake, many visitors enjoyed the plentiful and easy trout fishing. Some guests opted for a ride on the steamboat *Zillah*. Owned by the colorful and controversial concessionaire E. C. Waters, the steamboat was but one of several enterprises that the entrepreneur operated, including livestock near the hotel and a small zoo containing captive bison and elk on the lake's Dot Island, a *Zillah* stopover. In time, Waters's obnoxious personality and behavior coupled with negligence regarding his animals led to the suspension of his park contract in 1907.[26] Waters's livestock and zoo, however, were not the only troubling animal shows in the vicinity of the Lake Hotel. In the evenings, the hotel's garbage dump attracted bears, a sight also unnatural but nonetheless thrilling to many hotel guests.

Scenery, fine dining, and a menagerie of animals aside, the Lake Hotel, absent geysers or a canyon, needed something else, and Harry W. Child set out to find it. From his home state of California, Child recruited a rising young architectural star in 1903, the aforementioned Robert Reamer. A decade before Reamer designed the Grand Canyon Hotel and long before he designed the charming cabins to accompany the Mammoth Hot Springs Hotel, the young architect at the turn of the twentieth century worked in the West Coast hotel industry. Soon after Child introduced Reamer to Yellowstone, the architect at the age of twenty-nine relocated to the park to begin work on his first two major projects in Wonderland: the construction of the Old Faithful Inn and a major renovation of the Lake Hotel.

The latter, completed in 1904, transformed the simple, wooden, yellow hotel into a grand and luxurious Colonial structure featuring 210 rooms, four times the original total. Newly added Roman columns soaring fifty feet high supported three porticoes, on each side mirrored in style by false dormers and complemented with fifteen false balconies. New Colonial Revival windows came in three styles: rectangular, half-moon, and oval (oculus). Inside Reamer expanded the lobby, walls, and columns, while incorporating ceiling beams made from California redwood. So dramatic was the makeover that for several decades, the hotel was known by various names: Lake Colonial Hotel, Colonial Lake Hotel, or the Colonial Hotel.

Additional expansions in the 1920s, driven by a dramatic growth in tourism due to automobiles and a surging national economy, collectively added an East Wing and a North Wing, an enlarged dining room, a presidential suite (enjoyed by President Calvin Coolidge), and the iconic hotel lobby sunroom overlooking the lake. Some seven hundred feet long and boasting 323 rooms with baths by 1929, Lake Hotel was effectively finished, today looking virtually the same.

Then (and now), live entertainment in the massive lobby off the dining room included an evening string quartet. A well-stocked bar offered drinks for purchase. Board games and puzzles provided family-style recreation. Prior to the finishing touches of the 1920s, a 1913 guidebook's description of the grand hotel on the lake offered words that have withstood the test of time: "This is a good place to stop, to rest from your journey and wonder seeing, and to prepare for the scenic grandeur to come when you start out again."[27]

Old Faithful Inn

To architect Robert Reamer belongs the credit for shaping the elegant Lake Hotel as it stands today. Yet Reamer is far less remembered for his work on the Lake Hotel than he is as the mastermind behind the Old Faithful Inn, arguably the most famous hotel in the world. Yet the story of the Old Faithful Inn begins long before Reamer, for if not for Harry W. Child's determination, Reamer likely would have never set foot in Yellowstone, and the Old Faithful Inn as beloved by millions would not exist.

By the turn of the twentieth century more than ten thousand visitors arrived in Yellowstone annually, Old Faithful being the number one park destination, and the very place in which Harry W. Child floundered. Although his Northern Pacific–financed Yellowstone Park Transportation Company delivered travelers to the park's biggest attraction, and despite also operating the Northern Pacific–allied Yellowstone Park Association lodging company, Child lacked a real hotel in the Upper Geyser Basin.

Nor did the basin boast of any large-scale hotels. Few lodging options existed there at the turn of the century, none upscale. Most prominently, a large Wylie tent village near Daisy Geyser served the overnight needs of many visitors. In addition, a small, ramshackle wooden "hotel" that had replaced the 1885 Upper Geyser Basin Hotel—more commonly known as the Shack Hotel—when it burned in 1894, provided crude lodging rooms. Managed by Larry Mathews of lunch-station fame, the replacement hotel, also known as the Shack Hotel, consisted of a small and plain

Designed by architect Robert Reamer to complement the surrounding wilderness, the unique Old Faithful Inn, constructed of nearby natural materials, opened in 1904. The hotel inspired a new architectural movement, "Parkitecture," or "National Park Service Rustic." Today, the Old Faithful Inn is arguably the most famous hotel in the world. This undated image by JP Clum depicts the hotel's entrance area. NPS PHOTO

wooden building housing a dining room and surrounded by a dozen or so large tents divided into rooms.[28]

What then, might Harry W. Child do to capture more of the growing tourist market at Old Faithful?

Many visitors who stayed overnight, he observed, complained about the lack of a genuine hotel. Child's Yellowstone Park Association held the lease on the land occupied by the ramshackle Shack Hotel (the hotel that had replaced the former Upper Geyser Basin Hotel). A real hotel would certainly appeal to visitors, but no previous hotel in the Upper Geyser Basin had been successful. Undeterred nonetheless, Child at the turn of the century was determined to build a grand hotel near Old Faithful Geyser. Envisioning a rustic structure, he obtained permission from park officials to log trees in the nearby forest. And as he made plans, through

First-time visitors stepping through the front doors of the Old Faithful Inn often were—and are today—mesmerized. In this undated JP Clum image, the hotel's massive stone fireplace, constructed from rhyolite quarried nearby, soars far upward in the Old Faithful Inn's enormous open-air lobby. NPS PHOTO

a mutual friend Harry W. Child became acquainted with and hired the aforementioned architect Robert Reamer.[29]

Not only did Child stand to benefit from a hotel near Old Faithful Geyser, but so, too, the Northern Pacific Railway, which provided funding for the proposed project. Razing the (second) Shack Hotel provided a prime site for the new structure. Surveying the Upper Geyser Basin and its surroundings, Reamer crafted a design reflective of, and utilizing materials from, the natural environment of forests and exposed cliffs. For wood, Reamer turned to plentiful lodgepole pine trees in the vicinity. For the massive stone fireplace, he chose rhyolite, a hard, volcanic rock plentiful and close at hand, a product of the region's ancient volcanic history. Trees and rocks both were obtained mere miles from the building site.

With a unique and bold concept sketched out, Reamer and a crew of some forty to fifty men—probably locals, their names lost to history—in the summer of 1903 set to work. Some two hundred feet away from Old Faithful Geyser, a foundation of rock and cement was constructed, the Reamer-designed large log building thereafter taking shape and slowly rising skyward. Through the fall season and harsh winter, work on the Inn continued, months of snow cover facilitating the skidding of logs and stones to the work site. Imported nails and spikes held the great logs in place. Pine being unsuitable for the roof, redwood shingles were imported from the West Coast.[30]

In early 1904, with the structure enclosed, the attention of Reamer and his builders shifted to fixtures and furnishings. Again, Reamer turned to the surrounding forests for materials, this time for railings and decorative crosspieces—comprised of gnarled lodgepole limbs—and the large, wooden, front entrance doors. A forge operating on the construction site shaped much of the ironwork necessary for the steam-heated room vents, the front entrance doors, the dining room door, the massive clock on the fireplace facing the front door, and the electric lamp fixtures suspended from the ceiling. From afar, a myriad of furnishings arrived—beds, linens, tables, chairs, stoves, plates, and more—all positioned in place in time to accommodate guests nightly for the 1904 summer season.[31]

A towering marvel of logs crowned by a six-stories high, sloped gable roof, the majestic Old Faithful Inn captured the essence of Yellowstone's wilderness. Featuring three floors of rooms plus indoor balconies and a tree house, the hotel's open interior lobby soared upward over eighty feet, walls of exposed logs mirroring the nearby lodgepole forest. Dormer windows, rather than being arrayed in symmetrical fashion, from the outside perched out of balance in a seemingly haphazard arrangement that, in Reamer's eye, reflected the disorderliness of nature. Facing the geyser basin northward, Old Faithful Inn overlooked from a large, second-floor outdoor balcony the famous Old Faithful Geyser, which rose prominently to the right, with other popular geysers Beehive, Grotto, and Castle also visible. Beneath the outdoor balcony, a large porte-cochère (or coach gateway) brought stagecoaches to the front door.

Eager to capitalize on the first major park hotel located near Old Faithful Geyser and constructed in tandem with nature, the Northern Pacific Railway in February 1904 launched a national advertising campaign for the hotel's inaugural, upcoming summer season. Pairing the sitting President Theodore Roosevelt—America's foremost conservationist who had visited the park the year prior—with the hotel-in-progress, the railway "issued a handsome folder showing the Yellowstone Park Gateway [now known as the Yellowstone Arch], dedicated by President [Theodore] Roosevelt, April 24, 1903," alongside a rendering of the Inn.[32]

"Old Faithful Inn, modern in every respect, constructed of logs and boulders, located near Old Faithful geyser, is the most unique structure of the kind in the country," proclaimed the railway-friendly *Minneapolis Journal* newspaper as the Inn opened in June.[33] Days later Harry J. Horn, Northern Pacific Railway manager, visited Yellowstone and offered one of the earliest published descriptions of the building. "[U]ndoubtedly the most unique hotel in the world," he said of the hotel, expanding its architectural uniqueness globally. "It is constructed of rock and logs and rough lumber throughout, the braces, stairways and balconies being worked out from all sorts of odd shaped logs. The lobby of the hotel is made up of a series of log balconies extending from the floor to the roof, a distance of nearly ninety feet. The dining room in the hotel is similar to the magnificent dining room of the Washington hotel in Seattle, except that it is built entirely after the fashion of a log cabin."

"The hotel," he continued, "is furnished with arts and crafts specially designed furniture. The toilet seats are of old brown colonial patterns, the model of which was taken from a New Bedford sailor that sailed the ocean a hundred years ago. Old blue delft china and rag carpet rugs harmonize perfectly with the surroundings. The construction of the hotel is strictly on original lines, and I have no doubt that in time it will be extensively copied."[34]

Nor was Horn alone among Northern Pacific men in promoting the Inn. Near the close of the season A. M. Cleland, general agent of the railroad, also visited the Inn, further extolling the new hotel's unique charms. The Old Faithful Inn "is a wonder to all the tourists who visit it," he declared. "It is of enormous size, and built of logs throughout, the rustic appearance being preserved even in the guest rooms. The ax, saw and hammer built the entire structure. There isn't a yard of plaster in the entire building. The fireplaces are built of big boulders, and the hotel is simply the product of the forest. It is extremely beautiful, and has every comfort, such as private baths, hot and cold water, electric lights and all other conveniences."[35]

Cleland also focused on an exterior feature of the Inn that would mesmerize tourists for decades. "From the tower a search light is operated. I saw Old Faithful by searchlight; and the sight was magnificent. One of the features of the trip was to see the searchlight man chase the bears with the powerful beam of light. The bears are afraid of the electric glare, and ran like scared sheep whenever the rays were turned on them."[36] No ordinary searchlight in the early days of electricity, Old Faithful Inn's searchlight was a "battleship searchlight" powerful enough to illuminate "all the other geysers in the upper basin at play during the night."[37]

One would expect Northern Pacific Railway officials to speak glowingly of the Inn, but how did ordinary tourists perceive the hotel in its debut summer of 1904? A female visitor from Baltimore offered a helpful perspective and additional details. "Old Faithful Inn, a rustic hotel, built out of natural logs with the bark on, is not only unique and artistic, but very comfortable—a virtue not possessed by many artistic things—the dining room is also finished in the natural logs with the bark on, also all of the sleeping rooms and lobby." Meals were delightful, the dining room "enhanced by the immense fireplace in which glows a cheerful fire, over which a huge brass kettle is steaming merrily as if in invitation of its natural brothers—the geysers—outside."[38]

Of the lobby she spoke poetically. "The trusses are massive logs, artistically placed, giving an air of solidarity and beauty to the room, and a sense of serenity. A unique feature is the monster stone chimney with its eight fireplaces—a chimney which has no counterpart in the world—for whoever heard of a chimney with four large and four small fireplaces in it, each with a separate flue?" she marveled. "In the evening one is entertained by a Hungarian orchestra, which will make you wonder if you really are in the midst of Yellowstone Park." Of her tour of Yellowstone not a word did she offer of the other hotels, and far fewer words of Old Faithful Geyser.[39]

The original structure costing some $200,000 to construct,[40] several additions enlarged the Inn during the following two decades: an east wing (1913) and a west wing (1928) in total brought the room count to 390 rooms. An enlarged dining room roughly doubled seating capacity. Following Prohibition, the 1936 addition of a bar, the Bear Pit Lounge, pleased many guests. Originally located in the present-day snack room to the right of the dining room, the Bear Pit is now located immediately to the left of the dining room. By World War II, the Old Faithful Inn looked essentially as it does today, and after the war the hotel, access previously confined to paying customers, opened to the general public.[41]

In the present-day Old Faithful Inn still astonishes first-time tourists. Walking through the big red front doors, amazed visitors pause to gaze across the vast log lobby, momentarily fixating on the massive stone fireplace adorned by a huge cast-iron frame clock. Heads tilt upward to the second and third balconies, and still beyond to the roof far above, civilization and wilderness crowning in harmony. It is a moment, the first time one walks into the Inn's storied lobby and looks upward, that is not easily forgotten, a memory that endures and draws some visitors back year after year.

Standing apart from all other national park hotels as the first example of Parkitecture—also known as National Park Service Rustic—the Old Faithful Inn's opening in 1904 marked the beginning of America's enduring love affair with nature-inspired, western national park hotels and lodges. Soon, Parkitecture style found additional expression in the construction of other nature-inspired national park lodging facilities, including Paradise Inn in Mount Rainier National Park (1917); Zion Lodge in Zion National Park (1925; destroyed by fire in 1966, it was rebuilt in 1990); Bryce Canyon Lodge in Bryce Canyon National Park (1925); the Ahwahnee Hotel in Yosemite National Park (1927); and Grand Canyon Lodge in Grand Canyon National Park (1928; destroyed by fire in 1936, it was rebuilt the following year).[42]

Within Wonderland itself, the ongoing success of the Old Faithful Inn represented, and still today represents, the capstone of grand hotels' ascendancy in the park's four major tourist areas: Mammoth, the Grand Canyon and Lower Falls, Yellowstone Lake, and finally, the Upper Geyser Basin. Today, Robert Reamer's first Yellowstone hotel creation, the Old Faithful Inn, intact through a succession of operating companies, remains Yellowstone's most desirable lodging option.

Currently the Old Faithful Inn and all other park hotel properties—including at Grant Village, built in 1984 south of West Thumb, and Yellowstone's newest visitor complex—are managed by Xanterra Parks and Resorts, operating as Yellowstone National Park Lodges. Paying tribute to the heritage of the park's iconic hotels, public historians employed by Xanterra provide free narrated tours of the Old Faithful Inn, a position held by Ruth Quinn for some three decades before her retirement in 2020. Quinn never tired of her dream job, her contributions to Yellowstone's history spanning several generations of visitors and including a biography of architect Robert Reamer.[43] Said a fellow employee, historian Lee Whittlesey, "The power of the ending of her tour speech about the Inn made me literally cry."[44]

WYLIE CAMPING COMPANY

Despite the Old Faithful Inn's grand entrance in 1904, the Wylie Camping Company yet fared well serving visitors of more modest means throughout the park's stagecoach era. Founder of the foremost commercial camping outfit amid a changing landscape of operators in the park, William Wallace Wylie succeeded by arriving early and patiently building a tent empire in Wonderland.

An Ohio native, Wylie moved to Bozeman in 1878 from Iowa as the new superintendent of the fledgling town's schools, his family following the next year. Fascinated with Yellowstone, in the summer of 1880 with school out of session, he began conducting seasonal tours of the park for paying customers. Three years later Wylie formally named his business and conducted ten-day park tours, housing tourists in movable tents. A decade later with permission of the Interior Department he established semi-permanent tent camps in Yellowstone, and by the turn of the century was an approved operator of permanent canvas tent camps at Apollinaris Spring (relocated to Swan Lake Flat in 1906); near Daisy Geyser in the Upper Geyser Basin; a short distance from the Lake Hotel (now the site of Lake Lodge); and near the old Canyon Junction at Cascade Creek. He also operated a lunch station at West Thumb. Offering six-and-a-half-day guided tours in the park inclusive of lodging and dining, Wylie hired teachers during their summer school break to serve as tour guides, thereby educating his guests about Yellowstone's natural surroundings. In addition to the educational dimension, camaraderie among guests, campfire talks replete with popcorn, employee entertainment, and general informality (contrasted with the formal attire required for hotel guests) characterized the "Wylie Way." Whereas five-and-a-half-day hotel tours cost $50, Wylie charged a mere $35 for his one-day-longer, more informative, and relaxed tours.[45]

Nonetheless, William Wylie struggled financially and was looked down upon by hotel operators. By 1905, the former superintendent of schools had grown weary of the camping business after nearly twenty-five years of busy summers, as well as a discouraging failure to obtain more than an annual, one-year lease for his operation. Ending an era, Wylie put his business up for sale. Quietly, Harry W. Child through a straw purchaser acquired a two-thirds interest in the Wylie Camping Company, bringing the park's leading camping outfit into his Yellowstone Park Association portfolio alongside his extensive hotel and transportation businesses. Under the auspices of the Wylie Permanent Camping Company and soon minus Wylie himself, the well-financed Child and his Livingston business partner A. W. Miles thereafter acquired a long-denied ten-year camping lease.

Relocating some camps and opening new ones, the new owners continued for a decade serving much of the park's tent clientele, Harry W. Child thereby profiting from visitors of varied financial means while continuing to use the term "Wylie Way." But in 1917 the newly established National Park Service reordered the concessions businesses, leading to the consolidation of the park's two main camping companies—Wylie and the Shaw & Powell Camping Company—into the singular Yellowstone Parks Camping Company, bringing a formal end to the Wylie name in

Yellowstone. In addition to the mandate from the NPS requiring Child to divest himself of camping interests in the park, Child also closed the Fountain Hotel, its location in the Lower Geyser Basin no longer needed as a stagecoach stopping point. The company's namesake and his family, meanwhile, established a new generation of Wylie tent camps in Zion and Grand Canyon National Parks.[46]

For only a few years longer canvas tent camping remained in Yellowstone, the tents supplanted in the 1920s and 1930s by park lodges (some constructed as early as the 1910s) offering affordable cabins targeted at visitors of modest means. Among early lodges with cabins, Old Faithful Lodge, Lake Lodge, and Roosevelt Lodge all remain in operation in similar fashion to the present-day. Mammoth Lodge ceased operation in 1940, many of the cabins relocated to Roosevelt. The original Canyon Lodge closed in 1957, and today's Canyon village features luxurious lodge rooms as well as less expensive cabins.[47]

For visitors of even lesser means, and nature-loving tourists desirous of sleeping beneath the park's dark night skies, park administration by the 1920s and 1930s transitioned from makeshift open-air campsites to formally constructed, designated, and managed public campgrounds. One of them, the Mammoth Hot Springs campground, was built by the Civilian Conservation Corps during the Great Depression.

But lodging accommodations alone could not meet the needs and expectations of tourists. Emerging parallel to and complimentary of early hotels and tent camps, some additional visitor services provided for travelers' evolving tastes.

STORES AND SHOPS
In the late nineteenth century, many small shops and stores hawked souvenirs and supplies to Wonderland's tourists. Among early stores was Ole Anderson's tent store at Mammoth Hot Springs, a rudimentary enterprise selling "coated specimens," popular souvenirs such as combs, bottles, and horseshoes soaked in the runoff waters of Mammoth Hot Springs to produce an alabaster-like coating.[48]

On a larger scale, George L. Henderson—an assistant park superintendent from 1882 to 1885 and businessman in Yellowstone thereafter until

The Klamer Store in the Upper Geyser Basin, depicted here in 1907, was the second general store in Yellowstone. From souvenirs to food and dry goods, general merchandise stores in early Yellowstone supplied the various needs of tourists. NPS PHOTO

1905—and his family also sold merchandise in Wonderland. Leading the way, Jennie Henderson, daughter of George and his wife Jeanette, served as Mammoth Hot Springs postmaster for a number of years from the 1880s into the early twentieth century. From the post office she also sold tourist items. In 1896 Jennie and her husband (George Ash) opened Yellowstone's first general store. Selling dry goods, general merchandise, clothing, and souvenirs, Jennie's general store—the building still in operation today as a store and located between the Mammoth Hot Springs cafeteria and service station—remained in her name until 1907, after which she sold the business to her brother, Walter Henderson, and his business partner, Alexander Lyall.[49]

Yellowstone's second general store opened one year after Jennie's store commenced business. In 1897 Henry Klamer, husband of Jennie's sister Mary, set up shop in the Upper Geyser Basin. Selling general merchandise, Klamer's store serviced tourists visiting the popular Old Faithful Geyser, among other thermal features in the area.[50]

Both stores remained in the Henderson family into the second decade of the twentieth century when, within the space of two years, each transitioned to new ownership. In 1913 Walter Henderson and Alexander Lyall sold their Mammoth Hot Springs store to George Whittaker, previously a soldier stationed in the park, and later a civilian scout in Yellowstone. Whittaker operated the store for two decades, also opening a gas station in Mammoth village (1915), as well as a general store and gas station at Canyon later in the decade.[51]

One year after the Henderson family divested itself of the store business at Mammoth Hot Springs, Henry Klamer died in 1914. A native of Winnipeg, Canada, and having established himself in the park by working for Harry W. Child, Charles Hamilton in 1915 joined the growing ranks of major park concessionaires with his purchase of the Klamer General Store at Old Faithful. Renovating the building in a style similar to that of the Old Faithful Inn and renaming it Hamilton's Store, Hamilton enlarged the log structure in 1924, adding a porch the following year. In subsequent years the operation of the store became a family affair, with Hamilton's sisters and a cousin all employed in the enterprise. Located near Old Faithful Inn, Yellowstone's second general store exists today in essentially the same structural form as in the 1920s, albeit without the Hamilton name.[52]

Paralleling the Henderson family's Yellowstone businesses, F. Jay Haynes solidified his photography business in the park. By the late 1890s his photo shops at Mammoth and Old Faithful stood a cut above the clutter of the many unsightly—and sometimes hazardous—concessions-related buildings scattered throughout the park. Acting superintendent Captain George Anderson, for years having struggled to bring order out of the chaos of concessionaires' facilities, deemed Haynes's Upper Geyser Basin log photo shop "the most beautiful and appropriate in the park."[53]

For almost four decades Haynes extensively photographed Yellowstone, producing a massive catalog of park photographs that he parlayed into a vast assortment of tourist items, including postcards, a variety of other souvenir items, and the annual *Haynes Guide* to Yellowstone. His photography and guidebook, the latter introduced in 1890 and revised

Charles Hamilton purchased the Klamer Store, renamed it Hamilton's Curio Store (later Hamilton Store), and refashioned the building (shown here in a 1917 Haynes image) to reflect the rustic look of the Old Faithful Inn. Thereafter Hamilton added a log front porch to the building. NPS PHOTO

annually through 1960, endured beyond his death in 1921, managed and supplemented by the work of his successor, son Jack E. Haynes.

Then and now, the Haynes family name stands tall in the annals of Yellowstone. "The history of Yellowstone National Park is, in many ways, the history of F. Jay and Jack Haynes," declared historian Mary Shivers Culpin. Mount Haynes, located in Madison Canyon along the Madison River between the park's West Entrance and Madison Junction, is named in Haynes's honor. Son Jack grew up in Mammoth Hot Springs and received his father's photography business in 1916. Producing popular postcards numbering in the hundreds of thousands over some five decades, in time the junior photographer and career Yellowstone resident became known simply as "Mr. Yellowstone."[54]

Outlasting both the Henderson and the Haynes families, the Hamilton family name, beginning with Charles Hamilton's purchase of the Klamer store in 1915, also became a long-lasting, multi-generational presence in Yellowstone. Charles Hamilton acquired store business operations at Mammoth and Lake in 1917, thereafter expanding into a network of general stores and filling stations at Old Faithful, Lake, Fishing Bridge, West Thumb, and, beginning in 1953, Mammoth Hot Springs and Canyon. Founded by Hamilton in 1926 in partnership with Harry W. Child and George Whittaker, Yellowstone Park Service Stations became a fixture in the park. From 1933 to 1951 Hamilton also operated the bath house and pool at Old Faithful, the popular tourist attraction fed by warm water that ran downhill from distant Solitary Geyser. In the second half of the twentieth century, the family-operated Hamilton stores—affectionately known as "Ham" stores by family, friends, and employees—effectively controlled the general mercantile business in Yellowstone. But amid a shifting commercial landscape in early twenty-first century Yellowstone, in 2003 the Delaware North Companies secured the park's general store concessions contract, bringing an end to Hamilton stores.[55]

The Hamilton family also operated the popular Geyser Bath House during the facility's later decades. Located in the Upper Geyser Basin, the bath house was fed by water from Solitary Geyser. NPS PHOTO

Long gone today is the heady, colorful, and rapidly changing tourist store, shop, and service landscape of earlier park days. In addition to the present-day Delaware North Yellowstone General Stores, Xanterra's Yellowstone National Park Lodges now operates small gift shops within park hotels. Yellowstone Forever, the singular nonprofit establishment partnered with the National Park Service in raising funds for park improvements and providing in-park educational courses and activities for visitors, operates additional gift stores in National Park Service–operated visitor centers. On the other hand, Yellowstone Park Service Stations remain, under newer ownership servicing the needs of motorists with locations at Mammoth Hot Springs, Old Faithful, Canyon, Tower/ Roosevelt Junction, Grant Village, and Fishing Bridge.[56]

Today's Yellowstone concessions landscape reflects twenty-first century visitors' expectations in an expanding, diverse world of national parks. Above all, the Old Faithful Inn and the Lake Hotel have withstood the test of time intact, still thriving as famed edifices nestled in Yellowstone's remote wilderness. Also notable, lesser-celebrated hotels, lodges, stores, and service stations enrich visitors' experiences in a modern Wonderland.

CHAPTER TEN

Rangering in Yellowstone

Guardians, Interpreters, Administrators, and Specialists

*Do good, avoid evil; remember who you are and what you stand for;
and watch out for the company you keep.*
—JERRY MERNIN, YELLOWSTONE RANGER[1]

IN THE PROCESS OF SAVING EARLY YELLOWSTONE NATIONAL PARK FROM
harmful human schemes, the US Army established a workable model for
policing not only the park's vast domain, but other national parks as well.
Even so, the federal government did not intend for the Army to remain
in Wonderland long-term.

However, it would be thirty-two years after riding into Yellowstone
that the soldiers and guardians of Wonderland who faced headwinds
within and without, saw their duty drawing to a close in 1918. Stagecoaches no longer rolled along the park's roads, leaving horse-mounted
soldiers seemingly out of place in a new automobiles-only world. At the
same time, an escalating war in Europe threatened the world order and
ensnared America, requiring the services of the Army. In the absence of
the War Department's administration of Yellowstone, the newly established National Park Service (NPS) introduced new civilian leadership of
the nation's oldest national park.

Created within the Department of the Interior in 1916, the National
Park Service was charged with consolidating oversight and management
of the country's national parks and monuments. As the nation's first and
premier national park, Yellowstone served as a model and testing ground
for the federal park lands that followed. Against the backdrop of the

pioneering 1872 Yellowstone Act, Congress by the year 1918 had established dozens of new national parks and monuments, all but one in the American West, many of archaeological as well as wilderness value, and all designated during Yellowstone's Army years.

In Wonderland, the journey toward national park rangers began early. Army soldiers manned Yellowstone's entrance stations, protected the geyser basins from vandals, occasionally gave talks at Old Faithful Geyser and other major park attractions, and answered visitors' questions. Separately, hardy and experienced local frontiersmen served as scouts. Charged with preventing poaching in the park's vast wilderness, scouts on horseback patrolled summer and winter, pitting their wits and stamina against the crafty wiles of illegal hunters pursuing elk and bison for commercial profit.

British (Scotland) native Jack Baronett, a seaman and gold prospector prior to serving as an Army scout during the Civil War and for General George Armstrong Custer on the Great Plains, settled in the Yellowstone region and became a legendary frontiersman. A brush with fame in 1870 accompanied his discovery and rescue deep within Yellowstone of the lost and nearly dead Truman C. Everts of the Washburn Expedition. Sixteen years later in 1886 he became the first Yellowstone scout. A tough and colorful pioneer in the park's early history, Baronnette Peak (bearing a misspelling of his name) was named in honor of him.[2]

In 1915, the combined roles of soldiers and scouts led to the experimental hiring of six seasonal "park rangers" in Yellowstone. The first four operated entrance stations in the summer, supplementing soldiers' duties. Employed in the fall and winter offseason, the remaining two more closely resembled the scouts of old but were chosen not to hunt poachers, but ironically to kill certain animals—coyotes, cougars, and wolves—deemed undesirable within the people's pleasuring ground due to their predation of ungulates favored by tourists.[3]

From these early efforts to instill law and order in Wonderland, a permanent national park ranger force soon emerged. Assuming the responsibilities of the recently departed Army soldiers and civilian scouts, Yellowstone's early rangers collectively manned entrance stations, policed and controlled road traffic, served in interpretive roles with visitors, oversaw various studies within the park, pushed office paperwork, fought wildfires, and patrolled human and wildlife behavior in the park. Yellowstone's early park rangers, in turn, shaped the emerging National Park Service–wide park ranger force.

Often on horseback into the 1930s, park rangers became ubiquitous in Yellowstone, the public face of the nation's first national park. Then as now, most served seasonally, reflective of busy summer tourist seasons and much quieter winter months. But today, the winters are not quieter; there is an entire winter tourist season.[4]

The lure of living in Yellowstone drew plenty of applicants in the early decades of the park's ranger force and it still does today, no matter the meager pay. Although comprised largely of men, a growing number of women pioneers in the 1920s and 1930s joined the ranks of park rangers. Donning the ranger uniform and badge was a source of pride, the attire initially formal in appearance but in time trending more to comfort. Whether checking automobiles at entrance stations, cruising roads on motorcycles or by car, patrolling the backcountry on horse, or serving in an interpretive capacity in visitor centers or at popular points in the park, the distinctive park ranger uniform, standardized throughout the National Park System, commanded respect from visitors.

An account related by Yellowstone historian Aubrey Haines and penned by a visitor caught speeding in 1937 captures the high esteem with which many visitors held park rangers. Writing to the judge who heard his case in court, the Yellowstone visitor admitted he deserved a speeding fine. On behalf of himself and his family he also spoke positively about his experience with the park ranger who had fined him. "The high point for us in the whole affair was making the acquaintance of the Ranger, Lee Coleman," said the offender. "I don't think I have spent as enjoyable a day in recent years," the chastised visitor said of his time spent with the park ranger. Ranger Coleman "regaled me with the natural history of the Park in all its forms; geologically, the fauna, the flora, Indian lore, a myriad of subjects and he was remarkably well informed," the defendant recounted of his ride with Coleman to the courtroom.[5]

In his time spent with the speeding tourist, NPS Ranger Lee Coleman served not merely as a traffic officer, but also as a naturalist, the latter a role that first took shape in 1920s Yellowstone. With the exiting of the Army, National Park Service director Stephen Mather and Yellowstone superintendent Horace Albright realized the need for a museum to educate park visitors.

Stephen Mather, from New England and formerly a newspaper reporter and then a highly successful businessman, in 1914 on a tour of western national parks recoiled at disorderly conditions within the parks. Informing his friend Secretary of the Interior Franklin Lane of his disappointment, Mather received an invitation to move to Washington, DC, to address the problems. Appointed as an assistant to Lane, Mather worked for free. Organizing the nation's disparate federal park lands within a single government agency, the National Park Service, Mather served as its first director. Foregoing a salary, he went beyond merely advancing initial NPS lands. Using his own wealth and soliciting donations from other wealthy businessmen, Mather enlarged Park Service holdings by purchasing additional land for federal protection.[6]

A lawyer by training, Horace Albright gained employment with the Interior Department at an opportune time. Appointed as the assistant director of the National Park Service upon the agency's founding in 1916, for two years thereafter Albright served as acting director while director Stephen Mather was sidelined with a severe illness. In 1919 and with Mather well again, Albright assumed the helm of Yellowstone, while simultaneously retaining his role as NPS assistant director. Holding both positions until 1929, in the person of Horace Albright, Yellowstone and the National Park Service led the way in fleshing out the NPS's mission "to conserve the scenery and the natural and historic objects and the wild life therein [national parks and monuments] and to provide for the enjoyment of the same in such manner and by such means as will leave them unimpaired for the enjoyment of future generations."[7]

Proactively working to raise public awareness of national parks, Mather and Albright together promoted and educated Americans about federal park lands, Yellowstone serving as the foundation of their efforts.

In 1919, the two men turned to Milton P. Skinner, an ex-employee in Yellowstone's hotels and an avid, self-taught naturalist with experience in lecturing park visitors. Appointed as the park's first ranger naturalist,

Yellowstone's first post–US Army park superintendent, Horace Albright (1919–1929), left, oversaw many advancements in the park's administration and infrastructure. His duties also included the hosting of dignitaries, including fisherman and frequent visitor Secretary of Commerce Herbert Hoover. Hoover, holding a fly rod and string of fish, was elected US president in November 1928. NPS PHOTO

Skinner assumed the responsibility of developing an overarching educational program for tourists.

Beginning with a small office in park headquarters at old Fort Yellowstone in Mammoth, Skinner in 1922 established what one historian referred to as a "homemade museum," a single room containing several hundred geological, paleontological, botanical, and zoological specimens. Skinner then departed, and a permanent naturalist took his place. Soon thereafter in 1925, Albright appointed park concessionaire and photographer Jack E. Haynes, a second-generation Yellowstone resident and chronicler of the park through visual media, as acting director of the park's museum.[8]

From these simple beginnings and leading the way among national parks, Superintendent Albright and NPS Director Mather in 1926 called upon a handful of emerging naturalists to compile and internally publish Yellowstone's first *Ranger Naturalists' Manual*.

Comprised of a selection of "various lectures, guide-talks and special articles pertaining to Yellowstone National Park," the manual sought to assist rangers "assigned to guiding, lecturing, information and museum duty" by "avoiding conflicting statements and too much repitition [*sic*]." Albright recognized the need for a professional program of education in the park. "In the past the criticism has been made that rangers occasionally 'talk down' to their audiences, make sarcastic replies, and unintentionally give the impression that they think themselves superior to their audiences," he noted. Nonetheless, the small naturalist staff "as a whole . . . have done their work in such an admirable way as to be a real credit to the National Park Service and to themselves," he continued.[9]

Ranger naturalists, Albright declared, "represented the Secretary of the Interior and the National Park Service as hosts to the People of the World. Every tourist is our personal guest. And we are the faculty of the biggest summer school of nature study on earth,—a school of 150,000 pupils!" Far more numerous were visitors to Yellowstone in the mid-1920s than in the prior decade, and Albright and Mather wanted city visitors to both marvel at and learn about the natural beauty of the nation's first national park. In lofty language Mather, speaking for park naturalists, declared: "Our glorious task is, in John Muir's words, 'To entice people to look at Nature's loveliness.' Our statements must be exact and cautious beyond possibility of question. And we mustn't hesitate to show our boundless delight in the marvelous and beautiful world we have to interpret."[10]

Among Yellowstone's park rangers involved in naturalist responsibilities by 1926, Marguerite Lindsley stood out as the first full-time female park ranger in the entire National Park System. Lindsley had grown up in Mammoth, where her father, Chester Lindsley, first worked as a civilian clerk during the Army years, later serving as the interim superintendent of the park during the transition period from the Army to the National Park Service. From her love of Yellowstone, after obtaining a decree in bacteriology, the younger Lindsley returned to Yellowstone in 1921 as a

Yellowstone's park rangers performed many duties in the service of protecting the park, educating visitors, and policing tourist infractions. Pictured here are unnamed ranger station personnel at the Canyon Ranger Station, 1922. NPS PHOTO

seasonal park ranger, one of three initial women serving as rangers that year, and among the most educated of the park's rangers. In 1925, Lindsley became a full-time ranger, and the following year helped craft Yellowstone's first *Ranger Naturalists' Manual*.[11]

From these starting points, ranger naturalists and park museums—the personnel and institutional facilities charged with educating Yellowstone visitors—transitioned into an era of professionalization. Increasingly-educated park naturalists of the late 1920s and early 1930s delivered lectures to ever-larger numbers of visitors and staff. In addition, they managed the expanding museum at Mammoth, as well as new museums at Old Faithful, Madison Junction, and Norris. Roadside interpretive exhibits supplemented the museums, allowing motorists to easily learn bite-sized pieces of the park's history.[12]

Among Yellowstone's early female rangers, Herma Albertson Baggley, a botanist, in 1931 became the first full-time woman ranger-naturalist in the park. She later coauthored the first book on plants and wildflowers in Yellowstone, titled *Plants of Yellowstone National Park*. NPS PHOTO

Playing a central role in this early era of professionalization, Herma Albertson became Yellowstone's first permanent female naturalist. Far to the west of her home state of Iowa, Albertson graduated from the University of Idaho with undergraduate and graduate degrees in botany. During two summers between semesters, she worked in Yellowstone as a summer "pillow puncher" (maid) for Harry Child's Yellowstone Park Hotel Company at the Old Faithful Inn. When not cleaning rooms, she created a self-guided, interpretive trail for Upper Geyser Basin visitors and collected wildflowers for the Inn's dining room tables. Upon obtaining her graduate degree, Albertson in 1931 was hired as a full-time ranger naturalist specializing in interpretive activities, her popular walking tours and lectures drawing hundreds of visitors daily. During the same year she married Yellowstone's chief ranger, George Baggley, assuming his last name.[13]

Herma Albertson Baggley thereafter made another lasting contribution to Yellowstone in the publication of a hallmark book, the first tome on plants and wildflowers in Yellowstone. Written with coauthor and botanist Dr. Walter B. McDougal, *Plants of Yellowstone National Park* (1936) greatly advanced knowledge of the park's flora and remains in print to the present day.

Yellowstone's entire ranger force grew steadily throughout the Great Depression years, including some charged with supervising New Deal Civilian Conservation Corps (CCC) camps in the park. The 1930s also brought additional challenges, including an increase in wildfire activity during a prolonged period of regional and national drought. In response the NPS enacted a new policy of extinguishing all wildfires by 10:00 a.m. the day following. More manpower often required in order to fulfill the directive, Yellowstone's rangers commonly supplemented fire lines alongside local firefighters and CCCers.[14]

Peaking in number between 1936 and 1942, Yellowstone's park ranger staff declined in tandem with a sharp drop in park visitation during World War II. Afterward visitation again climbed dramatically, but ranger staffing lagged, hindered by inadequate funding. In the early 1950s, a shortage of personnel prevented park rangers from adequately policing bad tourist behavior—commonly expressed in throwing objects into hot springs

Franklin D. Roosevelt's administration promoted travel to national parks during the Great Depression. This 1938 poster, produced by the New Deal's Works Progress Administration, promoted Yellowstone's expanding ranger naturalist services. LIBRARY OF CONGRESS, PRINTS & PHOTOGRAPHS DIVISION, LC-DIG-PPMSCA-13399

such as the popular Morning Glory Pool, as well as defacing geyser formations—and breaking up seemingly ever-present bear jams. Eventually the pendulum swung back toward more funding and a larger park ranger staff during the 1960s, many of the additional personnel tasked with law enforcement.

New conservationist policies introduced in the 1970s incorporated more naturalists and biologists into the ranks of park rangers, transforming a park long known for its artificial management of wildlife into a place (and an era) of natural ecosystem management. New bear policies weaned grizzlies and black bears alike off human food and away from roadsides, hotels, and campgrounds and into the backcountry, initiating natural management of animals previously acclimated to humans. No longer were bison fed hay in the winter months at the Lamar Buffalo Ranch, nor elk and deer fed hay along roadsides, nor elk thinned by hunting when the population grew too large.

Although perhaps from a distance seemingly less taxing than the era of artificial management, the task of restoring and maintaining Yellowstone's natural ecosystem—or at least a semblance thereof, because ecosystems naturally change over time—required considerable effort. Time-consuming and detailed studies, long processes of implementing best practices, and constant vigilance continuously challenged a chronically understaffed park ranger force. Nor has that natural ecosystem management been free of controversy, efforts relating to grizzlies, wolves, bison, and winter use intersecting with federal mandates related to endangered wildlife and air pollution. Decisions in many cases today require federal and state interagency cooperation and citizen input, and frequently involve litigation from competing, special interest groups.[15]

From administrative personnel to park rangers in the field, today's complex managerial environment increasingly requires multi-disciplinary collaboration, diplomatic skills, and adaptability. More than a century has passed since stagecoaches exited Wonderland and the US Army handed the park over to a civilian superintendent and park rangers, and today Yellowstone visitation routinely tops four million, straining overburdened roadways and endangering the park's fragile ecosystem. Far removed from the railroads' charming marketing posters, contemporary tourist dynamics fueled by ubiquitous and ever-present social media amplify dangerous visitor behavior in geyser basins and in the presence of wildlife, often necessitating ranger intervention.

More than ever, Yellowstone's park ranger force is highly professional, knowledgeable, and diverse. Confronting complexities seemingly changing from year to year, today's park rangers, like generations previous, serve out of a passion for protecting and preserving the treasured place that is Yellowstone National Park.

CHAPTER ELEVEN

Yellowstone Savages

Adventure, Hospitality, Humor, and Romance

*College girls who earn books and tuition over the summer as guides,
waitresses and tent girls in the Yellowstone camps, [keep] the great
wonderland lively with their songs, plays and adventures.*
—EYRE POWELL, *NEW YORK TRIBUNE*, 1922

WITH THE 1883 OPENING OF THE NATIONAL HOTEL (LATER KNOWN AS
the Mammoth Hot Springs Hotel) in Mammoth Village, and, the same
year, the debut of the Wylie Camping Company, came a very large opportunity for summer jobs in Yellowstone National Park.

Requiring a sense of adventure and hard work, employment in the
remote national park consisted of working for lodging, dining, gift shop,
and transportation companies in servicing the needs of tourists. From
stagecoach drivers to maids and cooks and much more, jobs otherwise
ordinary in cities and towns throughout America took on an added
dimension of seeming importance amid the uniqueness of Wonderland.
Embedded within Yellowstone's wilderness, employees experienced the
park in a more intimate and longer-term way than did tourists. Forming bonds with fellow laborers in common lodging and dining facilities,
many seasonal employees during their off-time recreated and explored
Yellowstone with friends, departing at summer's end with memories of
a lifetime. More than a few returned for succeeding summers, and a fair
number made Yellowstone into long-term careers.

With the passing of years job openings expanded. Through advertising and word of mouth more and more college students and teachers,

The Wylie Permanent Camping Company published a map of Yellowstone with their tent camp locations clearly marked. This map was published in 1908. Wylie stagecoach tours offered an educational dimension lacking in hotel tours. USED BY PERMISSION BY JACK AND SUSAN DAVIS—ALL RIGHTS RESERVED

their summers rapturously free otherwise, learned of the opportunity to work in Wonderland. Applicant numbers often surpassed available positions, the securing of a summer Yellowstone job an occasion for joy. In late spring from across America came the successful applicants, traveling to the park by train. Many came not merely for work, but for the experience of wilderness, fun, and yes, even romance. Some

WYLIE SERIES No. 3. A WYLIE TWO-COMPARTMENT TENT INTERIOR—YELLOWSTONE PARK. HAYNES-PUB.

As depicted in this 1907 Haynes postcard, the "Wylie Way" consisted of camping tents with wooden floors and enclosed by canvas siding and a roof, the interior heated by a stove. Beds and chairs were comparable to a simple hotel room.

Yellowstone employees, then and today, met their "significant others" in Wonderland.

More than three decades into this inner, seasonal world of Yellowstone a transformative year arrived, both for America and the nation's first national park. In Washington, DC, President Woodrow Wilson worried over a growing war across the Atlantic Ocean. Europe's Western and Eastern powers, having been drawn into bloodshed that began two years before, by the spring of 1916 were aligned in an evolving morass of alliances and hostilities ensnaring a growing number of nations outside of the region.

As Americans, wary of the European war, wavered between preparedness and isolationism, President Wilson publicly advocated neutrality. At the same time and with travel curtailed to Europe, an emerging network of cross-country roads generated excitement on the home front among motorists, fostering a "See America First" domestic travel campaign. With coast-to-coast travel easier than ever, the "wanderlust of American tourists may be quenched at home," the chairman of one pro-roads committee declared of domestic travel aspirations. Amid the enthusiasm, calls for western, park-to-park road routes grew all the louder. Simultaneously, some advocated for better East to West highways. At Yellowstone's Canyon Hotel on July 24–25, 1916, the "Park-to-Park Highway Association held a most enthusiastic meeting and started a movement for good roads from all the contiguous States to the parks and within the States."[1]

Yellowstone, too, was on the mind of Wilson, who in 1916 lent his presidential signature to congressional legislation creating the National Park Service, thereby consolidating and streamlining the administration of federal parks and monuments.

In a year marked by international war, home-front uncertainty, newly minted cross-country highways, automobile enthusiasts, a domestic travel campaign, and a focus on national parks, many of Yellowstone's seasonal summer workers arrived, as customary, by special train cars.[2]

Carefree and eager for a summer of adventure and fun, hundreds of college students and college graduates at crossroads in their own lives arrived in Wonderland in early June. On the surface they came to wash dishes or serve meals, to cook food or attend store counters, to clean rooms or carry luggage, to chauffeur tourists or perform some other task. But whether eighteen or twenty-eight years of age, for many the work was, in part, a pretext for momentarily suspending their normal lives and the larger world in favor of an immersive experience with other young adults in Yellowstone's remote wilderness.

Summer employees in 1916 came to Yellowstone not knowing they would experience the last year of the park's iconic stagecoaches, the last year of the beloved Wylie Camping Company,[3] the beginning of the end of Wonderland's soldier guardians—due to the escalating war across the Atlantic Ocean—and the birth-year of the National Park Service. Some young men came not knowing that within less than a year their country, too, would call upon them to fight in World War I in Europe. Many young women, college students or teachers, came for fun and adventure during summer school break.

A bit older and perhaps more knowledgeable of world affairs than most of either gender, Beatrice Boedefeld of Elkhart, Indiana, came to

Yellowstone with notepad in hand, heart on her sleeve, and hope for a new future.

A college graduate with an English degree and tired of her job as a newspaper writer, Boedefeld cast her aspiring and venturesome gaze westward. Learning of the need for single women as seasonal workers for the Wylie Camping Company, she applied and was accepted. Leaving on June 11, she arrived three days later with other summer employees at the Union Pacific Depot in present-day West Yellowstone, then simply called "Yellowstone," Montana. Shortly thereafter "loaded into coaches like cattle," Boedefeld and her new friends rode in stagecoaches to the Upper Geyser Basin, their home for the summer.[4]

Settling into her new abode at the large Wylie campsite near Daisy Geyser, Boedefeld quickly absorbed the insider lingo of Yellowstone "savages," the local term applied for decades to hospitality workers. On her first day in Yellowstone she walked to the Old Faithful Inn with a new friend, Bill, whom she deemed "wonderful." Together at the majestic Inn, the duo "rubbered [looked] to our heart's content." Quickly smitten with nineteen-year-old Bill and fearful of rejection should she tell him her true age, Boedefeld, twenty-eight, passed herself off as a mere eighteen years of age. Bill seemingly took her at her word. By the end of the day, "we knew that we were going to be the best of friends," Boedefeld wrote in her diary.[5]

Surviving diaries of stagecoach-era Wylie Camping Company employees are few. Composed during the pivotal year of 1916, Beatrice Boedefeld's diary captured the essence of summer savage experiences of the stagecoach era: adventure, hospitality, humor, and romance.

For the summer and with five roommates, Boedefeld lived in an employee tent that the campers christened "Deaux Drop Inn." Per Wylie policies of hiring educated employees capable of interacting well with middle- to upper-class clientele, Boedefeld's roommates were likely college students or college graduates. A college graduate herself, the Indianan also filled a third category desired by the camp company: journalist, an occupation sometimes helpful with regard to publicity.[6]

If there were any doubt as to whether work or play most occupied the minds of summer employees, Boedefeld dispelled those misconceptions,

In addition to sleeping in tents, camp guests also dined in tents. In this Wylie dining tent chinaware plates accompanied by glasses, silverware, and flower-filled vases are neatly arranged on cloth-covered picnic tables. Meals were communal experiences. Savages, meanwhile, ate in employee dining tents.
NPS PHOTO

within five days acknowledging her need to keep the young men "in their places." Pairings in the Wylie camps took place quickly and fluidly, many of the boys eager to take romance ("rotten logging") as far as allowed. Evening dances afforded ample opportunity for flirting, and Boedefeld enjoyed dancing with many of the pack rats (porters) and stagecoach drivers during the summer, observing that "[T]he drivers and the pack rats don't mix." When boys were not available, Boedefeld was happy to dance with girls.[7]

In addition to dancing, Wylie savages hosted evening parties in their tents. Outside under the stars, campfire singalongs allowed for yet more socializing. As for work, far less interesting than play, Boedefeld's first full taste of pillow punching in the "dude" (tourist) tents took place on June 20, a snowy day that soaked her shoes. More enjoyable was her role as a reciter in an evening savage show, performed for guests.

Also of interest were the myriad of geysers and hot springs within easy walking distance that she and her friends visited during their free daylight hours. Magnificent Giant Geyser enthralled Beatrice Boedefeld with its beauty, but some lesser thermals proved useful. A hot spring near Grotto Geyser served as a washing machine for "dust rags." With girlfriends, Boedefeld enjoyed private hot baths piped from Punch Bowl Spring. In a more communal capacity, she sometimes hung out at the "Plunge," the public bath house sourced from Solitary Geyser.[8]

Meal times in the employee dining tent differed from guests' dining experiences, the needs of savages considered secondary to that of dudes. By July, so many tourists occupied the Old Faithful Wylie tent camp that there were not "enough cups to go around," Boedefeld observed, "so the Savages get their coffee in soup bowls; consequently, we can't have soup or mush." On one occasion something—beans, berries, or meat, perhaps— served in the employee dining tent but not the tourists' dinner tent "poisoned the camp." Nonetheless, savage meals were typically tolerable at the least. Sunday dinners included "pineapple and cakes," while popcorn and fudge were readily available for snacking throughout the week.[9]

As the weeks passed, Beatrice Boedefeld saw less and less of Bill, her first boyfriend of the summer, who had moved on to other interests. Evening dances occasioned new flings. Following a special July 4th masquerade party, Boedefeld strolled to Kepler Cascades with yet another boyfriend and in the company of another couple. But not all outings were ideal. Expressing disgust that so many of her dates demanded more and more liberties as the summer wore on, Boedefeld fought off one aggressive young man, refusing to be "mauled and pawed over." Enjoying dating but perplexed at the inappropriate behavior of many of the male employees, she lamented "I don't understand why the boys have to spoil things."[10]

Dangers other than misbehaving young men also lurked nearby, especially at night. On one occasion, a mountain lion "frightfully scared" a couple out for a walk. On some nights Boedefeld and her roommates heard bears at the "bear dump" fighting with one another, and the bruins often roamed through the Wylie camp and raided nearby garbage cans.[11]

In many ways, Boedefeld's summer was similar to that experienced by Wylie savages in prior years. But unlike summer employees in the past, the

During summers in early twentieth century Yellowstone, many young women, including the four pictured here circa 1908, worked as housekeepers in the park's tent camps. Dressed in housekeeping attire, the young women in this image are standing beside a linen cart while collectively holding brooms, linens, and candles. YELLOWSTONE NATIONAL PARK ARCHIVES, CATALOG #02884 YELL 228

class of 1916 witnessed Yellowstone's experiment of automobiles sharing park roads with stagecoaches, Boedefeld taking advantage of both. While she enjoyed rides in a friend's car to see Excelsior Geyser or other distant park attractions, "a trip to Lone Star Geyser in the Carpenter's coach" sitting atop alongside the driver made for a "special treat."[12]

Yet all too soon the end of the summer drew nigh. In her final weeks in Wonderland, one of Boedefeld's boyfriends proposed to her. (She was thrilled but noncommittal, and in time they broke up.) In the waning days of Yellowstone's summer she partook of a few final hikes, marveled at the northern lights one night, and listened to a visiting scholar give "a talk on the War," a sober reminder of the world lurking beyond Wonderland.[13]

Finally, the last day arrived. On the first of September, Boedefeld, sitting on the driver's bench, traveled by stagecoach from the Upper Geyser Basin to the Union Pacific Depot, one of the last persons to ride a stagecoach in Wonderland. Within hours speeding home by train, Beatrice Boedefeld summed up her summer in Yellowstone with words similar to what thousands of other savages—before and since 1916—have also said: "The most wonderful summer of my whole life."[14]

Alongside adventure and romance, Boedefeld's "savage summer" yielded an unexpected surprise: a chance encounter in Yellowstone with a visiting newspaperman in time led to a job at the *Natrona County Tribune* in Casper, Wyoming. In addition, Boedefeld, like many other savages, eventually returned to Wonderland for a reunion with several of her former coworkers.[15]

With the passing of the stagecoach era, the Wylie Camping Company also came to an end, its holdings consolidated in 1917—alongside the Shaw & Powell Camping Company—into the Yellowstone Park Camping Company. World War I and a deadly flu epidemic followed in 1918, curtailing park visitation that year. Emerging from the shadows of both, Yellowstone in 1922, the park's fiftieth year—and busiest to date— celebrated as never before. And according to at least one account, the female savages in Yellowstone's tent camps stole the show.

They are "as popular as Old Faithful itself," enthused a July 16, 1922, *New York Tribune* article that praised the young women beloved of park visitors. The "college girls who earn books and tuition over the summer as guides, waitresses and tent girls in the Yellowstone camps," the writer declared, keep "the great wonderland lively with their songs, plays and adventures."[16]

A mere four hundred selected from thousands of candidates, they represented "the best young American womanhood." A "happy and self-reliant creature . . . She'll sing you in, she'll feed you" and keep your tent "spotless and neat," the missive enthused. When leading visitors on a hike, "she'll tell you what makes the geysers gyse [*sic*] and introduce you to the bears. She'll sing you the quaint Yellowstone songs around the campfire at night . . . and tell weird and wonderful Yellowstone yarns," including geysers freezing in midair and "the one about the bear that ate a school teacher and the cubs that were born next spring with a college education." In mythical prose the writer continued: "She'll be climbing or hiking or fishing, holding a fish-fry by the river or a marshmallow roast on the mountain side, adventuring everywhere, and then turning up fresh as a daisy to take up her camp duties or help stage a dance or entertainment for the park's guests."[17]

An atmosphere of good times and celebration marked the entirety of the summer of 1922, the Yellowstone Park Camps Company hiring drama teacher and longtime summer savage Beulah Brown of Utah as the company's general amusement director. Throughout Wonderland at the company's tent camps employees performed outdoor theatrical productions of various time periods in the park's Euro-American history. As historian Elizabeth Watry has recounted, Mammoth employees commemorated "mountain men and other early explorers of the Yellowstone region"; Old Faithful savages focused on the 1870 Washburn-Langford-Doane Expedition; Lake Camp presented "a clever pantomime" of President Ulysses S. Grant signing the 1872 Yellowstone Act; and savages at Canyon put on a show about the stagecoaching days of old and the early automobile era, replete with "a parade of horse-drawn vehicles, a stagecoach hold-up, a minuet illustrating the spirit of the park's former days, and the arrival of several of Yellowstone's already famous yellow buses." Two years later, Brown published a book of "Songs of the Yellowstone Park Camps."[18]

All too soon, however, the tent camps became a relic of Yellowstone's past, replaced in some locations with rustic lodge cabins and a main lodge utilized for dining, social functions, and entertainment. Yellowstone's savage evening entertainment adapted accordingly, performances moving to indoor auditoriums.

In the new environment another veteran savage, Utahan Grace Johnson, took the lead. Following years of working in the summers as a waitress or maid, Johnson in 1932 took a position as the "hostess and supervisor of entertainment" at Canyon Lodge. A trained drama teacher with theatrical flair, Johnson wrote a succession of Yellowstone stage shows that for several years made Canyon Lodge "legendary for its extraordinary productions." Among her creations, the comedy *Savage* proved particularly popular, leading Johnson to obtain a copyright for the play and the title song, "Love Began in Yellowstone."[19]

Known for her longevity, savage Martha "Marty" Gorder, also a teacher who first worked in the park in 1929, succeeded Grace Johnson at Canyon and directed entertainment for most years from 1938 to 1956. Arranging and directing hundreds of shows during her nearly two decades at Canyon Lodge, Johnson's most popular production was *Fifty*

Romantic relationships often developed among Yellowstone's summer savages. This photo of unidentified Lake Hotel employees was captured about 1901. NPS PHOTO

Years in Review, performed in the decade of the 1950s. Featuring period music, song, and dance, the performance crowned some five decades or more of amazing savage summer performances.[20]

Sadly, with the closing of Canyon Lodge at the end of the 1956 season, Yellowstone's savage performances faded away, and summer employees focused their attention elsewhere.

Even so, to the present-day Yellowstone savages—from waitresses (heavers), gear-jammers (bus drivers), and porters (pack rats) readily visible, to dishwashers (pearl divers), laundry workers (bubble kings and queens), and maids (pillow punchers) often unnoticed—go the key to, and accolades for, the success of the park's tourist season, albeit a bit unsung compared to generations past.

Year after year still they come, the ranks of savages ever-swelling, job descriptions evolving over time. As always, modest pay accompanies hard work, the real payoff being the magic of living in Yellowstone.

Among today's young employees who typically work in the park's lodging and dining facilities, adventure, fun, and romance are every bit as common as a century ago, marriage proposals sometimes resulting. Some veteran savages make a summer-seasonal career of living and working in Yellowstone. Many retired senior citizens, following middle-class careers, also spend their summers working in the park. Lodging in their own recreational vehicles, they often staff gift shops and campgrounds. Enjoying on-the-job interaction with fellow seasonal workers as well as park visitors, these older employees, during their off hours and days, quietly enjoy the peaceful splendor of Yellowstone, a park for people of all ages.

It is no surprise that enduring bonds are often formed during summers spent living and working in Yellowstone. Following the stagecoach era and enabled by automobile and air travel, savage reunions in the park have rekindled friendships and memories for many decades. Beyond on-site reunions, social media has served in recent decades to keep savages of all ages in touch with friendships they forged earlier in America's Wonderland.

CHAPTER TWELVE

Coming of Age

How the Great Depression Transformed Yellowstone

> *Wanted: A job firing geysers!*
>
> —A LETTER WRITER SEEKING
> EMPLOYMENT IN YNP, JULY 1932[1]

IT WAS BY ALL ACCOUNTS A ROUTINE LATE OCTOBER IN YELLOWSTONE.

Superintendent Roger Toll, concluding his first tourist season, 1929, as Yellowstone's chief after former superintendent Horace Albright's promotion to National Park Service director, spent "several days in the office going through accumulated mail, writing reports, etc." related to end-of-season duties. More or less clearing his desk of critical paperwork and prior to the season-ending snows, Toll departed his office for a tour of the park. On Saturday the 26th he inspected road construction at the East Entrance, pronouncing the nearly completed work in "fine shape." The following day he reviewed remodeling projects undertaken by Harry Child's Yellowstone Park Hotel Company at Lake, Old Faithful, and Canyon. Thereafter taking a break from work, he hiked in and watched Imperial Geyser in action in the Lower Geyser Basin.[2]

The mechanisms of Yellowstone's magnificent geyser-shows at that time remained a puzzle, even to experts. Geologists were beginning to formulate theories, albeit lacking conclusive evidence. On his weekend tour of Yellowstone, Superintendent Toll stopped at Old Faithful and observed a "test hole" drilled by a team from the Geophysical Laboratory of the Carnegie Institute. Not a typical hole, the 406-feet-deep "special investigation borehole" sought data to substantiate theories "relative to geyser phenomena." At the bottom of the deep shaft and in "loose sand," the scientists recorded a temperature reading of a blistering 350 degrees Fahrenheit. The Carnegie Institute had planned to drill more test sites in the park, but a sudden "shortage of funds" brought their efforts to an abrupt end, an ill omen not yet fully understood.[3]

Nearby the Old Faithful Museum, recently established, stood to benefit from the dawning of scientific studies of geysers and hot springs. Already the museum's seasonal exhibits were packed and ready for transportation to storage in Mammoth during the winter offseason. A second museum, the Norris Museum under construction at Norris Geyser Basin, was slated for an opening the following season.[4]

Visitor education was evolving in Toll's Yellowstone, the park superintendent counting on chief ranger naturalist Dorr G. Yeager to elevate the latest scientific insights into the interpretive task. Currently en route

The Old Faithful Inn welcomed visitors even during the darkest days of the Great Depression. In the second half of the 1930s as the economy grew better, more Americans than ever visited the park annually, most driving their automobiles. This 1930s-era photo is titled *Old Faithful Inn, with automobiles parked in front, Yellowstone National Park, Wyoming.* NPS PHOTO

to the first ever Park Naturalists' Training Conference hosted by Horace Albright's alma mater, the University of California–Berkeley, Yeager, his naturalist team the largest of any national park, was charged with inspiring other western national park ranger staffs.[5]

Beyond the routine of the superintendent's paperwork in late October of 1929, these were heady times in the nation's first national park: major infrastructure improvements, the dawning of serious scientific inquiry, the first professionally designed museums, and the emerging professionalization of the park's visitor services. All told, Yellowstone's ranger personnel represented unprecedented advances in the growing realm of America's national parks.[6]

But even as Superintendent Toll labored to close out Yellowstone's 1929 season, a gathering storm in far-away New York City threatened America's financial prosperity. On October 23, the winds of fear sent automobile stocks into a deep dive, a glut of unsold cars weighing heavily on investors' minds. The singular consumer product most responsible for record visitation to Yellowstone during the decade, automobiles drove the American economy. However, automakers had failed to adjust production in light of a saturated automobile market, an indicator of industrial over-productivity.

Awaking from the stupor of a decade-long economic boom, panic ensued on Wall Street. A tsunami of stocks suddenly for sale found but few buyers. J. P. Morgan and other New York bankers, recognizing the disaster at hand, quickly stepped in and purchased millions of otherwise-unwanted stock shares, thereby cutting the day's market losses. But it would not last.

While Toll cheerfully made his end-of-season inspection of Yellowstone, an uneasy truce hovered over New York, as if it were in the eye of a storm. As the superintendent returned to his office in Mammoth, the full fury of a long-delayed financial disaster crackled in the air and darkened men's souls. October 28 witnessed another steep decline in stock prices, followed by the deluge of October 29, the two days collectively witnessing a 25 percent stock market drop. The next day, just as Yellowstone ranger naturalist Yeager prepared to address the park naturalists' conference, none other than legendary philanthropist John D. Rockefeller—primary funder of Yellowstone's newly opened Old Faithful Museum and successive museum facilities soon to follow—assured the nation that the economy was fine.

Even though Rockefeller's words soothed fears for a few months, the greatest financial crisis in American history had begun, a decade-long period of despair that eventually became known as the Great Depression.

Although located some twenty-two hundred miles from New York City and in a remote wilderness, Yellowstone National Park no longer existed in isolation from East Coast financial markets. A booming 1920s economy under the capitalistic-friendly Calvin Coolidge and Herbert Hoover presidential administrations had, in recent years, impacted Wonderland in the form of larger annual budgets and record numbers of tourists.

Yellowstone's prosperity as well as that of the nation, however, had been built upon an unstable foundation of economic inequality and middle-class debt. From houses and cars to washing machines, furniture, radios, vacuum cleaners, and phonographs, most Americans sank ever further into debt through consumer loans. Toppled in late 1929, the corporate and household financial house-of-cards spread outward from the stock market collapse, the leading edge of debris reaching Yellowstone within months.

Saddled with the misfortune of having assumed the helm of the nation's first national park just prior to national economic calamity, Yellowstone superintendent Roger Toll opened his annual report the following year with ominous words that voiced the park's connection to the national economy. "An unsettled state of affairs throughout the country had its effect on the travel and business in Yellowstone National Park during the summer season," he intoned about the darkening year of 1930. "The park operators found it necessary to retrench considerably as the expected business failed to materialize. The reduction in rail travel was larger than in private automobile travel," Toll noted.[7]

One year later the park's financial landscape shifted to an even darker tone. On the one hand, an increase in park visitation of about 2 percent offered cause for cautious optimism. On the other hand, rail travel, plunging by some 30 percent, indicated a sign of financial distress on the part of wealthier Americans. Among motoring visitors, meanwhile, were "an unusually large number" of unemployed "persons seeking jobs in the park." All told, the "general depression of the country," Toll reported, made for "a poor business season" for concessionaires as visitors tended "to spend as little as possible and to seek the cheapest type of accommodations." Near the end of the season the bottom dropped out, producing tourist numbers so low that Superintendent Toll acceded to requests from park concessionaires to close the Lake Hotel, Lake Lodge, and Roosevelt Lodge on August 31.[8]

Nonetheless, a silver lining remained. Robust federal funding, appropriated by Congress prior to the onset of the economic downturn, remained in place. Ongoing road improvements included grading and oiling, thereby allowing for dust-free travel. And in a sign of yet better things to come, the surfacing of a few miles of roadway represented a first step toward paving all major park roads. Also seemingly unaffected by the Great Depression in 1931, ranger interpretive activities carried on as usual, the park's newest museum, at Fishing Bridge, opening in August.

Nor did the park operators suffer enough to halt facility improvements. Expanding electricity and plumbing infrastructure to newly constructed tourist cabins throughout the park and completing a new wing on the Canyon Hotel, Harry Child's Yellowstone Park Hotel Company hoped optimistically for better days. In addition, a new Fishing Bridge store opened and eight new fourteen-passenger White Motor Company touring buses were placed into service for tour groups.[9]

It would have been merely human nature if Superintendent Roger Toll at the dawn of 1932 had hoped his park would be spared the full effect of the Great Depression. But it was not to be. As national unemployment soared and homelessness reached epic proportions, the bottom fell out in Yellowstone, startling Toll. Compiling his annual report at year's end, the superintendent spoke of the "unexpected extent" of the decline in Yellowstone's commercial business (some 60 percent down from the prior year), rail travel (a 55 percent drop), and overall travel (down 30 percent). Those who did visit the park did so quickly and cheaply by automobile, motor-car visitors vastly outnumbering rail visitors, 147,747 to 8,572. It was "a bad financial year," Toll summarized in retrospect.[10]

Absorbing the realities at hand, Yellowstone's superintendent and all of America saw little immediate hope for better times. "The experience of this past summer," Toll admitted, "will probably result in extensive changes in operations of the hotels and lodges in order to meet the wishes of the traveling public."[11]

Amid decreasing visitation and growing unease in Yellowstone, by the presidential election year of 1932 unemployment reached 25 percent. Even so, President Herbert Hoover, convinced that capitalism would right itself without help from Washington, rejected pleas from destitute families to provide relief funds. Homeless Americans seemingly everywhere, lines at city soup kitchens stretched for blocks. Desperate citizens with nowhere else to go constructed "Hoovervilles," shanty towns throughout the nation's urban centers comprised of cardboard, scrap tin, and whatever other materials the homeless could scrounge for shelter. While Hoover dawdled, New York governor Franklin Delano Roosevelt campaigned for president on promises to provide relief for ordinary Americans, his message connecting with voters and leading to an overwhelming win in the November presidential elections.

True to his word, within weeks of his inauguration President Roosevelt rolled out the first programs designed to provide work for and protect impoverished Americans. Collectively known as the New Deal, FDR's extensive economic and social programs during the Great Depression utilized federal funding to improve landscapes and infrastructure, advance public arts, and establish social safety-nets for vulnerable Americans.

An advocate of forests and a healthy natural environment at a time in which poor farming practices had depleted many of America's croplands, FDR established the Civilian Conservation Corps (CCC) on April 5, 1933. As a part of the New Deal, Roosevelt's "Tree Army" was charged with fighting forest fires, planting trees, improving roadsides, re-seeding overgrazed farm lands, and reducing soil erosion by training farmers in modern conservation practices. Young men, some three hundred thousand within the first few months, labored on the federal payroll, their muscles put to work protecting and improving America's natural landscape. Many were assigned to CCC camps on US Forest Service and National Park Service lands, including Yellowstone.

Yellowstone's initial Civilian Conservation Corps workers arrived in the spring of 1933. The CCC, employing thousands of laborers in Yellowstone over the course of a decade, made a significant and lasting impact in the park. Some CCCers and several barracks of YNP-1 are pictured in this winter scene dated 1/23/35. Photographer: Crowe. YELLOWSTONE NATIONAL PARK ARCHIVES, YELL 32294. OPEN PARK NETWORK, YELLOWSTONE PHOTO ALBUM 21, PAGE 19.

So quickly did President Roosevelt jump-start the Civilian Conservation Corps that Toll, caught by surprise, failed to comprehend the significance of the program. Nor was he particularly pleased, at least at first. Rather than employing many of the more than one thousand unemployed local men living in communities in proximity to the park, the program's administrators for Yellowstone's CCC camps initially recruited unemployed young men from far off New York City. Unexpectedly forced to quickly prepare for the arrival of hundreds of urban young men with no wilderness experience, park officials and staff set to the task, albeit with reservations.[12]

Construction of four CCC camps occupied the months of April and May. Located one each at Mammoth and Canyon, and two at Lake, each facility required accommodations for some two hundred enrollees. Fortunately, the government allowed for the hiring of twenty-five local men in a support capacity, with five in supervisory roles. Permanent park rangers, too, in some instances appointed to work alongside the CCCers, participated in hastily arranged staff meetings to "thoroughly" discuss "many of the problems" arising due to the unprecedented circumstances.[13]

With the arrival of Yellowstone's first CCC enrollees in June, a tension-filled meeting of West and East began. Still scrambling to put in place appropriate infrastructure and supervision, veteran park staff eyed the young New Yorkers with suspicion, the eastern urbanites returning the favor. Making matters worse for all involved, these poor young men, some having left New York City for the first time, struggled to adjust to their new wilderness surroundings. June snows and thin tents made for nightly misery, a novel but unwelcome experience. Adding to the discontent, initial food rations of poor quality failed to satisfy the new laborers, while for weeks job roles remained frustratingly unclear. Disputes and fights among some restless enrollees ensued, necessitating the establishment of supervisory methods and disciplinary actions in record time.

Before roles and responsibilities could be fully defined, some troublesome CCCers were sent home for infractions, while others, failing to adjust, left on their own. Finally, in July, work routines took hold, manual labors involving forestry work, fighting fires, roadside cleanup, trail maintenance, and more. Even then, an exasperated Superintendent Toll wondered if the experiment would work, by season's end merely acknowledging that the worst of the kinks had been worked out, and entertaining the possibility that in time Yellowstone's CCC labor force might prove beneficial. For their part, CCC workers who remained for the entirety of the summer benefited from an improvement in the quality and quantity of food at a time when many American families lived on the edge of starvation.[14]

Few likely realized that the park's CCC camps would remain for almost a decade as the Great Depression lingered year after year. Having survived the first summer season, Superintendent Roger Toll and his park staff refined the duties of a previously unanticipated annual seasonal workforce. In anticipation of an eventual return to growth in visitation, federally financed CCC muscle offered the opportunity to reshape the park's landscape and infrastructure to accommodate future visitor needs and expectations.

As road crews continued the arduous task of paving and otherwise improving park roads, and additional New Deal dollars funded locally sourced labor in the construction of a stately post office at Mammoth (operational to the present day), CCC labor improved the aesthetics of road shoulders. Working under a federal mandate to protect the beauty of the park's forests by quickly snuffing out wildfires, some Civilian Conservation Corps workers, alongside park rangers and local firefighters, manned fire lines, while others helped build fire towers. Reflecting the growing democratization of Yellowstone, CCCers, most of modest means, improved existing public campgrounds and from scratch constructed Mammoth Campground, each facility free to the public and helping make a Yellowstone vacation more affordable to families similar to theirs.

Other tasks included building telephone lines and constructing support buildings for park operations. Some laborers prepared for summer visitors by clearing snow, or assisted concessionaire operations by cutting firewood for hotel fireplaces. More visible were projects expanding tourist infrastructure, such as the construction of a boardwalk through Norris Geyser Basin. Many CCC projects, in addition to hard labor, required architects, also funded by the federal works program.[15]

Whether seeking to preserve or improve the park's viewscape or enhance the visitor experience otherwise, the presence of the Civilian Conservation Corps enlarged the human imprint upon Yellowstone's landscape, an ecological trade-off. The dozens of CCC camps during the decade required large-scale infrastructure in the form of many support buildings. So, too, the enhancement and expansion of public campgrounds and other public infrastructure encroached upon previously natural terrain.

Reflective of President Franklin D. Roosevelt's campaign to replant western landscapes denuded by poor farming practices, tree nurseries at Mammoth and in the Lamar Valley nurtured young seedlings for transport near and far, also altering Yellowstone's natural landscape. From suppressing naturally occurring wildfires to creating fire breaks, from cutting down pine beetle–infested trees to clearing space in forests for telephone lines and harvesting wood for park fireplaces, CCC workers' forestry labor accelerated a decades-long and park-wide commitment to beautification and infrastructure over preservation of forests in a natural state.[16]

Civilian Conservation Corps' workers, however, did more than labor. In the evenings and on the weekends they toured the wonders of Yellowstone, played ball on baseball diamonds built in the park, enjoyed various indoor games—including Ping-Pong—in camp recreation centers, occasionally joined park savages in evening dances, and sometimes visited the nearby community of Livingston, Montana.[17]

Apart from labor and fun, with the encouragement of the federal government many enrolled in educational classes taught in their camps. Whether academic or vocational in nature, the courses served to equip the young men with the tools to secure permanent employment in their home communities following their summer in Yellowstone. In many instances, the skills learned as well as discipline practiced in the Corps prepared the young men for service in the military during World War II.[18]

Similar to those of Yellowstone's summer savages, CCC workers' experiences in the park imprinted lasting memories. Many former enrollees in later years and after having settled down returned to visit Yellowstone with their families. In a broader sense the introduction to and experience of Yellowstone among thousands of poor Americans contributed to the accelerating democratization of the nation's first national park.

As federally employed CCC workers labored in Yellowstone at the behest of the Roosevelt Administration, FDR, an enthusiastic supporter of America's national parks, also led the way in promoting the parks as a salve for hard times. A years-long national parks marketing campaign included a series of national park postage stamps beginning in 1934, as well as an extensive promotional campaign in newspapers, on radio, and in film clips extolling the natural beauty and inspirational value of parks. In the late 1930s, the Roosevelt Administration's Works Progress Administration produced and distributed national parks promotional posters.[19]

Federal national park promotional efforts took place alongside New Deal programs reforming business practices and protecting workers, leading to more vacation time for middle-class and some lower-class families. Seizing a new opportunity to elevate the yet-struggling economy of the late 1930s, the Roosevelt Administration touted travel as a means of economic revival. Americans responded, visiting Yellowstone and other national parks at record levels.

From the renewed interest in travel, now accompanied by robust, nationwide highway infrastructure, FDR created the national parks–centric US Travel Bureau, giving a federal stamp of approval to an emerging, professional travel industry. Promoting national parks, in turn, conveniently served the administration's purpose of drawing public attention away from the growing war in Europe, not so subtly communicating nationalist sentiment alongside a government curtailing travel to Europe.[20]

Readily accessible, democratized, developed, and systemically promoted, Yellowstone National Park of the late 1930s became the long-envisioned "people's park." Efforts on the part of the Roosevelt Administration to end at least some discriminatory practices against African Americans led to more travel by Black Americans, albeit limited in scope due to state segregationist laws and norms yet embedded across much of America.

Alongside unparalleled tourism in the latter part of the Great Depression, scientific thought and disciplines came of age in America. Reflecting the ascendancy of science, professionally trained ranger naturalists engaged Yellowstone's visitors through museum exhibits, trailside lectures, one-on-one interactions, and self-guided interpretive guides, collectively educating visitors about the park's natural history.

Apart from the tourist experience, scientists increasingly conducted field studies, throughout the decade advancing knowledge of the park's geology. Primarily focused on thermal areas and the Grand Canyon of the Yellowstone River—the very wonders of the park that most entranced visitors—scientists developed theories about geyser mechanisms and the canyon's ancient history that would propel additional and more refined scientific insights in the late twentieth century and into the twenty-first century.[21]

An emerging emphasis on Yellowstone's natural ecosystem and biological health also characterized the decade, albeit briefly. A decades-long history of killing predators and artificially feeding ungulates and bears— the latter in the crowd-pleasing form of human food scraps at publicly viewable hotel garbage dumps as well as handouts from tourists along roadways and in campgrounds—remained the status quo as the 1930s arrived. By mid-decade, however, young biologist George Melendez Wright, allied with Yellowstone superintendent Roger Toll and studying the park's ecosystem, advocated for natural management of flora and fauna.

Proceeding cautiously upon environmental terrain in advance of the times, Wright began testing bear-proof trashcan concepts in the park's campgrounds. But this tentative step all too soon came to a halt in the wake of one of the greatest human tragedies in Yellowstone's history: the untimely death of both Roger Toll and George Wright in a 1936 highway accident, cutting short the life of a likely future National Park Service director and the promising career of a cutting-edge wildlife biologist. Absent Toll's administrative commitment and Wright's knowledge and passion, Yellowstone's brief foray into restoring the park's natural ecosystem receded from view by the end of the decade.[22]

With science on the rise but not yet significantly impactful upon a fractured Yellowstone ecosystem, World War II arrived, the global conflict bringing a close to the Great Depression and the Civilian Conservation Corps. Enrollees departed the park in the summer of 1942, their campsites soon dismantled. During the war years, few tourists visited the park, and many accommodations and services remained shuttered. Even so, as the war years passed and visitors returned, the Great Depression–era efforts in Yellowstone bore witness in the democratization of, infrastructure improvements within, and emerging scientific interest in America's first and foremost national park.

CHAPTER THIRTEEN

Back to the Past

Yellowstone's Cultural Heritage and Natural Ecosystem

A look into wolf eyes will make you think deeply about life.
—DOUG SMITH, SENIOR WILDLIFE BIOLOGIST, YNP[1]

IN ADDITION TO TRANSFORMING THE INFRASTRUCTURE OF YELLOW-stone National Park, the Great Depression era in time became a cultural touchstone in the park. A number of structures built during the era yet remain and, alongside many human-created structures from prior decades, have historical, architectural, and/or engineering significance. In many cases visitors can readily identify culturally important historical sites while traveling through the park. Stepping into the past is simply a matter of knowing where to look.

From the northern entrance via Gardiner, Montana, through the Roosevelt Arch (constructed 1903), a five-mile drive leads to Mammoth Hot Springs Village. Entering the developed area, the stately Depression-era Mammoth Post Office (1938) comes into view to the left. In Mammoth one is struck by the manicured lawns and well-ordered buildings of old Fort Yellowstone, constructed in the late nineteenth and early twentieth centuries and long serving as park headquarters. For those who wish, a self-guided walking tour of fort buildings is available via pathway interpretive displays. A few yards north and slightly to the west of Fort Yellowstone is the Mammoth Hot Springs Hotel (redesigned in 1913 and in the 1930s). In place of horses and stagecoaches of a bygone era, automobiles and buses pull up beneath the portico. Behind the hotel are cabins, also constructed in the 1930s. Due east of the Mammoth Hotel is

President Theodore Roosevelt, America's most prominent conservationist at the turn of the twentieth century, visited Yellowstone and dedicated the Roosevelt Arch on April 24, 1903. He also toured the park. In this 1903 American Stereoscopic Company image, the president is pictured, left, at Mammoth Hot Spring's Liberty Cap. AMERICAN STEREOSCOPIC COMPANY, MANUFACTURERS AND PUBLISHERS, C1903. COURTESY LIBRARY OF CONGRESS, PRINTS & PHOTOGRAPHS DIVISION, LC-USZ62-100949.

yet another culturally significant structure, the two-story Haynes Photo Shop (1929), the building currently utilized for non-public purposes.

From the eastern entrance visitors cross Sylvan Pass, the road then following the northern shore of Yellowstone Lake to the Fishing Bridge Museum (1932) and the Fishing Bridge (originally constructed in 1902 and rebuilt several times since). In decades past fishing from the bridge was a popular pastime, hence the name. Today, fishing is prohibited.

Turning left past the bridge and at the intersection with the park's lower loop roadway, a short drive southward brings one to Lake Hotel (1891). Although now much bigger, more expansive, and more attractive than in its earlier incarnation, the original structure remains. Outside facing the lake, yellow touring buses, some modern and some that have plied the park's roads at various times since the 1930s, pull up alongside the hotel and wide-eyed passengers pour out. As at Mammoth, the Lake Village also offers historic cabins (1930s) for more budget-conscious travelers, yellow cabins adjacent to the hotel, as well as rustic and western Lake Lodge cabins.

Among the park's early and iconic hotels, meanwhile, the Old Faithful Inn (1904) today most closely resembles its original incarnation. Most directly approached from the western or southern park entrances, the Old Faithful Inn remains virtually unchanged since a period of expansion and interior modifications in the 1920s and 1930s. The Inn is the most magnificent of Yellowstone's hotels. Today's first-time visitors awed every bit as those of the early twentieth century. This is the granddaddy of national park hotels, and arguably the most famous in the world.

From the less-traveled route over the Beartooth Mountains one passes through the remote Northeast Entrance Station (1935) through the Lamar Valley and to the rustic Roosevelt Lodge and Cabins (1920). To the lodge's namesake, conservationist and US president Theodore Roosevelt, goes much credit for helping birth and provide momentum for the early conservation movement that impacted Yellowstone National Park.

In addition, two small museum structures are of notable historical significance beyond their size. The Madison Museum (1930), now utilized for other purposes, is located near the junction of the Gibbon and

Firehole Rivers, the two waterways forming the Madison River. Here at the turn of the twentieth century Yellowstone's "Creation Myth" was born. A fictitious story perpetuated by the park's first superintendent, Nathaniel Langford, the myth credited the idea of setting Yellowstone aside as a national park to a campfire conversation among members of the 1870 Washburn Expedition while camping at the current site of the Madison Museum. In reality, the idea emerged earlier over time.[2]

Northward from the Madison Museum at Norris Campground, meanwhile, is the Norris Museum (1930), a museum devoted to park ranger history. The Norris Museum pays tribute to the thousands of men and women whose hard work for over a century has guided and provided oversight into Yellowstone's evolving story.

Particularly noteworthy among the structures identified in our road tour of Yellowstone National Park are five examples of Parkitecture, or park "rustic" architecture: the Old Faithful Inn, Northeast Entrance Station, and the Fishing Bridge, Madison, and Norris museums.[3]

Many other historical structures exist, albeit less visible and lesser known, many pre-dating the park's Euro-American history. More than four hundred historical indigenous sites, identified by tribal leaders as integral to the identity of the Native peoples who historically inhabited the Yellowstone plateau, are protected for their natural and cultural value. In addition, some one thousand buildings, roads, bridges, utility structures, grave markers, and other human-constructed structures have been identified and are protected for their historical, architectural, and/or engineering significance. Management of the many historical structures requires maintaining as much as possible the historical condition of the entity, while ensuring that any repairs or additions reflect the structures' original character.[4]

In Yellowstone's preserved historical structures, visitors can experience the park's cultural past. At the same time, today's park ecosystem, equally visible to park visitors, is arguably more naturally intact than during the late nineteenth and early twentieth century era of conflicting park priorities.

The 1872 Yellowstone National Park Act mandated a two-fold management responsibility for the newly created federal park. Maintaining

Yellowstone "as a public park or pleasuring-ground for the benefit and enjoyment of the people" evoked nineteenth-century domestic European gardens. Protecting the park's uniqueness via "the preservation, from injury or spoliation, of all timber, mineral deposits, natural curiosities, or wonders within said park, and their retention in their natural condition" as well as prevention of the "wanton destruction of the fish and game," on the other hand, conjured the stirrings of a conservationist movement in America.

From its inception as a federal park, remote and unpoliced, Wonderland drew the attention of well-connected and powerful capitalists, tilting the balance of stewardship toward the "pleasuring ground" mandate, against which an underfunded park administration struggled to adequately protect landscapes and wildlife from human greed and exploitation.

Fortuitously, the 1894 well-publicized apprehension of poacher Edgar Howell spurred Congress to pass legislation—the Lacey Act, named after park defender Ohio congressman John F. Lacey—providing the Department of the Interior with the power to prosecute violations of Yellowstone's laws. Nearly a decade later in 1903 America's most prominent conservationist, President Theodore Roosevelt, toured Yellowstone. During his visit and while presiding over the laying of the cornerstone of the entryway arch at the park's North Entrance, Roosevelt spoke in favor of the preservationist portion of the 1872 Yellowstone Act.

While "accessible to all visitors," the president declared of Yellowstone's wonders, "the scenery of the wilderness" and "wild creatures of the Park are scrupulously preserved." Enjoining both management dimensions of the congressional mandate, Roosevelt declared: "The creation and preservation of such a great natural playground in the interest of our people as a whole is a credit to the nation." A better road system was needed, he observed, for public access by all Americans. At the same time, enjoyment of Yellowstone by present and future generations necessitated "jealously safeguarding and preserving the scenery, the forests, and the wild creatures." Roosevelt praised park acting superintendent Major John Pitcher and the conscientiousness of area residents for working together "to prevent acts of vandalism and destruction." Development of pleasuring-ground infrastructure, Roosevelt insisted, should observe the preservationist mandate.[5]

Presidential encouragement notwithstanding, the intersection of human enjoyment within and careful guardianship of Wonderland remained weighted in favor of the former. America's early conservationist ethic, as voiced by Roosevelt, understood Yellowstone's wild land and animals as natural resources requiring human interference to produce certain outcomes: an aesthetically beautiful landscape populated by desirable animals easily viewed, accommodated by visitor infrastructure suitable for transporting, housing, feeding, and entertaining tourists primarily of financial means.

A refinement of the enjoyment versus the preservationist relationship emerged in the Organic Act of 1916 creating the National Park Service. Expanding the scope and reversing the order of the 1872 Yellowstone Act, the Organic Act created the National Park Service with a mandate "to conserve the scenery and the natural and historic objects and wild life therein and to provide for the enjoyment of the same and in such manner and by such means as will leave them unimpaired for the enjoyment of future generations."[6]

By placing conservation prior to enjoyment, the Organic Act effectively moved the needle toward preservation. On the ground in Yellowstone, the 1916 legislation ushered in a park ranger force empowered with stronger tools to police tourist behavior. At the same time, by the early 1930s professionally trained ranger naturalists and public museums educated visitors about the park's geology, thermal attractions, and wildlife, while reinforcing preservationist-oriented park rules and regulations.

Even so, the evolving concept of "conservation" remained at best irregular, particularly in regard to wildlife. Following the elimination of wolves in Yellowstone by the late 1920s, the National Park Service, responding to emerging ecological thought regarding holistic ecosystems, reversed course early in the next decade and placed predators under protection, alongside other wildlife. Although too late for wolves, the decision offered a reprieve for coyotes, animals for decades hated by ranchers on the park's northern border and often hunted and killed by rangers within park boundaries. Scientific studies, meanwhile, revealed that Yellowstone's

During World War II Yellowstone's remaining public bear feeding grounds closed, including the Old Faithful dump, pictured here, where grizzlies rummaged among rubbish for food. Even so, decades would pass before the park instituted natural management of bears. NPS PHOTO / R. ROBINSON

coyotes subsisted on a spectrum of small prey, rarely preying on livestock as wrongly believed by ranchers. Although Yellowstone Park naturalist C. Max Bauer touted the studies in defense of coyotes, for several decades park administration and ranching interests remained at odds over the fate of the canid. Amid ongoing controversy coyotes ranging along the park's northern border remained in danger of untimely death.[7]

For all the hardships of the war years in Yellowstone—few tourists, closures of many lodging and other visitor facilities, the rationing of tires, paper, and other items, and a shoestring budget—World War II represented a demarcation point in the park's history. Having transitioned from playground of the elite to a vacation destination for ordinary Americans during the Great Depression of the 1930s, Yellowstone soaked up a booming postwar economy that completed the makeover of the nation's premier national park. America's middle class expanded rapidly, as more and more families joined the ranks of summer vacationers. Simultaneously a growing interest in scientific knowledge found expression in grade school textbooks as well as the growth of scientific university degrees and academic journals. Stoking a hunger for understanding the natural world, the ascendancy of science furthered public and professional interest in the natural history and wildlife biology of Yellowstone.

In whipsaw fashion, the park's annual record visitation of 579,696 in 1941 on the eve of America's entry into World War II dropped precipitously two years later, only to surge dramatically upward into the stratosphere of a million-plus visitors in 1948. Through the decade of the 1950s visitation climbed yet further, thereby straining park facilities.[8]

More visitors, too, meant more handouts for bears, their roadside begging remaining despite the closure of the public garbage dumps. But alongside old practices carried over into postwar years, currents of new thinking emerged in Yellowstone in the form of systematic, scientific studies of wildlife populations. A key moment arrived in 1959 when conservationists Frank and John Craighead, brothers with extensive wildlife expertise, launched a decade-long study of the park's grizzly bears, the first comprehensive, scientific analysis of any large carnivore. Deploying path-breaking technology for the times, the Craighead brothers attached radio-tracking collars to select grizzlies. By monitoring the animals' movements the scientists learned that the bears often traveled into national forests surrounding Yellowstone. From this kind of collected data, the Craigheads mapped the scope of the grizzlies' range, the project giving birth to a transformative conceptualization of Yellowstone as not merely a boundaried park, but a larger region.[9]

From Yellowstone's early years, beginning with park advocate General Philip Sheridan in 1882, a number of voices had called for a significant enlarging of the park's boundaries to better protect wildlife. Although small additions to the park's northern and western boundaries took place in 1929 and 1932 during the Hoover Administration, calls for large-scale expansion of Yellowstone's boundaries met resistance. But armed with concrete data amid a rapidly expanding awareness of ecological dynamics, the Craigheads in the 1960s and 1970s made the same argument in a more persuasive and precise manner, utilizing the language of a Yellowstone "ecosystem" extending beyond park boundaries. Other Yellowstone advocates adopted the Craigheads' language, leading in 1983 to the birth of the concept of the Greater Yellowstone Ecosystem (GYE).[10]

An eleven-million-acre expanse including, and in total five times the size of, Yellowstone National Park, the GYE is today comprised of federal lands contiguously connected: national park, national forest, US Fish and Wildlife, and Bureau of Land Management lands. Anchored by Yellowstone National Park and collectively extending north to south from near Bozeman, Montana, to central Wyoming, and east to west from the vicinity of Cody, Wyoming, into Idaho, today's GYE is partially managed as a singular ecosystem.[11]

Within the GYE the Craigheads' research work with Yellowstone's grizzlies revealed a population in peril, the animals' health compromised and lives shortened by a diet of human food. Spurred on by the revelations, the National Park Service launched an initiative to re-acclimate Yellowstone's bears to their natural habitat: a life cycle independent of human activity and consisting of the animals' historical natural diet.

In addition to revising park rules and regulations to legally prohibit visitors from feeding bears, park officials simultaneously closed the last remaining garbage dump inside the park (a non-public dump located near Trout Creek). By the 1970s the park's bears, once ubiquitous along park roadways, were once again seeking sustenance from a natural and seasonally adjusted diet of winter-killed animals, stalked kills, pine nuts, trout, moths, blueberries, and other sources. Lest bears be tempted to return to the consumption of human food, park officials mandated the installation of bear-proof garbage cans that George Wright first envisioned in the 1930s. Even so, following a century of eradication outside of Yellowstone and artificial management within park boundaries, Yellowstone's grizzly population remained tenuous, their numbers too small for genetic self-survival. Recognizing the critical importance of a healthy grizzly population in the larger Yellowstone ecosystem, Congress in 1975 granted federal protection to the species through the 1973 Endangered Species Act.[12]

As the Craigheads researched grizzlies in the 1960s, another team of scientists working with the National Park Service examined "biotic associations"—interconnected communities of plants and animals—within national parks. In 1963, the scientists issued a report titled "Wildlife Management in the National Parks" (commonly known as the Leopold Report, named in honor of environmentalist and author Starker Leopold) and recommending the implementation of "natural regulation" resource management in national parks. In practical terms, the introduction of natural resource management brought an end to the artificial management of the park's elk and bison herds, including winter hay feeding and population culling.[13]

Soon the Leopold Act, refined by additional legislation, became a framework for national park management. Within Yellowstone the report provided a blueprint for setting and achieving goals through policies requiring the use of "high quality science from inventory, monitoring, and research to understand and manage park resources."[14]

Alongside the Leopold Act and in addition to the Endangered Species Act, a succession of national environmental laws enacted by Congress further shaped the increasingly complex task of resource management in Yellowstone and other national parks. The Wilderness Act of 1964 impacted wilderness lands in national parks by recognizing the value of preserving "an area where the earth and its community of life are untrammeled by man, where man himself is a visitor who does not remain," in practice creating laws requiring that human visitors "leave no trace" of their presence upon wilderness-designated lands.[15]

In 1970, the National Environmental Policy Act required the federal government to assess potential human-caused damage to the environment in decision-making processes, subsequently necessitating environmental assessments and impact statements in national parks. During the same year the Clean Air Act, passed in an era of poor air quality due to high pollution levels throughout much of the country, mandated the protection of air quality at the highest level in national parks. In similar fashion and in response to widespread contamination of rivers and lakes, the 1972 Clean Water Act required restoration and maintenance of "chemical, physical and biological integrity of the Nation's waters" through the elimination of pollution discharges.[16]

Soon Yellowstone became a model for emerging environmental stewardship. World leaders took notice. Recognizing the park's successes in preserving cultural resources and protecting ecosystems while acknowledging the yet fragile nature of the park's landscape and wildlife, the United Nations designated Yellowstone National Park as a World Heritage Site and Biosphere Reserve in 1976.[17]

Nonetheless, challenges remained in the task of reversing artificial management policies yet harmful to the park's ecosystem. From the 1930s into the 1970s, in an effort to maintain forest aesthetics, National Park Service fire policies mandated the rapid extinguishing of all conflagrations. Reflective of a shift toward the prioritization of forest health, revised fire protocols in 1972 allowed some natural wildfires to burn under controlled conditions. Years later world-headlining and record-breaking fires in the dry summer of 1988 trained the spotlight on fire management policies as never before. The massive wildfires, many started by lightning and fueled by dry dead-fall, burned roughly one-third of Yellowstone, barely sparing the Old Faithful Inn. Extensive studies of the 1988 fires led to modification of park policies four years later, including greater monitoring of natural wildfires and increased funding for fire management. Further refinement of policies in ensuing years established comprehensive guidelines for determining whether natural wildfires should be allowed to burn, or should be suppressed.[18]

Other major policy reversals followed, none more storied than the 1995 reintroduction of wolves into Yellowstone. First proposed by Aldo Leopold in the 1940s, the idea of restoring wolves to the park later received affirmation in studies conducted by biologist John Weaver (1970s) and elk researcher Douglas Houston (1980s). More than two decades after the 1995 reintroduction of wolves, Yellowstone senior wildlife biologist Doug Smith and coauthors of a post-restoration study reflected on the leadership team who carefully implemented the long process of wolf restoration. "Looking back, the process to restore wolves to Yellowstone went surprisingly smoothly," Smith recalled of the effort opposed by many in the nearby ranching community. "Early U.S. Fish and Wildlife Service work, combined with the vision of National Park Service (NPS) Director William Penn Mott, the quiet leadership of Yellowstone Superintendent Robert Barbee, the detailed planning of the Recovery Team, support from the Clinton administration and Secretary of the Interior Bruce Babbitt, and final implementation by Edward Bangs and Steven Fritts of the U.S. Fish and Wildlife Service, with big assists from Yellowstone planners John Varley and Wayne Brewster, were the reasons for the success."[19]

Barbee, Yellowstone superintendent from 1983 to 1994, in addition to initiating and shepherding the wolf restoration project to the brink of completion, also received acclaim for his handling of the aftermath of the 1988 fires. Michael Finley, appointed park superintendent in 1995 during the final months of the wolf restoration project, spearheaded the implementation of the more than decade-long project.[20]

Many others, including historians, archaeologists, and paleontologists wrote papers and books that undergirded the project and documented the history of wolves in Yellowstone. The National Park Service selected historians Paul Schullery and Lee Whittlesey to document the history of wolves in the Greater Yellowstone Ecosystem, based upon all known literature; chose paleontologist Kenneth P. Cannon to examine the presence of wolves in the region in ancient times; and designated biologists John A. Mack and Francis J. Singer to examine elk, mule deer, and moose as potential for wolves' food sources in the region. The studies of many others in the areas of economics, sociology, taxonomy, genetics, and the fields related to potential interactions of wolves with other parts of the ecosystem buttressed the aforementioned studies. All of these papers, several of them book-length, were published in the volumes appropriately named *Wolves for Yellowstone? A Report to Congress.*[21]

The return of wolves to Yellowstone marked a major step toward the reestablishment of the park's historic ecosystem, the apex predator restoring a more traditional balance to the ecosystem's flora and fauna. Forced to adjust to the presence of wolves, the park's fluctuating northern elk herd, for some seven decades preyed upon only by grizzlies and experiencing boom-and-bust population numbers marked by cyclical mass starvation, changed movement and grazing patterns as the wolves stalked and often killed weak and young animals. Now stabilized, the northern elk herd numbering from six thousand to eight thousand exists in symbiotic relationship with a wolf population of between 300 and 350.[22]

In 1995 wolves were reintroduced into Yellowstone, roughly seventy years since their eradication from the park in the 1920s. Wolf #10, pictured here in February 1995 in a temporary enclosure in the park, became a favorite of wolf biologists and the public alike. Released into Yellowstone's wilderness in March, weeks later #10 and his mate, #9, wandered out of park boundaries into Montana, where #10 was illegally killed and mutilated by a hunter. PHOTO JIM PEACO/NPS

Far from a local event, the return of wolves symbolized the coming of age of ecosystem-restoration efforts across the globe. Often visible today from park roadways in the Lamar Valley and sometimes elsewhere, wolves are the living star of a renewed Yellowstone, as year after year the animals' pack dynamics fascinate tourists and scientists alike.

On the heels of wolf reintroduction, a geological threat to Yellowstone's ecosystem also garnered much attention. In the late nineteenth century, the discovery of gold near the northeast corner of Yellowstone touched off a prolonged battle between corporate and conservationist interests over commercial mining of the site, conservationists eventually winning the day. A century later, however, another mining company sought to extract gold from the already-scarred landscape. Concerned that pollution from new mining would leach into park waters, environmentalists battled the mine developer in court. In 1996, President Bill Clinton signed legislation thwarting the ecological threat, the federal government purchasing the proposed New World Mine site and setting in motion the cleanup and restoration of the damaged land. Finally resolving a long-standing threat to the Lamar Valley's Soda Butte Creek and other nearby waterways, this federal legislation represented a critical step forward in protecting the integrity of the Yellowstone ecosystem.[23]

Notable victories aside, ecosystem challenges remain to the present day, the underlying issues often being complex. Prolonged court battles over the protected status of Yellowstone's grizzly and wolf populations are ongoing. In addition to ranchers' opposition to the expanding presence of the park's predatory animals upon livestock terrain, both species are also threatened by rapid, urban growth on the perimeter of the Greater Yellowstone Ecosystem.[24]

For other reasons bison, their population currently robust, generate controversy. Yellowstone's natural capacity for accommodating the animals within park boundaries is limited. In addition, there are lingering fears, despite the lack of documented evidence, that the disease brucellosis, common in the park's wild bison, may infect domestic cattle herds near the park. An illness that can cause cows to abort fetuses, brucellosis detected in a single cow triggers federal restrictions on an entire herd of cattle. Addressing both issues, an agreement between the National Park Service and the state of Montana requires the annual capture and slaughter of some bison that wander outside park boundaries to the north and northwest during the winter months. Animals killed in this program are processed in slaughter plants, and the meat and hides given to Native tribes. Additionally, some bison straying beyond park boundaries into Montana are legally killed by Native and state hunters.[25]

In addition to slaughter and hunting, a third option for managing the park's bison that wander outside of park boundaries into Montana is a "Bison Conservation Transfer Program." In this program, co-developed and administered with the InterTribal Buffalo Council, some captured bison are placed into pens in or near the park and tested for brucellosis. Over a lengthy period of time a series of brucellosis tests are administered to the animals. Yellowstone's wild bison that test negative for the disease

America's wild bison, hunted to near extinction by the 1890s, in the twentieth century recovered within Yellowstone's sanctuary. Today, the park's iconic mammal numbers in the thousands and is a favorite of visitors. In this image bison wander through a meadow. Steam from thermal features in the Lower Geyser Basin is visible in the background. COPYRIGHT BRUCE GOURLEY

throughout the testing stages are eligible for shipment to tribal entities throughout the United States to strengthen the genetics of small tribal herds of bison.[26]

Apart from wildlife and geological controversies, winter visitors' motorized impact upon the park—originating with snowplane trips in 1949 and giving way to snowcoaches in the 1950s, joined by snowmobiles in the 1960s—is increasingly regulated to reduce pollution emissions and noise levels in the twenty-first century. Summer visitation, now numbering over four million annually on essentially the same two-lane road system in place for nearly a century, also presents long-term challenges in terms of traffic congestion, parking, and pollution.[27]

Today, the preservation of the park's cultural heritage and restoration and protection of the natural ecosystem together dramatically enhances visitors' Yellowstone experience. Whether standing awestruck in the lobby of the Old Faithful Inn or thrilling at the sight of wolves in the Lamar Valley, today's park visitors simultaneously stand in both the present and the past. This timeless privilege is made possible by the devoted work and caretaking of generations of administrators, naturalists, biologists, historians, archaeologists, law-enforcement rangers, backcountry maintenance workers, entrance station operators, winter keepers, and other park staff members who faithfully steward the world's most famous national park.

CHAPTER FOURTEEN

Mysteries of Life and the Universe

How Yellowstone's Thermal Waters Unlocked a Scientific Revolution

Look deep, deep into nature, and then you will understand everything better.

—ALBERT EINSTEIN, 1951[1]

WHAT IS LIFE? DOES LIFE EXIST BEYOND PLANET EARTH?

From ancient thinkers to early philosophers, from medieval theologians to bloggers, from wise elders to young children, from bar rooms to college classrooms, humanity has long pondered life's biggest questions.

But not until the modern age of science, a discipline devoted to the discovery and understanding of ever-expanding knowledge, have the big mysteries of life come into clearer focus.

In the 1950s, a watershed moment arrived when James D. Watson and Francis Crick, pioneering American geneticists and biophysicists, discovered the building blocks of life: the molecular structure of deoxyribonucleic acid, popularly known as DNA. Inside each cell of a living organism is a spiral of DNA containing pairs of chromosomes carrying the genetic codes of life. First discovered with the aid of a microscope in the late nineteenth century, DNA and chromosomes remained little understood until Watson and Crick identified DNA, comprised of chromosomes, as the basis of life.

Even so, decoding DNA, and hence understanding life's biggest questions, remained elusive.

Elusive, that is, until an extraordinary discovery in Yellowstone National Park.

For centuries Native peoples had marveled at the contrasting beauty and harshness of Yellowstone's thermal waters. Heated by underground volcanic forces, the beguiling rainbow hues of the park's hot springs masked certain death for wildlife and humans alike who fell into the hottest of the natural cauldrons. Early Euro-American explorers wandering onto the Yellowstone plateau struggled to describe the dangerous but colorful hot springs and towering columns of water erupting from the ground. Early tourists gaped, gawked, and often got too close, some suffering painful injuries, a few from carelessness or misfortune meeting the horrible fate of death by boiling. None realized that the super-heated waters capable of snuffing out one's life in mere seconds also harbored invisible life forms of great variety in seemingly infinite numbers.

Here matters stood until the summer of 1964 and a scientist's chance trip to Yellowstone.

While Watson and Crick toiled in labs unraveling the structure of DNA, Thomas Dale Brock studied microbes. A native of Cleveland, Ohio, Brock worked as an assistant professor of bacteriology at Indiana University. Also a prolific writer, he published his findings in numerous scientific articles as well as books. Ever inquisitive, Brock in the 1950s and early 1960s traveled from coast to coast in search of understanding the world of microorganisms. A hiker, Brock in his travels sometimes made side trips to satiate his craving for wilderness experiences. On a cross-country trek in the summer of 1964, he took time off to backpack in Grand Teton National Park.

Although from a distance long enamored of the Grand Tetons, Brock was not as interested in Yellowstone, his image of that famous place reflecting lingering public perceptions of the iconic park as a pleasuring ground rather than a nature preserve. In his own words, Brock had "no desire to go to Yellowstone because of its reputation as a heavily-visited 'amusement' park, rather than a natural area." Little did he know that even then the park was beginning to turn a corner away from the primacy of entertaining visitors and toward an overriding focus on restoring ecological balance.[2]

Following his backpacking trip in the Tetons, Brock drove north into Yellowstone, his expectations low. Like explorers of the early nineteenth century who knew not what to expect, Brock stood stunned at the sight of an exciting world of thermal waters. Unlike the fur trappers and gold prospectors of old, however, Brock arrived in Yellowstone with a frame of reference for understanding the otherworldly sights he beheld. Although viewing natural hot springs for the first time, with a mind honed by his studies of invisible organisms in other watery environments the microbiologist saw the park's thermal waters in a different light than had any of the millions of visitors who preceded him. "I had not expected," Brock wrote of his first trip to Yellowstone, "such enormous developments of microorganisms as were present in the runoff channels of the Yellowstone hot springs." During a return trip to the park late in the summer, Brock collected samples from several hot springs, later in the lab comparing the warm water bacteria to commonly known organisms living in sulfur springs of which he was currently studying.[3]

Intrigued, Brock returned yet again, his visit in 1965 soon becoming "one of the more exciting two weeks of my career." This time he examined the colorful bacterial mats commonly formed on the perimeter of geysers and hot springs, searching for thermal algae, or cyanobacteria, the most ancient of life forms. At Octopus Spring in the Lower Geyser Basin Brock saw "pink gelatinous masses of material, obviously biological, at surprisingly high temperatures." He recognized that the filaments shared similarities with an organism he had previously studied at Friday Harbor on Washington State's coast. In his field book, Brock noted that the hot spring microorganisms were "definitely living." Deducing that he was witnessing bacteria "living at temperatures near boiling," Brock's observations led him "to commit early to the idea of what I later called extreme thermophiles."[4]

Brock next secured a grant from the National Science Foundation to formally study Yellowstone's hot springs during the following year, 1966. Leading a team of young scientists, Brock and his assistants obtained a sample of a particular microbe in Mushroom Pool in Lower Geyser Basin, an organism they named *Thermus acquaticus*. Researching the organism in the months and years following, Brock's team realized they

Bacterial mats in Yellowstone's hot springs, such as pictured here in a closeup image, are teeming with ancient, microscopic, extreme thermophilic life forms that have revolutionized our understanding of life itself. Nonetheless, scientists remain in the early stages of identifying the vast numbers of living organisms collectively living in the park's ten-thousand-plus thermal features. COPYRIGHT BRUCE GOURLEY

had discovered a previously unknown form of life, the first identified hot-water organism among an immense number of extreme thermophiles living in Yellowstone's thermal waters.

Continuing his work in Yellowstone, Brock published several hall-mark scientific papers in the years following. His research provided evidence of bacteria living not only at near-boiling temperatures, but also microbial organisms thriving in temperatures above the boiling point, an even more astonishing discovery. From his work in Yellowstone, Brock embarked on a successful search for extreme thermophiles in hot springs in other parts of the world, including heated deep-sea vents.[5]

Thomas Brock's discoveries opened a new avenue in the exploration of Yellowstone's natural ecosystem. Soon hundreds of references to *Thermus acquaticus* appeared in scientific journals, microbiologists increasingly focused on extreme life forms previously unknown. Not until the 1980s, however, did Brock and his colleagues' work suddenly emerge as one of the most pivotal scientific breakthroughs in history.

Since Watson and Crick's discovery of the structure of DNA, scientists had been unable to find an enzyme capable of withstanding the extreme heat required for replicating DNA for analytical purposes. Not until 1983 did a scientist, biochemist Kary Mullis of the biotechnology firm Cetus Corporation, derive a solution: the polymerase chain reaction, or PCR. A methodology of rapidly copying and exponentially replicating DNA samples, PCR utilized thermal cycling—repeated cycles of cooling and heating—enabled by an enzyme, Taq polymerase, from the heat-resistant *Thermus acquaticus*. A tiny revolution of immense proportions was born: the ability to unlock the genomes of life forms.[6]

Launching the modern genetics revolution, the extreme abilities of Yellowstone's *Thermus acquaticus* led to the sequencing of the human genome in the early twenty-first century. From that remarkable achievement, scientists discovered that all modern human beings are roughly 99 percent genetically identical. Turning the clock backward in time, DNA sequencing of ancient organic material dramatically expanded knowledge of evolutionary branches of humanoids and other life forms. *Thermus acquaticus* also revolutionized criminal forensics, enabling investigators to solve crimes by collecting crime scene genetic evidence unique to a single individual—DNA fingerprints extracted from substances such as blood or hair—and comparing the genetic evidence to that of suspects or genetic records stored in criminal databases. Within and beyond Yellowstone, DNA fingerprinting allowed park rangers, researchers, and scientists to match tufts of hair to a specific species or singular animal, such as the rarely sighted nocturnal wolverine, for purposes of studies. In the arena of human health, scientists discovered processes to edit, repair, and tweak DNA sequences to design cures for rare genetic illnesses, and create vaccines for highly contagious and deadly pathogens such as SARS-Cov-2 (or COVID-19).

In addition to opening a door to understanding the fundamentals of life, the scientific contributions of Yellowstone's extreme thermophiles paved the way for scientists to develop a growing suite of tools for modifying and creating life. Utilizing advanced DNA techniques, scientists are now editing the genetic composition of life forms and creating new life forms, beginning with simple organisms. In addition, biologists are now working toward the restoration, or re-creation, of certain life forms—a process known as "de-extinction"—with future hope of potentially bringing back to life key extinct species, from birds to mammoths. Success in the arena would mark perhaps the greatest human achievement ever.[7]

Beyond Earth, the discovery of extreme life in Yellowstone's hot springs, long thought inhospitable to living organisms, launched an interstellar revolution. With the knowledge that life is far more diverse and hardy than ever before imagined, astrobiologists now search for life in the extreme hot, cold, and seemingly inhospitable environments of deep space. Today, the search for life on distant planets in "habitable zones" orbiting host stars is carried out by analyzing chemical signatures deduced from a planet's light waves. Many scientists feel certain that it is merely a matter of time before humanity discovers extraterrestrial life elsewhere in the Milky Way Galaxy. Perhaps the first discovery of life in deep space will be of a simple organism similar to those dwelling in Yellowstone's thermal waters.[8]

Today the search for life in Yellowstone, and in turn future medical cures and potential life on other planets, continues. In partnership with the National Park Service, microbiologists, including some from Montana State University's (Bozeman) Thermal Biology Institute, are carefully examining some of the more than 98 percent of the park's extreme, thermophilic life-forms yet to be identified. At the same time and carrying on a long heritage of educating park visitors, National Park Service interpretive displays physically placed alongside some hot springs, as well as interpretive exhibits in the Old Faithful Visitor Center, provide opportunities for park visitors to learn more about the unfolding story of Yellowstone's extreme, microscopic wildlife.[9]

A land of enduring mystery and fascination, Yellowstone National Park remains on the frontier of human understanding. Today, millions of visitors from throughout the world each year stand in awe of the natural glory of this unique place of never-ending discovery.

The epic saga of Yellowstone National Park continues.

Come. See. Hear. Learn. Connect.

NOTES

CHAPTER ONE

1. George W. Wright, Joseph S. Dixon, and Ben H. Thompson, *Fauna of the National Parks of the United States* (Washington, DC: US Government Printing Office, 1933), 44.
2. For more information about the seasonal cycles and general ecology of Yellowstone National Park see Frank C. Craighead Jr., *For Everything There Is a Season: The Sequence of Natural Events in the Grand-Teton Yellowstone Area* (Falcon, 1970); George Wuerthner, *Yellowstone: A Visitor's Companion* (Stackpole Books, 1992); and Sharon Eversman and Mary Karr, *Yellowstone Ecology: A Road Guide* (Mountain Press, 1992).

CHAPTER TWO

1. John Muir, *Our National Parks* (Boston: Houghton, Mifflin and Company, 1901), 83. Muir is describing the ancient geological forces that shaped Yellowstone National Park.
2. "Precambrian Time," National Geographic, https://www.nationalgeographic.com/science/prehistoric-world/precambrian-time/; "NPS Geodiversity Atlas—Grand Teton National Park, Wyoming," National Park Service, https://www.nps.gov/articles/nps-geodiversity-atlas-grand-teton-national-park-wyoming.htm.
3. "Geological History of the Yellowstone Region," USGS Geological Bulletin 1347, https://www.nps.gov/parkhistory/online_books/geology/publications/bul/1347/sec2.htm.
4. Sara Tulga and David Smith, "Fossils in Our Parklands: Yellowstone National Park—Wyoming, Idaho, Montana," https://ucmp.berkeley.edu/science/parks/yellowstone.php.
5. *Yellowstone Resources and Issues Handbook: 2016* (Yellowstone National Park, WY), 107; "Geological History of the Yellowstone Region," USGS; Zachery M. Seligman, Anna E. Klene, and Frederick E. Nelson, "Rock Glaciers of the Beartooth and Northern Absaroka Ranges, Montana, USA," *Permafrost and Periglacial Processes*, October/December 2019, 249–59, https://onlinelibrary.wiley.com/doi/10.1002/ppp.2019; "Geology of Wyoming: Absaroka Volcanic Province," https://www.geowyo.com/absaroka-volcanic-province.html.
6. "Geological History of the Yellowstone Region," USGS. *Yellowstone Resources and Issues Handbook: 2016*, 107; "Discovery of Two New Super-Eruptions from the Yellowstone Hotspot Track (USA): Is the Yellowstone Hotspot Waning?", *Geology*, Vol. 48, no. 9 (2020), 934–38, https://pubs.geoscienceworld.org/gsa/geology/article/48/9/934/586793/Discovery-of-two-new-super-eruptions-from-the.
7. *Yellowstone Resources and Issues Handbook: 2016*, 109; "Geological History of the Yellowstone Region," USGS.

8. *Yellowstone Resources and Issues Handbook: 2016*, 109–10; "Geological History of the Yellowstone Region," USGS.
9. "Grand Canyon of the Yellowstone," National Park Service, https://www.nps.gov/yell/learn/nature/grand-canyon.htm; *Yellowstone Resources and Issues Handbook: 2016*, 107–10, 121–22; "Geological History of the Yellowstone Region," USGS.
10. *Yellowstone Resources and Issues Handbook: 2016*, 121–22; "Glaciers," National Park Service, https://home.nps.gov/yell/learn/nature/glaciers.htm; "Yellowstone Lake Geology," National Park Service, https://www.nps.gov/yell/learn/nature/yellowstone-lake-geology.htm; Kenneth L. Pierce, "History and Dynamics of Glaciation in the Northern Yellowstone National Park Area," Geological Survey Professional Paper 729 F, https://pubs.usgs.gov/pp/0729f/report.pdf.
11. "Hot Water and Stream Phenomena," USGS Geological Survey Bulletin 1347, https://www.nps.gov/parkhistory/online_books/geology/publications/bul/1347/sec5.htm; Jacob B. Lowenstern, Shaul Hurwitz, and John P. McGeehin, "Radiocarbon Dating of Silica Sinter Deposits in Shallow Drill Cores from the Upper Geyser Basin, Yellowstone National Park," *Journal of Volcanology and Geothermal Research*, Vol. 310, January 15, 2016, 132–36, https://www.sciencedirect.com/science/article/abs/pii/S0377027315004114; "60 Years Since the 1959 M7.3 Hebgen Lake Earthquake: Its History and Effects on the Yellowstone Region," USGS, August 5, 2019, https://www.usgs.gov/center-news/60-years-1959-m73-hebgen-lake-earthquake-its-history-and-effects-yellowstone-region. For more information on the Hebgen Lake earthquake, sometimes referred to as the Yellowstone Earthquake, see Larry Morris, *The 1959 Yellowstone Earthquake* (Columbia, SC: History Press, 2016).

CHAPTER THREE

1. Richard Grant, "The Lost History of Yellowstone," *Smithsonian*, January-February 2021, 36.
2. "Tracking the First Americans," *National Geographic*, https://www.nationalgeographic.com/magazine/2015/01/first-americans/; Michael Greshko, "Ancient DNA Reveals Complex Migrations of the First Americans," *National Geographic*, November 8, 2018, https://www.nationalgeographic.com/science/2018/11/ancient-dna-reveals-complex-migrations-first-americans/; Ker Than, "Oldest Burial Yields DNA Evidence of First Americans," *National Geographic*, February 12, 2014, https://www.nationalgeographic.com/news/2014/2/140212-anzik-skeleton-dna-montana-clovis-culture-first-americans/; Michael Balter, "Native Americans Descend from Ancient Montana Boy," *Science*, February 12, 2014, https://www.sciencemag.org/news/2014/02/native-americans-descend-ancient-montana-boy.
3. Tamsen Emerson Hert, "Yellowstone, the World's Wonderland," https://www.wyohistory.org/encyclopedia/yellowstone-worlds-wonderland; "Hunter-Gatherers," https://www.history.com/topics/pre-history/hunter-gatherers; "The Earliest Humans in Yellowstone," https://www.nps.gov/yell/learn/historyculture/earliest-humans.htm; "Archeology," https://home.nps.gov/yell/learn/historyculture/archeology.htm; *Yellowstone Resources and Issues Handbook: 2016*, 14, 15.

4. Charles Q. Choi, "Climate Change Wiped Out Woolly Mammoths, Saber-Toothed Cats," *LiveScience*, May 24, 2010, https://www.livescience.com/6506-climate-change -wiped-woolly-mammoths-saber-toothed-cats.html; William J. Ripple and Blaire Van Valkenburgh, "Linking Top-down Forces to the Pleistocene Megafaunal Extinctions," *Bioscience*, July/August 2010; *Yellowstone Resources and Issues Handbook: 2016*, 14; Sarah Tulga and David Smith, "Yellowstone National Park—Wyoming, Idaho, Montana," https://ucmp.berkeley.edu/science/parks/yellowstone.php; Richard Grant, "The Lost History of Yellowstone," 50.
5. *Yellowstone Resources and Issues Handbook: 2016*, 14; Richard Grant, "The Lost History of Yellowstone," 38.
6. *Yellowstone Resources and Issues Handbook: 2016*, 14–16; Alysa Landry, "Native History: Yellowstone National Park Created on Sacred Land," *Indian Country Today*, May 1, 2017, https://indiancountrytoday.com/archive/native-history-yellowstone-national-park -created-on-sacred-land-Vu5ywco8VU66zGmghrlQvw.
7. *Yellowstone Resources and Issues Handbook: 2016*, 16–17; Richard Grant, "The Lost History of Yellowstone," 54.
8. "Historic Tribes," https://www.nps.gov/yell/learn/historyculture/historic-tribes.htm; "Timelines of Early Human History in Yellowstone," National Park Service, https:// www.nps.gov/yell/learn/historyculture/timeline.htm; Alysa Landry, "Native History: Yellowstone National Park Created on Sacred Land"; *Yellowstone Resources and Issues Handbook: 2016*, 16–18.
9. Lee Whittlesey citing Peter Nabokov and Lawrence Loendorf, "Native Americans, the Earliest Interpreters," 272, 274, www.georgewright.org/01yp_whittlesey.pdf; Richard Grant, "The Lost History of Yellowstone," 54.
10. Doug MacDonald quoted in Richard Grant, "The Lost History of Yellowstone," 34. For more information see Doug MacDonald, *Before Yellowstone: Native American Archaeology in the National Park* (Seattle: University of Washington Press, 2018).
11. For the story of the forced removal and suppression of Native peoples, see Roxanne Dunbar-Ortiz, *An Indigenous Peoples' History of the United States* (Boston: Beacon Press, 2015). For a map of the early Crow Reservation, see Pierre-Jean De Smet's 1851 Map of the Upper Plains and Rocky Mountain Region, https://www.loc.gov/resource/g4050.ct0 00883/?r=0.318,0.309,0.166,0.084,0.
12. See Gary Clayton Anderson, *Ethnic Cleansing and the Indian: The Crime That Should Haunt America* (Norman: University of Oklahoma Press, 2014); Richard Grant, "The Lost History of Yellowstone," 55.
13. See Peter Nabokov and Lawrence Loendorf, *Restoring a Process: American Indians and Yellowstone National Park* (Norman: University of Oklahoma Press, 2004).
14. Richard Grant, "The Lost History of Yellowstone," 117.

CHAPTER FOUR
1. "The Explorers: Pierre Gaultier de Varennes et de La Verendrye 1732–1739," Canadian Museum of History, https://www.historymuseum.ca/virtual-museum-of-new -france/the-explorers/pierre-gaultier-de-varennes-et-de-la-verendrye-1732-1739/.

2. Robert A. Saindon, ed., *Explorations into the World of Lewis and Clark*, Vol. 1/ 3 (Great Falls, MT: Lewis and Clark Trail Heritage Foundation, 2003), 62–65.

3. Saindon, 66–67; "The Place Where Hell Bubbled Up," https://www.nps.gov/parkhistory/online_books/yell/clary/sec3.htm.

4. Saindon, "The Place Where Hell Bubbled Up."

5. Whittlesey, "Native Americans, the Earliest Interpreters," 274, www.georgewright.org/01yp_whittlesey.pdf.

6. For more information about Colter's possible route, see Merrill J. Mattes, *Colter's Hell and Jackson's Hole: The Fur Trappers' Exploration of the Yellowstone and Grand Teton Park Region* (Yellowstone Association and Grand Teton Natural History Association, 1962), https://www.nps.gov/parkhistory/online_books/grte1/chap3.htm and David A. Clary, *"The Place Where Hell Bubbled Up": A History of the First National Park* (National Park Service, US Department of the Interior, 1972), https://www.nps.gov/parkhistory/online_books/yell/clary/sec3.htm.

7. Alexander Ross, *The Fur Hunters of the Far West; a Narrative of Adventures in the Oregon and Rocky Mountains*, Vol. 1 (London: Smith, Elder and Co., 1855), 266–67.

8. E. S. Topping, *Chronicles of the Yellowstone* (St. Paul: Pioneer Press Company, 1883), 14–15.

9. J. W. Gunnison, *The Mormons, or, Latter-day Saints: in the Valley of the Great Salt Lake: a History of Their Rise and Progress, Peculiar Doctrines, Present Condition, and Prospects; Derived from Personal Observation, During a Residence Among Them* (Philadelphia: Lippincott, Grambo & Co., 1852), 150–51.

10. *Philadelphia Gazette*, September 27, 1827. Potts wrote under the pseudonym/initials DTP. Also see Clary, *"The Place Where Hell Bubbled Up"*; "West Thumb Geyser Basin," NPS, https://www.nps.gov/yell/learn/nature/west-thumb-geyser-basin.htm; and Mattes, *Colter's Hell*, https://www.nps.gov/parkhistory/online_books/grte1/chap6.htm.

11. Warren Angus Ferris, *Life in the Rocky Mountains: A Diary of Wanderings on the Sources of the Rivers Missouri, Columbia, and Colorado from February, 1830, to November, 1835* (Denver: F. A. Rosenstock, 1940), 150–51.

12. Ferris, *Life in the Rocky Mountains*, 150–51.

13. Ferris, *Life in the Rocky Mountains*, 150–51.

14. Ferris, *Life in the Rocky Mountains*, 150–51.

15. A digital reproduction of Warren Angus Ferris's 1836 map of Yellowstone is at https://cdm15999.contentdm.oclc.org/digital/collection/p15999coll31/id/14973. For more information about Ferris's western trek see "Rocky Mountain Geysers," *Western Literary Messenger*, Vol. 2 (July 13, 1842), 12–13. In 1841 Ferris also made a name for himself as surveyor of the town that became Dallas, Texas; see "Ferris, Warren Angus (1810–1873?)," Texas State Historical Association, https://www.tshaonline.org/handbook/entries/ferris-warren-angus.

16. Aubrey L. Haines, *The Yellowstone Story: A History of Our First National Park*, Vol. 1, Revised Edition (Niwot: University Press of Colorado, 1996), 7.

17. Nearly one hundred thousand books have been written about slavery and/or the American Civil War. Readers interested in slave autobiographies may wish to visit "North American Slave Biographies," a digital compilation edited by William L.

Andrews and published by the University of North Carolina "Documenting the American South" project, https://docsouth.unc.edu/neh/biblintro.html. Regarding the story of the role of slavery as an economic institution prior to the Civil War, a good starting point is Edward E. Baptist, *The Half Has Never Been Told: Slavery and the Making of American Capitalism* (New York: Basic Books, 2016). Finally, one of the most esteemed single-volume surveys of the American Civil War is James M. McPherson, *Battle Cry of Freedom: The Civil War Era* (Oxford University Press, 1998, 2003).

18. Haines, *Yellowstone Story*, Vol. 1, 64–68.

19. Haines, *Yellowstone Story*, Vol. 1, 89–90. A digital rendering of DeLacy's 1865 Montana map is at https://www.loc.gov/resource/g4251h.ct001859/.

20. Joy Porter, *Native American Environmentalism: Land, Spirit and the Idea of Wilderness* (University of Nebraska Press, 2014), 27. Also see "George Catlin," National Park Service, https://www.nps.gov/people/george-catlin.htm.

21. Haines, *Yellowstone Story*, Vol. 1, 81; Barry MacIntosh, "The National Park Service: A Brief History," https://www.nps.gov/parkhistory/hisnps/NPSHistory/briefhistory.htm.

22. "The Great Yellowstone Wonder—The Valley and Pass of Hell," *Weekly Trinity Journal*, Weaverville, California, February 1, 1868, 1, https://chroniclingamerica.loc.gov/lccn/sn85025202/1868-02-01/ed-1/seq-1.pdf.

23. "The Upper Yellowstone," *Montana Post*, August 31, 1867, 1, https://chronicling america.loc.gov/lccn/sn83025293/1867-08-31/ed-1/seq-6.pdf.

24. "Hell on the Yellowstone River," *New York Herald*, September 14, 1867, 8, https://chroniclingamerica.loc.gov/lccn/sn83030313/1867-09-14/ed-1/seq-8.pdf.

25. "Niagara Eclipsed," *Daily Phoenix*, Columbia, South Carolina, October 10, 1867, 1, https://chroniclingamerica.loc.gov/lccn/sn84027008/1867-10-10/ed-1/seq-1.pdf.

26. See "Niagara Eclipsed," *Pulaski* (TN) *Citizen*, December 6, 1867, 1, https://chronicling america.loc.gov/lccn/sn85033964/1867-12-06/ed-1/seq-1.pdf.

27. Louis C. Cramton, *Early History of Yellowstone National Park and Its Relation to National Park Policies* (Washington, DC: Government Printing Office, 1932), 10–12; Haines, *Yellowstone National Park: Exploration and Establishment* (Washington, DC: US Department of the Interior, National Park Service, 1974), 140–48. For brief biographies of Folsom, Cook, and Peterson go to https://www.nps.gov/parkhistory/online_books/haines1/iee4.htm.

28. Haines, *Exploration and Establishment*, 47–51.

29. Haines, *Exploration and Establishment*, 47–51. "Mr. Hubbel" was A. H. Hubbel, who settled later in Big Timber, Montana.

30. Haines, *Exploration and Establishment*, 47, 51–54.

31. Haines, *Exploration and Establishment*, 47, 48.

32. Haines, *Exploration and Establishment*, 47, 48, 54, 55, 140, 141, 150–52.

33. Haines, *Exploration and Establishment*, 142, 143; Cramton, *Early History*, 12–21; Richard West Sellars, *Preserving History in the National Parks* (New Haven, CT: Yale University Press, 1997), Chapter One.

34. For a biography of Jay Cooke and the Northern Pacific Railroad, see *Jay Cooke's Gamble: The Northern Pacific Railroad, The Sioux, and the Panic of 1873* (Norman: University of Oklahoma Press, 2006).

35. Amanda Shaw, "The Superintendents—Nathaniel Langford," https://www.nps.gov/yell/blogs/the-superintendents-nathaniel-langford.htm; Haines, *Yellowstone Story*, Vol. 1, 105; Sellars, *Preserving History*, Chapter One.

36. Cramton, *Early History*, 12–21; Haines, *Yellowstone Story*, Vol. 1, 105–38.

37. Nathaniel P. Langford, *The Discovery of Yellowstone National Park: Diary of the Washburn Expedition to the Yellowstone and Firehole Rivers in the Year 1870* (St. Paul, MN: 1905); "Letter from Secretary of War Communicating the Report of Lieutenant Gustavus C. Doane Upon the So-Called Yellowstone Expedition of 1870," 1871, 37–38, https://babel.hathitrust.org/cgi/pt?id=njp.32101079825236&view=plaintext&seq=39; Walter Trumbull, *The Washburn Yellowstone Expedition*, 1870, www.yellowstone-online.com/history/trumbull/trumbull1. See also Paul Schullery and Lee Whittlesey, *Myth and History in the Creation of Yellowstone National Park* (Lincoln: University of Nebraska Press, 2003).

38. Truman Everts, "Thirty Seven Days of Peril," *Scribner's Monthly*, Vol III, November 1871.

39. Everts, "Thirty Seven Days"; "Marvels of Montana," *The States and Union*, Ashland, Ohio, February 1, 1871, 2, https://chroniclingamerica.loc.gov/lccn/sn83035174/1871-02-01/ed-1/seq-2.pdf.

40. "Scribner's Monthly," *The Manitowoc* (WI) *Pilot*, November 2, 1871, 3, https://chroniclingamerica.loc.gov/lccn/sn85033139/1871-11-02/ed-1/seq-3.pdf.

41. "Scribner's for November," *The Cecil Whig*, Elkton, Maryland, October 28, 1871, 1, https://chroniclingamerica.loc.gov/lccn/sn83016348/1871-10-28/ed-1/seq-1.pdf.

42. "Magazines," *Chicago Tribune*, November 13, 1871, 2, https://chroniclingamerica.loc.gov/lccn/sn82014064/1871-11-13/ed-1/seq-2.pdf.

43. "The Yellowstone Expedition," *Helena Weekly Herald*, October 27, 1870, 4, https://chroniclingamerica.loc.gov/lccn/sn84036143/1870-10-27/ed-1/seq-4.pdf.

44. For more analysis, see Schullery and Whittlesey, *Myth and History*.

45. *"Letter from Secretary of War Communicating the Report of Lieutenant Gustavus C. Doane Upon the So-Called Yellowstone Expedition of 1870*," 1871, 37–38, https://babel.hathitrust.org/cgi/pt?id=njp.32101079825236&view=plaintext&seq=39.

46. Haines, *Exploration and Establishment*, 1974, 40; See also Aubrey Haines, ed., "The Yellowstone Diaries of A. Bart Henderson," *The Yellowstone Interpreter*, Vol. 2, nos. 1–3, January–June 1964.

47. Haines, *Exploration*, 1974, 40; James Gourley, "A Reminiscence of James Gourley, Prospector of 1870," photographed copy in author's collection, original located at the Yellowstone Heritage and Research Center in Yellowstone National Park; "James Gourley, Montana Pioneer of 1862, Saw Exciting Times Along the Yellowstone," *Bozeman* (MT) *Courier*, October 7, 1927, https://chroniclingamerica.loc.gov/lccn/sn86075113/1927-10-07/ed-1/seq-11.pdf.

48. Doane Report, 28.

49. "Dashed to Pieces," *The Evening Telegraph*, Philadelphia, June 3, 1870, 1, https://chroniclingamerica.loc.gov/lccn/sn83025925/1870-06-03/ed-1/seq-1.pdf.

50. "Art and the Hayden Geological Survey," Smithsonian American Art Museum, https://americanexperience.si.edu/wp-content/uploads/2015/02/Art-and-the-Hayden -Geological-Survey-of-1871_.pdf.

51. F. V. Hayden, *Preliminary Report of the United States Geological Survey of Montana and Portions of Adjacent Territories* (Washington, DC: US Government Printing Office, 1872), 4–5, https://quod.lib.umich.edu/cgi/t/text/text-idx?c=moa&cc=moa&view=text& rgn=main&idno=AGM5641.0001.001.

52. Hayden, *Preliminary Report*, 4–5, 115; Stephen B. Jackson, "Joshua Crissman: Yellowstone's Forgotten Photographer," *Montana: The Magazine of Western History*, Vol. 49, no. 2 (Summer 1999), 24–37. See also "Joshua Crissman," The Yellowstone Stereoview Page, https://yellowstonestereoviews.com/publishers/crissman.html. The same year Thomas Hines also photographed in Yellowstone, but his images were destroyed in the Great Chicago Fire mere months later, October 8–10, 1871. See James S. Brust and Lee H. Whittlesey, "Thomas J. Hines: One of Yellowstone's Earliest Photographers," *Montana: The Magazine of Western History*, Vol. 49, no. 2 (Summer 1999), 14–23.

53. Haines, *Yellowstone Story*, Vol. 1, 188.

54. Haines, *Exploration and Establishment*, 110.

55. Haines, *Exploration and Establishment*, 110.

CHAPTER FIVE

1. George P. Marsh, "Address Delivered Before the Agricultural Society of Rutland County," September 30, 1847, https://todayinsci.com/M/Marsh_George/MarshGeorge -RutlandAgSoc.htm.

2. Frederick Law Olmsted, "Preliminary Report Upon the Yosemite and Big Tree Grove, 1865," https://www.yosemite.ca.us/library/olmsted/report.html.

3. *Helena Herald*, January 16, 1872, cited in Cramton, *Early History*, 24.

4. *Helena Herald*, March 1, 1872; Cramton, *Early History*, 25.

5. "An Act to Set Apart a Certain Tract of Land Lying Near the Head-waters of the Yellowstone River as a Public Park," March 1, 1872, Forty-Second Congress, Session II, Ch. 21–24, 32, https://memory.loc.gov/cgi-bin/ampage?collId=llsl&fileName=017/ llsl017.db&recNum=73. Although the legislative act did not use the phrase, politicians in the nation's capital and some newspaper editors across America in early 1872 sometimes referred to "the Yellowstone National Park." See the *Cheyenne Daily Leader*, April 8, 1872, 4, https://chroniclingamerica.loc.gov/lccn/sn84022149/1872-04-08/ed -1/seq-4/, and the *Alexandria* (VA) *Gazette*, May 13, 1872, 4, https://chroniclingamerica .loc.gov/lccn/sn85025007/1872-05-13/ed-1/seq-4/. For background information, see Haines, *Yellowstone Story*, Vol. 1, 166–73.

6. 1872 Yellowstone Act.

7. 1872 Yellowstone Act.

8. 1872 Yellowstone Act.

9. Aubrey L. Haines, *Yellowstone Story*, 178–79.

10. Haines, *Yellowstone Story*, Vol. 1, 179. For the story of the financial struggles of Jay Cooke and the Northern Pacific Railroad, see M. John Lubetkin, *Jay Cooke's Gamble: The Northern Pacific Railroad, the Sioux, and the Panic of 1873* (Norman: University of Oklahoma Press, 2006). Also see 1873 railroad map at https://www.loc.gov/resource/g3700.rr000540/?r=0.272,0.054,0.318,0.154,0.

11. Haines, *Yellowstone Story*, Vol. 1, 185–86. McCartney's log hotel was located at Hymen Terrace.

12. Haines, *Yellowstone Story*, Vol. 1, 182–89.

13. Nathaniel P. Langford, *Report of the Superintendent of the Yellowstone National Park for the Year 1872, Annual Report of the Secretary of the Interior for 1872* (Washington, DC: Government Printing Office, 1873), 1–4. Copies of annual and monthly superintendent reports are available at the Yellowstone Heritage and Research Center in Yellowstone National Park. In many instances, digital copies are available online.

14. Langford, *1872 Report*, 1–4.

15. Langford, *1872 Report*, 4–9.

16. Langford, *1872 Report*, 4–9.

17. Mary Shivers Culpin, *For the Benefit and Enjoyment of the People: A History of Concession Development in Yellowstone National Park, 1872–1966* (Yellowstone National Park, WY: National Park Service, Yellowstone Center for Resources), 2, https://www.nps.gov/yell/learn/historyculture/upload/ConcessionDevelopment.pdf.

18. Haines, *Yellowstone Story*, Vol. 1, 193–96.

19. Haines, *Yellowstone Story*, Vol. 1, 195–98.

20. William Ludlow, *Report of a Reconnaissance from Carroll, Montana Territory, on the Upper Missouri, to the Yellowstone National Park, and Return, Made in the Summer of 1875* (US Army, 1875), 27, 36; Haines, *Yellowstone Story*, Vol. 1, 203–4, https://quod.lib.umich.edu/m/moa/ADQ3957.0001.001?rgn=main;view=fulltext.

21. For more information, see John Taliaferro, *Grinnell: America's Environmental Pioneer and His Restless Drive to Save the West* (New York: Liveright, 2019) and Michael Punke, *Last Stand: George Bird Grinnell and the Battle to Save the Buffalo, and the Birth of the New West* (New York: Harper Perennial, 2020).

22. Haines, *Yellowstone Story*, Vol. 1, 204–5.

23. W. E. Strong, *A Trip to the Yellowstone National Park in July, August and September 1875, From the Journal of General W. E. Strong* (Washington, DC: 1876), https://archive.org/details/GR_4014.

24. Strong, *Trip*, 16–26.

25. Strong, *Trip*, 27–91.

26. Strong, *Trip*, 91–93.

27. Flight of Nez Perce; P. W. Norris, *Report Upon the Yellowstone National Park for the Year 1877, to the Secretary of the Interior* (Washington, DC: Government Printing Office, 1877), 842.

28. For more information about the Nez Perce Flight in Yellowstone, see M. Mark Miller, *Encounters in Yellowstone: The Nez Perce Summer of 1877* (Guilford, CT: TwoDot, 2019). For Chief Joseph's October 5, 1877, speech, see https://www.biography.com/news/chief-joseph-quotes-surrender-speech. For the Nez Perce's view of Oklahoma, see

Rich Wandschneider, "Writing the Nez Perce Story: An American Epic Told in Books," *Oregon Historical Quarterly*, Vol. 119, no. 4 (Winter 2018), 528–37.

29. Harry Yount, "Report of the Gamekeeper," Yellowstone National Park, September 30, 1881, in Annual Report of the Secretary of the Interior, 1881 (Washington, DC: Government Printing Office), 807–8; William R. Supernaugh, "Enigmatic Icon: The Life and Times of Harry Yount," https://www.nps.gov/parkhistory/hisnps/npshistory/yount.htm.

30. Haines, *Yellowstone Story*, Vol. 1, 255–60; Haines, *Yellowstone Story*, Vol. II, 450.

31. For more information see Chris J. Magoc, *The Creation and Selling of an American Landscape, 1870–1903* (Albuquerque: University of New Mexico Press, 1999). Also see Langdon Smith, "The Contested Landscape of Early Yellowstone," *Journal of Cultural Geography*, Vol. 22, no. 1 (Fall-Winter 2004), 3, https://www.people.iup.edu/rhoch/ClassPages/EnvPlanningSeminar_X/Readings/2018_Readings/Week1/The_contested_landscape_of_....pdf.

32. Richard A. Bartlett, "The Concessionaries of Yellowstone National Park," *The Pacific Northwest Quarterly*, Vol. 74, no. 1 (January 1983), 5. See also Bartlett, *Yellowstone: A Wilderness Besieged* (Tucson: University of Arizona Press, 1985), 122–35.

33. Haines, *Yellowstone Story*, Vol. 1, 260–64.

34. Haines, *Yellowstone Story*, Vol. 1, 262–69; Tina Schlaile, "Ambition, Aspirations and Arrogance: A Concessioner and a Superintendent in Early Yellowstone," *Yellowstone History Journal*, Vol. 2. no. 1 (2020), 57–59.

35. Magoc, *Creation and Selling*, 53–77.

36. Culpin, *Benefit and Enjoyment*, 11; Schlaile, "Ambition," 59–66; Bartlett, "The Concessionaires," 7–10.

CHAPTER SIX

1. Captain Moses Harris, *Report of the Acting Superintendent of the Yellowstone National Park, 1886* (Washington, DC: Government Printing Office, 1886), 11.

2. David W. Wear, *Report of the Superintendent of the Yellowstone National Park, 1886* (Washington, DC: Government Printing Office, 1886), 3; Kiki Leigh Rydell and Mary Shivers Culpin, *Managing the Matchless Wonders: A History of Administrative Development in Yellowstone National Park, 1872–1965* (Yellowstone National Park, WY: National Park Service, Yellowstone Center for Resources, 2006), 19.

3. "Situations Offered," *St. Paul* (MN) *Globe*, June 27, 1884, 3, https://chronicling america.loc.gov/lccn/sn90059522/1884-06-27/ed-1/seq-8.pdf; "Fire in the Park Hotel," *Livingston Enterprise*, July 25, 1885, 3, https://chroniclingamerica.loc.gov/lccn/sn860752 61/1885-07-25/ed-1/seq-3.pdf.

4. Wear, *1886 Superintendent Report*, 3–4. Culpin, *Benefit and Enjoyment*, 12, 27.

5. Culpin, *Benefit and Enjoyment*, 29–30.

6. Culpin, *Benefit and Enjoyment*, 29–30.

7. Wear, *1886 Superintendent Report*, 4–5.

8. Wear, *1886 Superintendent Report*, 4–5; Culpin, *Matchless Wonders*, 23.

9. Culpin, *Matchless Wonders*, 23.

10. Culpin, *Matchless Wonders*, 20–21, 25. For the ascension of the growing movement among civilian sportsmen beginning in 1882 to provide adequate protection for Yellowstone, see Sarah Ellen Broadbent, "Sportsmen and the Evolution of Conservation Idea in Yellowstone: 1882–1884," Thesis (Montana State University, April 1997), https://scholarworks.montana.edu/xmlui/bitstream/handle/1/7478/31762102370598.pdf?sequence=1.

11. Wear, *1886 Superintendent Report*, 5; Harris, *1886 Superintendent Report*, 6.

12. Harris, *1886 Superintendent Report*, 6; Amanda Shaw, "The Superintendents—Captain Moses Harris," https://www.nps.gov/yell/blogs/the-superintendents-captain-moses-harris.htm.

13. Harris, *1886 Superintendent Report*, 6–7.

14. Harris, *1886 Superintendents Report*, 7–8. For the early history of wildlife in Yellowstone see Lee H. Whittlesey, "Abundance, Slaughter, and Resilience of the Greater Yellowstone Ecosystem's Mammal Population: A View of the Historical Record, 1871–1885," *Montana: The Magazine of Western History*, Vol. 70 (Spring 2020), 3–26, 90–93. And see generally, Lee H. Whittlesey and Sarah Bone, *The History of Mammals in the Greater Yellowstone Ecosystem, 1796–1881: A Multi-Disciplinary Analysis of Thousands of Historical Observations* (Seattle: Kindle Direct Publications, 2020) (two volumes; 1305 pages).

15. Harris, *1886 Superintendent Report*, 8.

16. Harris, *1886 Superintendent Report*, 8–11.

17. Harris, *1886 Superintendent Report*, 11–13.

18. Harris, *1886 Superintendent Report*, 3–14.

19. Captain Moses Harris, *Report of the Superintendent of the Yellowstone National Park, 1887* (Washington, DC: Government Printing Office, 1887), 3–14.

20. Harris, *1887 Superintendent Report*, 13–14.

21. See "Explore the Fort Yellowstone Historic District," https://www.nps.gov/thingsto do/yell-tour-fort-yellowstone.htm.

22. "Explore the Fort Yellowstone Historic District."

23. Aubrey L. Haines, *The Yellowstone Story: A History of Our First National Park*, Vol. 2 (Yellowstone National Park, WY: Yellowstone Library and Museum Association, 1977), 34–38.

24. Haines, *Yellowstone Story*, Vol. 2, 38–41.

25. H. Duane Hampton, *How the US Cavalry Saved Our National Parks* (Bloomington: Indiana University Press, 1971), https://www.nps.gov/parkhistory/online_books/hampton/chap5.htm and https://www.nps.gov/parkhistory/online_books/hampton/chap6.htm.

26. Hampton, *US Cavalry*, https://www.nps.gov/parkhistory/online_books/hampton/chap6.htm.

27. Haines, *Yellowstone Story*, Vol. 2, 60–67.

28. Haines, *Yellowstone Story*, Vol. 2, 68–88.

29. Mary Shivers Culpin, *The History of the Construction of the Road System in Yellowstone National Park, 1872–1966* (National Park Service, Rocky Mountain Region, 1994), https://www.nps.gov/parkhistory/online_books/yell_roads/hrs1-12f.htm.

CHAPTER SEVEN

1. Becoming law on July 1, 1862, the Pacific Railroad Act provided for the use of federal lands to subsidize the construction of railroads and telegraph lines across a northern route to the Pacific Ocean. A digital copy of the Act is available at https://www.senate.gov/artandhistory/history/resources/pdf/PacificRailwayActof1862.pdf. A transcribed version is available at https://www.digitalhistory.uh.edu/disp_textbook.cfm?smtID=3&psid=4004.

2. Haynes images from Dakota Territory can be found at the North Dakota State University and Montana State University, Bozeman archives.

3. Railroads' marketing of Yellowstone has been explored in a number of books, theses, and papers, including: Magoc, *Creation and Selling*, 1999, and Ellen Rae Kress, "Wonder and Spectacle in the World's First National Park: Railroad Imagery of Yellowstone National Park," Thesis (Montana State University, Bozeman, 2011); Kathryn McKee, "Union Pacific Bears: Tourism Advertising and Yellowstone as the American Playground," *Yellowstone History Journal*, Vol. 4. no. 1 (2021), 48–54. See also "Alice's Adventures in the New Wonderland," National Park Service, https://www.nps.gov/yell/blogs/alices-adventures-in-the-new-wonderland-brochure.htm. For a broader but brief description of historical railroad marketing related to national parks at large, see Peter Blodgett, "Defining Uncle Sam's Playgrounds: Railroad Advertising and the National Parks," *Historical Geography*, Vol. 35 (2007), 81–113.

4. Magoc, *Creation and Selling*, 24–52.

5. See Bill Yenne, *The History of the Burlington-Northern* (New York: Random House, 1991). Also see Ronald M. Greenberg, ed., *Historic Railroads: A Living Legacy* (Cultural Resource Management, Washington, DC: National Park Service, Vol. 22, no. 10, 1999), https://www.nps.gov/crmjournal/CRM/v22n10.pdf.

6. See Maury Klein, *Union Pacific: Volume 1* (Minneapolis: University of Minnesota Press, 2006), and Maury Klein, *Union Pacific: Volume II* (Minneapolis: University of Minnesota Press, 2006). Also see Greenberg, *Historic Railroads*.

7. "English Writings About the Park," *Livingston* (MT) *Daily Enterprise*, August 18, 1883, 2, https://chroniclingamerica.loc.gov/lccn/sn85053382/1883-08-18/ed-1/seq-2/.

8. "English Writings About the Park," 2.

9. L.C. [G.L. Henderson], "Among the Geysers," *Livingston* (MT) *Daily Enterprise*, October 16, 1884, 1, https://chroniclingamerica.loc.gov/lccn/sn85053382/1884-10-16/ed-1/seq-1/.

10. "Among the Geysers," *Livingston Daily Enterprise*.

11. "Wonderful Grand Canyon," *Arizona Republican*, March 9, 1895, 3, https://chroniclingamerica.loc.gov/lccn/sn84020558/1895-03-09/ed-1/seq-3/. The story was retold from the "*Philadelphia Press.*"

12. See Lee H. Whittlesey, *Death in Yellowstone: Accidents and Foolhardiness in the First National Park*, Second Edition (New York: Roberts Rinehart, 2014).

13. "Fell Into a Geyser Pool," *Alexandria* (VA) *Gazette*, August 25, 1897, 2, https://chroniclingamerica.loc.gov/lccn/sn85025007/1897-08-25/ed-1/seq-2/.

14. "Fell Into a Geyser," *Topeka* (KS) *State Journal*, August 25, 1897, 5, https://chronicling america.loc.gov/lccn/sn82016014/1897-08-25/ed-1/seq-5/; *The Boston Medical and Surgical Journal*, Vol. CXXXVI, no. 20 (1897), 504.

15. Lee H. Whittlesey and Elizabeth A. Watry, *Ho! For Wonderland: Travelers' Accounts of Yellowstone, 1872–1914* (Albuquerque: University of New Mexico Press, 2009), 198–216.

16. Whittlesey and Watry, *Ho!*, 204–5.

17. Whittlesey and Watry, *Ho!*, 206.

18. Whittlesey and Watry, *Ho!*, 206–7.

19. Whittlesey and Watry, *Ho!*, 211–21.

20. Whittlesey and Watry, *Ho!*, 248.

21. Whittlesey and Watry, *Ho!*, 247.

22. Major John Pitcher, *Report of the Acting Superintendent of the Yellowstone National Park, 1902* (Washington, DC: Government Printing Office, 1902), 6.

23. Whittlesey and Watry, *Ho!*, 265–75.

24. Pitcher, *1902 Superintendent Report*, 6–7; Paul Schullery, *Yellowstone Bear Tales* (Niwot, CO: Roberts Rinehart, 1991), 55–58.

25. Ibid.

26. Pitcher, *1902 Superintendent Report*, 7.

CHAPTER EIGHT

1. Truman C. Everts, *Thirty-Seven Days of Peril: A Narrative of Early Days of the Yellowstone* (San Francisco: Grabhorn, 1923), 3–7.

2. Lee H. Whittlesey, *Death in Yellowstone: Accidents and Foolhardiness in the First National Park*, Second Edition (New York: Roberts Rinehart, 2014), 143.

3. Whittlesey and Watry, *Ho!*, 41.

4. Whittlesey and Watry, *Ho!*, 41–42.

5. Whittlesey and Watry, *Ho!*, 43.

6. Whittlesey and Watry, *Ho!*, 43.

7. Whittlesey and Watry, *Ho!*, 44–46.

8. Whittlesey and Watry, *Ho!*, 46–56.

9. See Mary Shivers Culpin, *The History of the Construction of the Road System in Yellowstone National Park, 1872–1966: Historic Resources Study, Vol. 1* (National Park Service: Division of Cultural Resources, Rocky Mountain Region, 1994), https://www.nps.gov/parkhistory/online_books/yell_roads/hrs1-1.htm.

10. Aubrey L. Haines, *Yellowstone Story*, Vol. 2, 1977, 100. In 1913 the Monida -Yellowstone line was renamed Yellowstone-Western.

11. Haines, *Yellowstone Story*, Vol. 2, 101–8; See also "'Tally-Ho' Stage Coaches," https://www.nps.gov/yell/learn/historyculture/stagecoaches.htm.

12. C. Van Tassell, *Truthful Lies of Yellowstone Park and a Thousand Laughs* (Bozeman, MT: Chas. Van Tassell, 1920), 8–11. The first edition of this small booklet was published in 1912.

13. Tassell, *Truthful Lies*, 16; Haines, *Yellowstone Story*, Vol. 2, 101–8.

14. Tassell, *Truthful Lies*, 21–22.

15. Lee H. Whittlesey, "You Count Only One Here: Larry Mathews and Democracy in Yellowstone, 1887–1904," *Yellowstone History Journal*, Vol. 1, no. 1 (2018), 2–27.

16. Haines, *Yellowstone Story*, Vol. 2, 108–23.

17. Haines, *Yellowstone Story*, Vol. 2, 123–27. Authorities refused to license the *E. C. Waters* after 1904, although there is evidence that it was used during the 1905 season.

18. Haines, *Yellowstone Story*, Vol. 2, 127–29.

19. Haines, *Yellowstone Story*, Vol. 2, 129–33.

20. Haines, *Yellowstone Story*, Vol. 2, 129–33.

21. Haines, *Yellowstone Story*, Vol. 2, 153–57. Haines cites a string of evidence leading to Trafton's eventual arrest. Not included in Haines's account is a published claim that several of the holdup victims took photographs of the bandit; see "Caught: The Young Highwayman of the Yellowstone," *Richmond Times Dispatch*, January 2, 1916, 49, https://chroniclingamerica.loc.gov/data/batches/vi_teal_ver02/data/sn83045389/00296020163/1916010201/0521.pdf.

22. Whittlesey, *Death in Yellowstone*, 141–42.

23. For the history of America's early highways, see Stephen H. Provost, *America's First Highways* (Martinsville, VA: Dragon Crown Books, 2020). For an overview of Yellowstone and the Panama-Pacific International Exposition, see Elizabeth Watry, "Westward Ho! The 1915 Panama Pacific International Exposition: And the Transformation of Yellowstone National Park Tourism," *Yellowstone History Journal*, Vol. 4, no. 1 (2021), 4–23.

24. See Watry, "Westward Ho!", 19–21.

25. Whittlesey, *Death in Yellowstone*, 149–50.

26. Horace Albright, *Report of the Superintendent of the Yellowstone National Park, 1923* (Washington, DC: Government Printing Office, 1923), 5, 15, 16, 21, 22.

27. In West Yellowstone, Montana, the town's Union Pacific historic buildings are preserved. Administered by the Yellowstone Historic Center, the town's Union Pacific Historic District, including the Museum of the Yellowstone, housed in the Union Pacific Deport, is open to the public from May through October. Visit http://museumoftheyellowstone.org for more information.

28. Haines, *Yellowstone Story*, Vol. 2, 84, 101, 106, 112, 134, 257, 352–55.

29. Haines, *Yellowstone Story*, Vol. 2, 273. See "1936 National Park Bus," https://www.nps.gov/yell/learn/historyculture/1936bus.htm, and "Historic Park Vehicles," Buses of Yellowstone Preservation Trust, busesofyellowstonepreservationtrust.org.

CHAPTER NINE

1. "Park Prices," *Livingston Daily Enterprise*, July 21, 1883, 1, https://chroniclingamerica.loc.gov/lccn/sn85053382/1883-07-21/ed-1/seq-1.pdf.

2. "Arrival of the Hatch Party," *Livingston Daily Enterprise*, August 23, 1883, 3, https://chroniclingamerica.loc.gov/lccn/sn85053382/1883-08-23/ed-1/seq-3/.

3. "Wealthy British Beats," *The New Northwest*, Deer Lodge, Montana, September 14, 1883, 1, https://chroniclingamerica.loc.gov/lccn/sn84038125/1883-09-14/ed-1/seq-1.pdf.

4. "The Yellowstone Visitors," *Daily Astorian*, Astoria, Oregon, September 9, 1883, 1, https://chroniclingamerica.loc.gov/lccn/sn96061149/1883-09-09/ed-1/seq-1.pdf.

5. "Pranks in the Park," *Semi-Weekly Miner*, Butte, Montana, September 5, 1883, 2, https://chroniclingamerica.loc.gov/lccn/sn84036033/1883-09-05/ed-1/seq-2.pdf.

6. "Pranks in the Park," 2.

7. For a detailed analysis of President Arthur's 1883 Yellowstone Expedition, see Robert E. Hartley, *Saving Yellowstone: The President Arthur Expedition of 1883* (Xlibris, 2007).

8. Hartley, *Saving Yellowstone*.

9. "The Yellowstone Visitors," 1.

10. "A Pitiful Sight," *Daily Globe*, St. Paul, Minnesota, September 10, 1883, 4, https://chroniclingamerica.loc.gov/lccn/sn83025287/1883-09-10/ed-1/seq-4.pdf.

11. "Death of Rufus Hatch," *New York Times*, February 24, 1893, 1, https://timesmachine.nytimes.com/timesmachine/1893/02/24/109694034.pdf?pdf_redirect=true&ip=0.

12. For a timeline of Yellowstone Park Company operations, see Lee Steiner and Cara Bertram, "Yellowstone Park Company Records 1884–1979," Yellowstone National Park, Wyoming, Yellowstone National Park Archives, 2012, 2015, https://www.nps.gov/yell/learn/historyculture/upload/MSC019YPC-04-2015.pdf. For more information about the Northern Pacific Railroad turned Northern Pacific Railway, see "Northern Pacific Railway Company Records, 1870–1968," Archives West, https://archieswest.orbiscascade.org/ark:/80444/xv68060.

13. Lee H. Whittlesey, *"This Modern Saratoga Wilderness!": A History of Mammoth Hot Springs and the Village of Mammoth in Yellowstone National Park* (Yellowstone National Park, WY: Yellowstone National Park Archives, 2020), 23, 24.

14. Major Moses Harris, *1889 Acting Superintendent's Report*, 5, https://mtmemory.org/digital/collection/p16013coll95/id/194.

15. "Rambling in Wonderland," *West Virginia Argus*, Kingwood, West Virginia, August 6, 1891, 2, https://chroniclingamerica.loc.gov/lccn/sn86092245/1891-08-06/ed-1/seq-2.pdf; "Glimmers of History," Yellowstone Gateway Museum, https://yellowstonegatewaymuseum.org/online-exhibits/glimmers-of-history/; *General Information Regarding Yellowstone National Park* (Washington, DC: Department of the Interior, 1912), 9.

16. "Seeing the Yellowstone," *Capital City Courier*, Lincoln, Nebraska, August 15, 1891, 1, https://chroniclingamerica.loc.gov/lccn/2010270510/1891-08-15/ed-1/seq-1.pdf.

17. Tamsen Emerson Hert, "Luxury in the Wilderness: Yellowstone's Grand Canyon Hotel, 1911–1960," *Yellowstone Science*, Vol. 13, no. 3 (Summer 2005), 23, https://www.academia.edu/2572648/Luxury_in_the_Wilderness_Yellowstones_Grand_Canyon_Hotel_1911_1960.

18. Hert, "Luxury in the Wilderness," 23.

19. Ruth Quinn, *Weaver of Dreams: The Life and Architecture of Robert C. Reamer* (Gardiner, MT: Leslie & Ruth Quinn, 2004), 73–74.

20. *Anaconda Standard*, August 4, 1911, https://geyserbob.org/hot-canyon.html.

21. Hert, "Luxury in the Wilderness," 24–29.

22. Hert, "Luxury in the Wilderness," 21, 27.

23. Hert, "Luxury in the Wilderness," 28–34.

24. Michelle Trappen, *Grand Lady of the Lake: The Remarkable Legacy of Yellowstone's Lake Hotel* (Red Fox Publications, 2016), 7.

25. Trappen, *Grand Lady*, 26.

26. For the story of E. C. Waters, see Mike Stark, *Wrecked in Yellowstone: Greed, Obsession, and the Untold Story of Yellowstone's Most Famous Shipwreck* (Helena, MT: Riverbend Publishing, 2016).

27. Trappen, *Grand Lady*, 31–37, 51–60.

28. For more information on early hotels in the Upper Geyser Basin, see Lee H. Whittlesey, *A History of the Old Faithful Area with Chronology, Maps, and Executive Summary* (National Park Service, 2007), http://npshistory.com/publications/yell/old-faithful-area -history.pdf. Also see Whittlesey, "You Count Only One Here," 17.

29. For more information see Karen Wildung Reinhart and Jeff Henry, *Old Faithful Inn: Crown Jewel of National Park Lodges* (Emigrant, MT: Roche Jaune Pictures, 2004); Quinn, *Weaver of Dreams*; Ruth Quinn, "Overcoming Obscurity: The Yellowstone Architecture of Robert C. Reamer," *Yellowstone Science*, Vol. 12, no. 2 (Spring 2004), 33–36; and Haines, *Yellowstone Story*, Vol. 2, 119–20.

30. For more information see Haines, *Yellowstone Story*, Vol. 2, 119–20; Quinn, *Weaver of Dreams*; and Susan C. Scofield, *The Inn at Old Faithful: The Last Word in Hotel Building* (Crowsnest Associates, 1979).

31. Haines, *Yellowstone Story*, Vol. 2, 119–20.

32. *Dickinson* (SD) *Press*, February 20, 1904, 3, https://chroniclingamerica.loc.gov/lccn/ sn88076013/1904-02-20/ed-1/seq-3.pdf.

33. "Reduced Rates to Yellowstone Park," *Minneapolis Journal*, June 10, 1904, 11, https://chroniclingamerica.loc.gov/lccn/sn83045366/1904-06-10/ed-1/seq-11.pdf.

34. "Yellowstone Park Improvements," *The Teton Peak*, St. Anthony, Idaho, June 30, 1904, 1, https://chroniclingamerica.loc.gov/lccn/sn86091134/1904-06-30/ed-1/seq -1.pdf.

35. "The Yellowstone Park," *Fargo Forum and Daily Republican*, Fargo, September 10, 1904, 16, https://chroniclingamerica.loc.gov/lccn/sn85042224/1904-09-10/seq-16 .pdf.

36. "The Yellowstone Park," 16.

37. "Searchlight Now Reveals the Geysers," *St. Paul Globe*, June 1, 1904, 4, https:// chroniclingamerica.loc.gov/data/batches/mnhi_plymouth_ver01/data/sn90059523/0020 6537826/1904060101/0006.pdf.

38. "Through Yellowstone Park," *The Cecil Whig*, Elkton, Maryland, October 15, 1904, 4, https://chroniclingamerica.loc.gov/lccn/sn83016348/1904-10-15/ed-1/seq-4.pdf.

39. "Through Yellowstone Park," 4.

40. "The Yellowstone Park," *Fargo* (ND) *Forum and Daily Republican*, September 10, 1904, 16, https://chroniclingamerica.loc.gov/lccn/sn85042224/1904-09-10/ed-1/seq-16 .pdf.

41. See Haines, *Yellowstone Story*, Vol. 2, 119–20; Quinn, *Weaver of Dreams*; Reinhart and Henry, *Old Faithful Inn*; Scofield, *The Inn at Old Faithful*.

42. For more information about Parkitecture embodied in western national park lodges and hotels, see "Parkitecture in Western National Parks: Hotels and Lodging," National Park Service, http://npshistory.com/publications/parkitecture/lodg/index.htm.

43. Bruce T. Gourley, "An Interview with Ruth Quinn: Official Old Faithful Inn Interpreter," *Yellowstone History Journal*, Vol. 2, no. 1 (2019), 25–27.

44. As conveyed to the author.

45. Elizabeth Ann Watry, *More Than Mere Camps: The Wylie Camping Company and the Development of a Middle Class Leisure Ethic in Yellowstone National Park, 1883–1916*, Master of Arts Thesis (Bozeman: Montana State University, 2010), 10–63, https://studylib.net/doc/13475247/more-than-mere-camps-and-coaches—the-wylie-camping-company; Haines, *Yellowstone Story*, Vol. 2, 134–37.

46. Watry, *More Than Mere Camps*, 78–103.

47. For an overview of historical lodges and cabins in Yellowstone, see Robert V. Goss, "Hotels and Cabins," https://geyserbob.org/hotels.html. For a more detailed analysis, see Mary Shivers Culpin, *A History of Concession Development in Yellowstone National Park, 1872–1966* (Yellowstone National Park, WY: National Park Service, Yellowstone Center for Resources), 2003.

48. For more about Ole Anderson and other early park souvenir vendors, see Robert V. Goss, "Coated Specimens and Colored Sands: Yellowstone's Early Curio Trade," *Yellowstone History Journal*, Vol. 3, no. 1, 39–45.

49. Robert V. Goss, "Yellowstone's First General Store: A Legacy of Jennie Henderson and Her Family," *Yellowstone Science*, Vol. 13, no. 2 (Spring 2005), 16–28.

50. Ibid., 22; Whittlesey, *Old Faithful Area*, 44–46.

51. Goss, "Yellowstone's First General Store," 26.

52. Ibid., 26.

53. See Culpin, *Concession Development*, 44.

54. Culpin, *Concession Development*, 12–13, 54–55.

55. Gwen Peterson, *Yellowstone Pioneers: The Story of the Hamilton Stores and Yellowstone National Park* (Hamilton Stores, 1985), 22–24, 31–32, 62–73; Culpin, *Concession Development*, 62, 66, 71, 79, 84.

56. Delaware North's Yellowstone General Stores website is https://www.delawarenorth.com/venues/yellowstone-general-stores. Xanterra's Yellowstone National Park Lodges website is https://www.yellowstonenationalparklodges.com/. The Yellowstone Forever website is https://www.yellowstone.org/. The Yellowstone Park Service Stations website is http://ypss.com/.

Chapter Ten

1. Jerry Mernin, *Yellowstone Ranger: Stories from a Life Spent with Bears, Backcountry, Horses, and Mules from Yosemite to Yellowstone* (Helena, MT: Riverbend Publishing, 2016), 7. Jerry Mernin, now deceased, rangered in Yellowstone for thirty-two years.

2. Haines, *Yellowstone Story*, Vol. 2, 442, 443, 445.

3. Timothy R. Manns, "History of the Park Ranger in Yellowstone National Park," National Park Service: Yellowstone National Park, 2–3, www.npshistory.com/publications/yell/ranger-history.pdf.

4. Haines, *Yellowstone Story*, Vol. 2, 286–95.

5. Haines, *Yellowstone Story*, Vol. 2, 302.

6. For more information about Stephen Mather, see Robert Shankland, *Steve Mather of the National Parks* (New York: Alfred A. Knopf, 1970).

7. Organic Act 1916, https://www.nps.gov/grba/learn/management/organic-act-of -1916.htm.

8. Ralph Lewis, *Museum Curatorship in the National Parks* (Washington, DC: National Park Service, 1993), 9–11.

9. *Ranger Naturalists' Manual: Yellowstone National Park* (Washington, DC: Department of the Interior, National Park Service, 1926), Preface, 1, https://archive.org/details/1926r angernatura00unit.

10. *Ranger Naturalists' Manual*, 1–2.

11. Hailey Galper, "Marguerite Lindsley: The First Permanent Female Ranger," National Park Service, https://www.nps.gov/yell/blogs/marguerite-lindsley-the-first -permanent-female-ranger.htm; Elizabeth A. Watry, *Women in Wonderland: Lives, Legends and Legacies of Yellowstone National Park* (Helena, MT: Riverbend Publishing, 2012), 151–84; Watry, *More Than Mere Camps*.

12. Lewis, *Museum Curatorship*, 42–49.

13. Elizabeth A. Watry, *Women in Wonderland: Lives, Legends and Legacies of Yellowstone National Park* (Helena, MT: Riverbend Publishing, 2002), 204ff.

14. For more information about park rangers and CCC enrollees during the Great Depression, see Matthew A. Redinger, "The Civilian Conservation Corps as a Tool of the National Park Service: The Development of Glacier and Yellowstone National Parks, 1933–1942," Thesis (Missoula: University of Montana, 1988), 31ff, https://scholarworks .umt.edu/etd/10983/.

15. Manns, "History of the Park Ranger," 4–7.

CHAPTER ELEVEN

1. For more information about President Woodrow Wilson and World War I, see Robert Striner, *Woodrow Wilson and World War I: A Burden Too Great to Bear* (Lanham, MD: Rowman & Littlefield, 2016); "See America First in 1915: The National Old Roads Trail Part 2," Federal Highway Administration, https://www.fhwa.dot.gov/infrastructure/not2b .cfm; "To Organize Park-to-Park Highway," *Northern Wyoming Herald*, Cody, Wyoming, May 26, 1916, 1, https://chroniclingamerica.loc.gov/lccn/sn92066926/1916-05-26/ed -2/seq-1.pdf; Lloyd M. Brett, *Superintendent's Annual Report for Yellowstone National Park*, 1916, 6–7.

2. "Park Employes Are On a Special Train," *Ogden* (UT) *Standard*, June 5, 1916, 4, https://chroniclingamerica.loc.gov/lccn/sn85058396/1916-06-05/ed-1/seq-4.pdf.

3. See Jane Galloway Demaray, *Yellowstone Summers: Touring with the Wylie Camping Company in America's First National Park* (Pullman: Washington State University Press, 2015).

4. "Diary of a Wylie Savage," Part 1, June 11, 1916, https://beyoublithe-n-bonny .blogspot.com/2015/05/diary-of-wylie-savage-part-1.html.

5. "Diary of a Wylie Savage," Part 2, June 15, 1916, https://beyoublithe-n-bonny .blogspot.com/2015/05/diary-of-wylie-savage-part-2.html; Find a Grave, "Beatrice Boedefeld Andrews," https://www.findagrave.com/memorial/7088400/beatrice-andrews.

6. See Demaray, *Yellowstone Summers*.

7. "Diary of a Wylie Savage," Part 2.

8. "Diary of a Wylie Savage," Part 2.

9. "Diary of a Wylie Savage," Part 3, https://beyoublithe-n-bonny.blogspot.com/2015/05/diary-of-wylie-savage-part-3.html.

10. "Diary of a Wylie Savage," Part 3, and Part 4, https://beyoublithe-n-bonny.blogspot.com/2015/05/diary-of-wylie-savage-part-4.html.

11. "Diary of a Wylie Savage," Part 4.

12. "Diary of a Wylie Savage," Part 4.

13. "Diary of a Wylie Savage," Part 4.

14. "Diary of a Wylie Savage," Part 5, https://beyoublithe-n-bonny.blogspot.com/2015/05/diary-of-wylie-savage-part-5.html.

15. "Diary of a Wylie Savage," Part 4.

16. Eyre Powell, "The Sophisticated Savage of Yellowstone," *New York Tribune*, July 16, 1922, 5, https://chroniclingamerica.loc.gov/lccn/sn83030214/1922-07-16/ed-1/seq-55.pdf.

17. "Sophisticated Savage of Yellowstone," 5.

18. Elizabeth A. Watry, "Yellowstone Follies: Entertaining Guests at Yellowstone National Park Lodges and Camps, 1896–1956," *Yellowstone History Journal*, Vol. 1, no. 1 (2018), 31–32.

19. Watry, "Yellowstone Follies," 34.

20. Watry, "Yellowstone Follies," 34–36.

CHAPTER TWELVE

1. Roger W. Toll, Superintendent, Yellowstone National Park, *Monthly Report for July 1932*, Press Release 1932-57.

2. Roger Toll, "Monthly Report for October 1929" (Yellowstone National Park), 1–2.

3. Toll, October 1929 Report, 3–5.

4. Toll, October 1929 Report, 6.

5. See *Proceedings of the First Park Naturalists' Training Conference, November 1 to 30, 1929* (Washington, DC: Department of the Interior, National Park Service, 1932), https://www.nps.gov/parkhistory/online_books/symposia/conference-pn1/proceedingst.htm.

6. Toll, Report October 1929, 3–5, 9–10.

7. Roger Toll, *Annual Report for Yellowstone National Park, 1930* (Yellowstone National Park), 1.

8. Roger Toll, *Annual Report for Yellowstone National Park, 1931* (Yellowstone National Park), 1–3. Roger Toll, "Monthly Report for August 1933" (Yellowstone National Park), 51.

9. Toll, *Annual Report, 1931*, 1–3, 6, 15.

10. Roger Toll, *Annual Report for Yellowstone National Park, 1932* (Yellowstone National Park), 1, 5.

11. Toll, *Annual Report, 1932*, 1.

12. Guy D. Edwards, Acting Superintendent, Monthly Report for March 1933 (Yellowstone National Park), 5; Guy D. Edwards, Acting Superintendent, Monthly Report for April 1933 (Yellowstone National Park), 5; John C. Paige, *The Civilian Conservation Corps and the National Park Service, 1933–1942: An Administrative History* (National Park Service, US Department of Interior, 1985), 123.

13. Roger Toll, "Monthly Report for March 1933" (Yellowstone National Park), 3, 14. Roger Toll, "Monthly Report for April 1933" (Yellowstone National Park), 3. Roger Toll, "Monthly Report for May 1933 (Yellowstone National Park), 6.

14. This sketch of the first summer of Yellowstone's CCC camps is compiled from monthly Yellowstone Superintendent reports for the months of March through August 1933, as well as the diary of a CCCer, "Life in the Civilian Conservation Corps 1933," Michael C. LoMonico Diary, 1933, http://ccc1933.blogspot.com/2010/10/explanation.html.

15. For more information see Matthew A. Redinger, "The Civilian Conservation Corps as a Tool of the National Park Service: The Development of Glacier and Yellowstone National Parks, 1933–1942," Thesis (Missoula: University of Montana, 1988), 31ff, https://scholarworks.umt.edu/etd/10983/.

16. Redinger, "Civilian Conservation Corps."

17. Redinger, "Civilian Conservation Corps," 92. Also see "LoMonico Diary."

18. Redinger, "Civilian Conservation Corps," 41–43, 93–94, 100.

19. For more information about the Roosevelt Administration's Great Depression era promotion of national parks, see Donald C. Swain, "The National Park Service and the New Deal, 1933–1940," *Pacific Historical Review*, Vol. 41, no. 3 (August 1972), 312–332; Robert Grogg, "Stamps, Parks, and a President: Franklin D. Roosevelt Approves Ten Postage Stamps to Celebrate National Park Year," The White House Historical Association, https://www.whitehousehistory.org/stamps-parks-and-a-president; and "WPA Posters," Library of Congress, https://www.loc.gov/collections/works-progress-administration-posters/?fa=subject%3Anational+parks+%26+reserves.

20. For a history of the US Travel Bureau, see Mordecai Lee, *See America: The Politics and Administration of Federal Tourism Promotion, 1937–1973* (Albany: SUNY Press, 2020).

21. One example of scientific literature produced from studies in Yellowstone during the Great Depression is E. T. Allen and Arthur L. Day, *Hot Springs of the Yellowstone National Park* (Washington, DC: Carnegie Institution, 1935).

22. George M. Wright and Ben H. Thompson, *Fauna of the National Parks of the United States: Wildlife Management in the National Parks* (Washington, DC: United States Printing Office, 1935), 21–24, 60–62, 84–87. See also Roger Toll, *Annual Report for Yellowstone National Park, 1935* (Yellowstone National Park), 13–14. For more information about George Melendez Wright, visit the website of the George Wright Society at https://www.georgewrightsociety.org/.

CHAPTER THIRTEEN

1. Douglas W. Smith, "My Time with 'Male 911': This Yellowstone Wolf Was Safe from People, but Not from Nature," *Washington Post*, June 1, 2019, https://www.washington

post.com/health/my-time-with-male-911-this-yellowstone-wolf-was-safe-from-people
-but-not-from-nature/2019/05/31/fbbbf8a8-7cda-11e9-8ede-f4abf521ef17_story.html.

2. The most authoritative analysis of Yellowstone's campfire creation story is Paul Schullery and Lee H. Whittlesey, *Myth and History in the Creation of Yellowstone National Park* (Lincoln: University of Nebraska Press, 2003).

3. *Yellowstone Resources and Issues Handbook: 2016* (Yellowstone National Park, 2016), 33–45.

4. *Yellowstone Resources and Issues Handbook: 2016*, 29–33.

5. Speech of President Roosevelt at Laying of the Cornerstones of Gateway to Yellowstone National Park, Gardiner, Montana, April 24, 1903, Theodore Roosevelt Center, https://www.theodorerooseveltcenter.org/Research/Digital-Library/Record?libID=o289720.

6. "NPS Organic Act of 1916," https://www.nps.gov/foun/learn/management/upload/1916%20ACT%20TO%20ESTABLISH%20A%20NATIONAL%20PARK%20SERVICE-5.pdf.

7. James A. Pritchard, *Preserving Yellowstone's Natural Conditions* (Lincoln: University of Nebraska Press, 1999), 138–62.

8. Historic Yellowstone visitation statistics, https://irma.nps.gov/STATS/SSRSReports/Park%20Specific%20Reports/Annual%20Park%20Recreation%20Visitation%20(1904%20-%20Last%20Calendar%20Year)?Park=YELL.

9. Pritchard, *Preserving*, 237–47. Frank Craighead tells the story of he and his brother John's pathbreaking scientific studies in Frank C. Craighead Jr., *Track of the Grizzly* (Sierra Club Books, 1982).

10. For an early history of the Greater Yellowstone Ecosystem, see Robert B. Keiter and Mark S. Boyce, eds., *Greater Yellowstone Ecosystem, Redefining America's Wilderness Heritage* (New Haven, CT: Yale University Press, 1991).

11. For a more recent analysis of the Greater Yellowstone Ecosystem, see Robert B. Keiter, "The Greater Yellowstone Ecosystem Revisited: Law, Science and the Pursuit of Ecosystem Management in an Iconic Landscape," *University of Colorado Law Review*, Vol. 91, no. 1 (2020), 1–181.

12. Pritchard, *Preserving*, 245–46. For a history of Yellowstone's grizzlies and the Endangered Species Act to 2006, see Kelley Ann McLandress, "Fates and Footprints: Yellowstone Grizzly Bears and the Endangered Species Act," Thesis (University of Montana, 2006), https://scholarworks.umt.edu/cgi/viewcontent.cgi?article=3346&context=etd. A timeline of Yellowstone's grizzlies and the ESA is available at https://www.nps.gov/yell/learn/nature/bearesa.htm. But the fate of the bears remains in the courts. As of late 2020 the animals are yet on the ESA: see Marie Fazio, "Grizzly Bears Around Yellowstone Can Stay on Endangered Species List, Court Rules," July 10, 2020.

13. See the Leopold Report, https://www.nps.gov/parkhistory/online_books/leopold/leopold.htm. See also *Yellowstone Resources and Issues Handbook: 2016*, 26.

14. *Yellowstone Resources and Issues Handbook: 2016*, 27.

15. *Yellowstone Resources and Issues Handbook: 2016*, 27.

16. *Yellowstone Resources and Issues Handbook: 2016*, 27.

17. "Yellowstone National Park," UNESCO, https://whc.unesco.org/en/list/28/.

18. Monica G. Turner, William H. Romme, and Daniel B. Tinker, "Surprises and Lessons from the 1988 Fires," *Frontiers in Ecology and the Environment*, Vol. 1, no. 7 (2003), 351–58; "Fire Management," National Park Service, https://home.nps.gov/yell/learn/management/fire-management.htm.

19. Douglas W. Smith, Daniel R. Stahler, Matthew C. Metz, Kira A. Cassidy, Erin E. Stahler, Emily S. Almberg, and Rick McIntyre, "Wolf Restoration in Yellowstone: From Reintroduction to Recovery," *Yellowstone Science*, Vol. 24, no. 1, https://www.nps.gov/articles/wolf-restoration-in-yellowstone-reintroduction-to-recovery.htm.

20. For detailed information about the reintroduction of wolves to Yellowstone, see Thomas McNamee, *The Return of the Wolf to Yellowstone* (New York: Henry Holt, 1997).

21. There is much more to the story of Paul Schullery and Lee Whittlesey's search for as many more of the historical animal observations as could be found, but those historical reports took twenty-eight additional years to find and publish. The two historians used 168 historical sources in their original (1992) book-length study. In 2006, they added Sarah Bone to their team who began inputting their findings into a permanent, NPS computer, and in 2015 Paul Schullery retired from the National Park Service. Whittlesey and Bone continued searching for those elusive, historical accounts for twenty-eight years, expanding the number of known historical accounts from 168 to 511. In 2020, Whittlesey and Bone published their massive, two-volume study. Entitled *The History of Mammals of the Greater Yellowstone Ecosystem, 1796–1881: A Multi-Disciplinary Study of Thousands of Historical Observations*, it contained 1,305 pages, including over eighty historical observations of wolves, 475 observations of bison, and thousands of observations of thirty-eight other mammals in the Greater Yellowstone Ecosystem. Important in the study was the discovery of naturalist George Bird Grinnell's 1875 trip to Yellowstone, during which time he saw and reported that "The 'so-called Mountain Buffalo' was abundant in the Yellowstone Park." There is literally no other historical and geographical study like it for any other location on Earth.

22. Doug Smith, "Ten Years of Yellowstone Wolves," *Yellowstone Science*, Vol. 13, 7–33; W. J. Ripple and R. L. Beschta. "Trophic Cascades in Yellowstone: The First 15 Years After Wolf Reintroduction," *Biological Conservation* Vol. 145 (2012), 205–13; Christine Peterson, "25 Years After Returning to Yellowstone, Wolves Have Helped Stabilize the Ecosystem," *National Geographic*, July 10, 2020, https://www.nationalgeographic.com/animals/2020/07/yellowstone-wolves-reintroduction-helped-stabilize-ecosystem/. For a longer treatment see Douglas W. Smith, Daniel R. Stahler, and Daniel R. Macnulty, *Yellowstone Wolves: Science and Discovery in the World's First National Park* (University of Chicago Press, 2020).

23. "President Clinton Signs Yellowstone / New World Mine Agreement," August 26, 1995, https://clintonwhitehouse2.archives.gov/CEQ/Record/081296tp.html.

24. See Michael J. Yochim, *Protecting Yellowstone: Science and the Politics of National Park Management* (Albuquerque: University of New Mexico Press, 2015).

25. "Brucellosis and Yellowstone Bison," US Department of Agriculture, https://www.aphis.usda.gov/animal_health/animal_dis_spec/cattle/downloads/cattle-bison.pdf; "History of Bison Management in Yellowstone," National Park Service, https://www.nps.gov/articles/bison-history-yellowstone.htm. Also see Yochim, *Protecting Yellowstone*;

"Interagency Bison Management Plan," www.ibmp.info/ and Rachel Cramer, "Bison Transfer Expands to Sixteen Native Tribes," Montana Public Radio, August 13, 2020, https://www.mtpr.org/post/bison-transfer-expands-sixteen-native-american-tribes.
26. Brett French, "Groups Raising Funds for New Quarantine Facility in YNP," *Bozeman Daily Chronicle*, A1, A12.
27. Studies of snowmobiling in Yellowstone are available at https://pubmed.ncbi.nlm .nih.gov/15696297/. For a more recent analysis, see Jen Miller, "Snowmobiles in Yellowstone National Park: An American Right, or Wrong?", Carleton College, https://serc .carleton.edu/research_education/yellowstone/snowmobiles.html.

CHAPTER FOURTEEN

1. Letter to Margot Einstein, after his sister Maja's death, 1951; quoted by Hanna Loewy in A&E Television Einstein Biography, VPI International, 1991.
2. Thomas D. Brock, "The Road to Yellowstone—and Beyond," *Annual Review of Microbiology*, Vol. 49 (1995), 1–28.
3. Brock, "Road to Yellowstone," 10.
4. Brock, "Road to Yellowstone," 11–12.
5. Brock, "Road to Yellowstone," 12–22.
6. Camille Barr, "Thermus Acquaticus," *Montana Naturalist*, February 25, 2018, https:// www.montananaturalist.org/blog-post/thermus-aquaticus/; *Yellowstone Resources and Issues Handbook: 2016* (Yellowstone National Park, 2016), 84–85; Daniel L. Dustin, Keri A. Schwab, and Kelly S. Bricker, "Thermus Acquaticus and You: Biodiversity, Human Health, and the Interpretive Challenge," *Rural Connections*, September 2010, 47, https:// digitalcommons.calpoly.edu/cgi/viewcontent.cgi?article=1038&context=rpta_fac. Mullis won the Noble Prize in Chemistry for creating the PCR methodology.
7. For more information, see "De-Extinction," Encyclopedia Britannica, https://www .britannica.com/science/de-extinction.
8. For more information about Yellowstone's contribution to the search for extraterrestrial life, see "Yellowstone Discovery Bodes Well for Finding Evidence of Life on Mars," National Science Foundation, April 20, 2005, https://www.nsf.gov/news/news_summ .jsp?cntn_id=104083; Aomawa L. Shields, Sarah Ballard, and John Asher Johnson, "The Habitability of Planets Orbiting M-Dwarf Stars," *Physics Reports*, Vol. 663, December 5, 2016, 1–38, https://www.sciencedirect.com/science/article/abs/pii/S0370157316303179; "A Yellowstone Guide to Life on Mars: A University of Cincinnati Geology Student Is Helping NASA Determine Whether Life Existed on Other Planets," *Science Daily*, April 25, 2018, https://www.sciencedaily.com/releases/2018/04/180425195618.htm; Dirk Schulze-Makuch, Rene Heller, and Edward Guinan, "In Search of a Planet Better Than Earth: Top Contenders for a Superhabitable World," *Astrobiology*, Vol. 20, no. 12 (December 2020), 1394–1404, https://www.ncbi.nlm.nih.gov/pmc/articles/ PMC7757576/; "Geysers on Earth and in Space: How Astrobiology Studies in Yellowstone Might Teach Us About Life on Other Planets!," US Geological Survey, March 8, 2021, https://www.usgs.gov/center-news/geysers-earth-and-space-how-astrobiology -studies-yellowstone-might-teach-us-about-life?qt-news_science_products=4#qt -news_science_products; and "Thermophiles in Time and Space," National Park Service,

Yellowstone National Park, https://www.nps.gov/yell/learn/nature/thermophiles-in-time
-and-space.htm.
9. For more information about ongoing research in the world of Yellowstone's thermal
microbes, see Thermal Biology Institute, Montana State University, https://tbi.montana
.edu/Extrememicrobiology.html. For a brief introduction to Yellowstone's world of
thermophiles, see "Thermophilic Communities," National Park Service, https://www.nps
.gov/yell/learn/nature/thermophilic-communities.htm.

Index